THE PRESIDENTIAL DILEMMA

THE
PRESIDENTIAL
DILEMMA

Leadership in the American System

SECOND EDITION

MICHAEL A. GENOVESE
Loyola Marymount University

Longman

New York San Francisco Boston
London Toronto Sydney Tokyo Singapore Madrid
Mexico City Munich Paris Cape Town Hong Kong Montreal

Vice President and Publisher: Priscilla McGeehon
Executive Editor: Eric Stano
Marketing Manager: Megan Galvin-Fak
Senior Production Manager: Bob Ginsberg
Project Coordination, Text Design, and Electronic Page Makeup:
    Sunflower Publishing Services
Cover Design Manager and Cover Designer: John Callahan
Cover Photo: PhotoDisc
Jr. Manufacturing Buyer: Kara Frye
Printer and Binder: RR Donnelley & Sons Company
Cover Printer: Lehigh Press, Inc.

Library of Congress Cataloging-in-Publication Data

Genovese, Michael A.
    The presidential dilemma: leadership in the American system/Michael
A. Genovese.—2nd ed.
        p. cm.
    Includes bibliographical references and index.
    ISBN 0-321-10898-1
    I. Title
                                                            2002028669

Please visit our website at http://www.ablongman.com

ISBN 0-321-10898-1

12345678910—DOH—05040302

To Gabriela, and a love that has lasted, endured, grown, strengthened. You are my everything.

Contents

Preface
Officeholders but Not Leaders ix

1 The Dilemma of Presidential Leadership 1
The Devolution of the Presidency 4
Failing the Leadership Test 33
Governing a Leaky Ship 42
The Finitude of Presidential Power 44

2 America's Leadership Aversion System 47
The Intent of the Framers 49
The Structure of American Government 52
Individual Skills 57
America's Political Culture 59
The Moods and Cycles of American Politics 63
The Decline of Intermediaries 69
Presidential Selection 71
The Market as Prison 73
The Politics of Globalization 77
Conclusion 79

3 Presidential Power-Maximizing Strategies 81
Presidential Leadership 84
The Building Blocks of Presidential Leadership 86
Political Timing 94
Controlling the Agenda 100
Coalition *and* Consensus Building 101
Popularity 104

The Media   112
Congress   118
Management   125
Policy Arenas: Foreign versus Domestic   133
The Supreme Court   137
Moving Beyond the Law   139
The President's Emergency Power   141
Presidential Action in Times of Emergency   146
Conclusion   148

4   **Making the Presidency Effective
     and Accountable**   151
     Jefferson's Vision of Democratic Leadership   155
     A Powerful and Accountable President?   157
     The Ends and Means of Presidential Power   160
     Separation or Syncopation?   161
     Reforming the Presidency   163
     Making the Presidency Work   165
     Conclusion   169

Endnotes   175
Internet Links   197
Bibliography   199
Index   217

Officeholders but Not Leaders

We give the President more work than a man can do, more responsibility than a man should take, more pressure than a man can bear. We abuse him often and rarely praise him. We wear him out, use him up, eat him up. And with all this, Americans have a love for the President that goes beyond loyalty or party nationality; he is ours, and we exercise the right to destroy him.

—JOHN STEINBECK,
AMERICA AND AMERICANS

In the 1981 movie *The History of the World, Part I,* Mel Brooks, playing King Louis of France, walks around an opulent garden, insulting his guests by squeezing the backsides of ladies of the court. Is he called to task for this gross behavior? No, in fact after pinching one especially voluptuous woman, Brooks turns to the camera and says with great satisfaction, "It's good to be da king!"

And indeed, it must have been good to be the king, especially in the days when the accepted paradigm was the Divine Right of Kings. Talk about POWER! The king claimed that his authority derived from the "fact" that God had anointed him king. To disobey the king was tantamount to disobeying God. As long as the vast major-ity of the people were willing to buy into that myth, the king could rule, or command, perched on the shoulders of God and fully expect to be obeyed.

Over time, the divine right of kings gave way to a new myth: the divine right of the people, or democracy. The ground beneath the king's authority collapsed and was replaced by a secular legitimacy based on the will or consent of the people. Few followed the commands of the ruler! Now people had to be persuaded to follow, or they believed that the "elected" leaders were to follow *their* will. The grounds of authority and legitimacy were weakened. If it was good to be the king, it was exceedingly difficult to be president.

To understand the great difficulty of governing in an age of mass democracy, stripped of the lubricating assistance of divine power, take a short trip with me to the beautiful Getty Museum in Los Angeles. Perched on a hill overlooking the city on one side and the Pacific on the other, the Getty is a gorgeous venue for art and culture.

One of the paintings—James Ensor's *Christ's Entry into Brussels in 1889* (1888)—holds special interest for students of politics. Believed to be the first "expressionist" painting, Ensor's painting is mad, magnificent, complex, claustrophobic, confused, confusing, anarchistic, and beautiful. Rich and colorful, it depicts Christ's entry into the city, but in a way that is unorthodox, even shocking to our sensibilities.

Picture in your mind's eye what a painting entitled "Christ's Entry into Brussels" *should* look like: Christ with a halo aglow sits on top of a donkey—the center of attention, with adoring followers lining the streets, bowing in respect, laying palm leaves on the path.

But in Ensor's dystopian version, Christ is barely visible. Lost amid a garish, cluttered, colorful anarchy of people and puppets, one has to squint and work hard to find Christ, who is lost in the crowd. There is a marching band, clowns, costumed characters, masked figures, performers, self-important officials, skeletons, and clerics. From the pompous to the pitiful, it is a mad cacophony of the leering mob.

This painting is relevant to our understanding of the presidency because Ensor's allegorical work of art portrays the dilemma of leadership in a mass democracy. Rather than deferring to Christ, the mob barely pays attention to him. There are too many distractions, too many entertaining diversions to pay attention to, not to mention defer to, this leader of the Christian movement. There is a party going on, a carnival—do not bother me with the boredom of authority. If the choice is party or piety—let the parade begin!

In our world today this Christ is not the center of attention, not the recipient of worshipful respect; this Christ must compete with the entertaining party of the human parade. The chaos of fun trumps worship. Self indulgence trumps hierarchy; individualism trumps obedience; party trumps followership. As James O'Toole notes:

> Ensor understood that social chaos would soon arise from the secular democracy then aborning in Europe. A hundred years ago, he foresaw the seeds of the tradition-destroying trend that would eventually germinate and produce, among countless other cultural horrors, seventy-six channels of cable television. The painting forces the viewer to think about the unprecedented obstacles to effective leadership in a world that has grown, in the subsequent century, even more turbulent than Ensor's frenetic Brussels street scene. . . . Ensor saw that henceforth leaders would face the challenge of having to lead without the traditional powers of station, sanction, or threat of suppression. Instead, like Christ, leaders would have to appeal to the minds and hearts of their followers.
>
> Ensor causes us to wonder how anyone could lead from the middle of an inattentive crowd of individualists, each a political and social equal, and every last one bent on demonstrating that fact. Though people have always resisted efforts to bring about changes, even those in their own self-interest, Ensor suggests that modern times would be characterized by widespread resistance to being led at all.[1]

The emergence of democracy as the new social and political paradigm, the imposition of the Divine Right of People, undermined authority and legitimacy. No longer would subjects automatically follow; now citizens had to be persuaded. They could choose to follow or not, they might give to a leader their authority and power, or not. It was no longer automatic but had to be earned, won.

And in a world of mass consumerism, those wishing to lead seemed to have precious little to offer by way of inducement. Why follow the leader when the carnival was going in the other direction? Why sacrifice for the cause when my comrades offer intoxication? Why give to the community when I can further my own pocket? And so, instead of kings commanding, in the new world elected officeholders had to "lead."

Yes, as the Mel Brooks character told us, it truly must have been good to be the king—commanding is so much easier than persuading. But democracies are not like that—and herein rests the difficulty of leading in a world where the deference, hierarchy, authority, and legitimacy of the old order have evaporated, and the new order requires this thing called *the consent of the governed.*

Presidents can rarely command. They have to generate and maintain support, build coalitions and consensus, persuade, influence, coax, cajole, push, and prod. And even then Congress might say NO. The people might turn a deaf ear. Interest groups might actively oppose. Business interests might seek to counter. Courts might demur.

Although the president has some constitutional authority, it does not match the high expectations and expressive demands placed upon the office. Is it any wonder that we are so often disappointed with our presidents?

We live in an age of weakened leaders. In politics, business, religion, and education, those who hold positions of status and power very often seem to let us down. As our problems grow, our politicians seem to shrink. As circumstances call for leadership, we may instead get pandering and petty rankling. Why? What is wrong?

This book is an effort to understand and explain the failure of the American presidency to meet the needs, expectations, and responsibilities placed upon leaders in the past forty years. The goal is to evaluate the modern presidents, examine the reasons why their performance has been underwhelming, discuss how presidents might maximize their opportunities for leadership, and ask a key question: Can presidents be powerful and accountable? The book follows a clear format and tries to show why our officeholders have so rarely been leaders and how—within the bounds of democratic accountability—presidents can become leaders instead of mere officeholders.

Three decades ago, David Mayhew presented an elegant theory of congressional behavior in his book, *Congress: The Electoral Connection:*[2] Members of Congress seek to maximize their chances for reelection. Since that time Mayhew's "theory" has become all but accepted wisdom in political science. I would like to suggest a "theory" of presidential politics, less elegant but hopefully as persuasive as Mayhew's: *Presidents, facing a system of multiple veto points, seek to maximize power and influence.*[3] Successful presidents use their power and influence to serve the public good. That they usually fail reflects the strength of the president's rivals, the limited resources at his disposal, and the many veto points a president must overcome to gain power. This book is about the roadblocks presidents face, the (limited) avenues of power available to them, and how the presidency "fits" into the American political system. Thus the "presidential dilemma" is that expectations and demands are high but resources and power are limited. With demands so high, but resources so limited, it should not surprise us that presidents so often "fail"—fail to meet our exceedingly high expectations of what they should deliver.

While this theory of presidential behavior focuses on power (the ability to get others to conform to your wishes), in a democratic political system *power* cannot be divorced from *purpose*. The American president is not simply a leader. To be seen as successful, he must be a *democratic leader*. Merely focusing on power might mean that presidents who got their way—for example, Lyndon Johnson and Richard Nixon—were successful presidents. But power must be linked to purpose in a democratic arena, which means that success is more than merely accumulating power; it also includes the *ends* to which power is used.

Throughout this book I refer to presidents with the pronoun "he" because all presidents to date have been men. Increasingly, women are rising to positions of political power and have served as chief executives of a number of nations,[+] but thus far the United States has lagged behind in affording women equal opportunity to rise to the top position of political leadership.

The first edition of this book was published at the midpoint of the Clinton presidency. Since that time we have witnessed sex scandals, the collapse of Newt Gingrich, impeachment, the 2000 election and its bizarre aftermath, the beginnings of a new Bush presidency, and the tragedy of September 11.

This new edition includes all of these events and more. It has also benefited from a careful reading and critiques from presidency scholars in the field who have been using the book. This book is designed to present an argument, perhaps even to start an argument. It has a point of view. While I am not objective, I have tried to be fair. Readers will find their favorite presidents praised for one thing, then called to task for another. I play no favorites but try to let the theme—that presidents of the past forty years have overall been underwhelming partly due to their own faults but largely due to the weak conditions or circumstances for leadership—drive the analysis.

I am indebted to many people who have been of help in the completion of this book. Typist Kelli Lee was extraordinarily cooperative and professional. Research assistants Amy Montes, Kirsten Oester, and Gina Semenza never once complained (to my face, at least) when I sent them back to the library for "more." As always, I owe a debt to friends and colleagues in the Presidency Research Group of the American Political Science Association, who have been welcoming and supportive over the years, especially Thomas Cronin and the late William Lammers. To all of you, my deepest thanks. But most of all I wish to thank Gaby for being the true love of my life. I hope every reader of this book is fortunate enough to find a love half as sweet as this.

MICHAEL A. GENOVESE

CHAPTER 1

The Dilemma of Presidential Leadership

Item 1: On a recent visit to Disney World in Orlando, Florida, I noticed a sign advertising the "Hall of Presidents"—a patriotic show celebrating American presidents and the presidency; an unapologetic Valentine to the men who occupied the office from Washington to Bush the Second. One could easily emerge from this exhibit of lifelike, life–size presidents with the impression that all good things in America are the result of what these robotic figures did.

Item 2: On a hill overlooking the Simi Valley in suburban Los Angeles, a lovely Spanish-style hacienda, serves as the home to the Ronald Reagan Presidential Library. It is one of nearly a dozen opulent palaces devoted to preserving and promoting the memory and reputation of former presidents—Gerald Ford, Jimmy Carter, Franklin D. Roosevelt, Richard Nixon, and others.

Item 3: The president's plane has been hijacked in the movie *Air Force One*. But our macho superhero (aka, the President, played by Harrison Ford) uses brains and brawn to defeat the thugs who outnumber and outarm him, and the presidential superman saves the day!

Item 4: Taking a leisurely stroll through the nation's capitol, one is struck by the sheer power and force of the architecture. Large, imposing, impressive buildings line the streets; the city oozes power. Sprinkled here and there one finds the Washington Monument, the Jefferson Memorial, the Lincoln Memorial, the FDR Memorial . . . grand tributes to our presidential icons.

All four of these examples are connected to a celebration of the presidency. Why have a Disney attraction devoted to

1

presidents? Why build libraries to honor occupants of one branch of government? Why do presidents so often appear as stars in film and more recently on television? And why do we devote monuments to presidents? Why do we honor the presidency so? Why don't we do the same for Congress,—the peoples' branch—or the Courts—the great defenders of our rights and liberties? Why not "the people"? What makes the presidency so special?

And in so honoring presidents at the expense of others, what message are we sending to the public? Does the public, exposed as it is to homages to the presidency, begin to view the president as a genuine Superman, powerful and good? Does this image accurately reflect the political world which presidents occupy? Do we "think" the president is more powerful than is in fact true? By ignoring the separation of powers and the other roadblocks faced by presidents, do we give a false impression of both the power of the office and the systemic realities of the separation of power? Are we building the presidential image up well beyond what can realistically be accomplished?

The point of this book, and the central dilemma faced by presidents, is precisely this expectation resource gap. We expect and demand that presidents perform like Superheroes, and culturally we get cues that indeed they may be Supermen. But constitutionally and politically they rarely resemble heroes but are more likely to be Gullivers enchained. The received message is that the presidency is powerful, but the reality (except in a crisis or on some foreign policy issues) is that presidents are far weaker than we are led to believe. Thus, we are often disappointed by presidents who "underperform."

Most Americans looking at the performance of modern presidents conclude that something is very wrong. The presidency, once seen as the great engine of American democracy, now seems to be "the little train that can't!" Where have all the leaders gone?

From the heady days of presidential power in the 1930s, when Franklin D. Roosevelt was both powerful and purposeful, we now face a system characterized by gridlock and roadblocks, paralysis and deadlock, pettiness and recriminations. When the modern presidency rose out of the ashes of the Great Depression, FDR embodied a president of power, leadership, and ideas. He was a leader who led, not merely an officeholder who presided. But the presidency of the past quarter century has been anything but effective. From Lyndon Johnson to Bill Clinton, the recent presidents have either failed, or performed inadequately. This has created "the crisis of the modern presidency."

The recent presidents have been either strong but pigheadedly wrong (Johnson), strong but corrupt (Nixon, Reagan, and Clinton), weak but honorable (Ford and Carter), or just plain lost in a changing world (Bush, I). Poor performance characterizes the modern presidents; failure to perform up to expectations is their common bond. For a variety of reasons, the recent presidents have been unable to provide the nation with the leadership necessary to fulfill the Constitution's pledge "to form a more perfect union, establish justice, insure domestic tranquillity, provide for the common defense, promote the general welfare, and secure the blessings of liberty to ourselves and our posterity. . . ."

As Phil Williams, an observant British analyst of American politics has noted, "The history of the American presidency since the early 1960s is one of failure, scandal, and disaster."[1] Presidency scholar Thomas E. Cronin reminds us that "presidential frustration is far more the rule than presidential triumph."[2] And political scientists Theodore J. Lowi and Benjamin Ginsberg begin their book *Democrats Return to Power* with this assertion: "Over the past thirty years, the history of the American presidency has been one of disappointment and failure."[3] Presidents of the Republican and Democratic parties, whether from the left or the right, have faced a similar fate: the inability to successfully perform the admittedly difficult tasks of the presidency.

The United States has come a long way from its founding, when in one generation, with a population of only five and a half million people, in a tiny emerging nation nestled on the eastern seaboard, this country produced a wealth of great leaders: Washington, Jefferson, Franklin, Hamilton, Madison, Paine, Adams, Henry, Morris, and others. Today, our list of "leaders" includes Lyndon Johnson, Richard Nixon, Gerald Ford, Jimmy Carter, Ronald Reagan, George Bush I, and Bill Clinton, a distinctly undistinguished lot. What has happened? In slightly over 200 years we have gone from the highest mountain of leadership to the deepest valley of despair (with a lot of peaks and valleys in between).

What have our recent presidents wrought? Lyndon Johnson escalated a war in Vietnam that tore the nation (and the presidency) apart;[4] Richard Nixon, possibly the most corrupt president in the nation's history, gave us the disgrace of Watergate;[5] Gerald Ford was a decent man but politically inept;[6] Jimmy Carter, another decent man, was also politically inept;[7] Ronald Reagan successfully played the role of Wizard of Oz, but when Toto pulled the curtain on his policies, it became clear that he had left the nation with the Iran-Contra scandal, and buried in debt;[8] George Bush turned out to be a president lost in space, as the dramatic changes of the post–Cold War era left him speechless and idealess;[9] and Bill Clinton gave us a series of embarrassing sex scandals culminating in his impeachment.[10]

When three of the past five incumbents lost in their bids for reelection, and seven of the past eight presidents left office under circumstances less than desirable, it should be obvious that something is wrong. And yet, when one inquires into the source(s) of these repeated failures, the personalistic explanation is usually offered. While convenient, blaming failure on the individual tells only part of the tale. Other forces of a systemic and institutional sort weigh heavily in our analysis. That the recent presidents have been disappointing seems clear; the multiple reasons for substandard performance may be less evident. Our task is to explore the multiple reasons for presidential inadequacy. Thus an examination of the ebb and flow of presidential fortunes will give us an insight both into the heady days of presidential greatness and into the decline of presidential performance in the past forty years.

The Devolution of the Presidency

Public and scholarly attitudes about the presidency have fluctuated dramatically in the past sixty years. When Franklin D. Roosevelt brought his unique style and political skill to meet the challenge of the Great Depression, then of World War II, the presidency was transformed into a "modern institution," and the White House became the vital center of the American political process. FDR, considered by presidential scholars to be one of the nation's greatest presidents, was a powerful and effective chief executive. Under his leadership, the presidency became the prime mover of the American system, and people began to look to the federal government and to the presidency as the nation's problem solver. The federal government had grown, and with it presidential responsibilities, ending the era during which a president such as Calvin Coolidge could claim that his greatest accomplishment was "minding my own business." Big government led to a big presidency.

Roosevelt was very successful. In fact, he was so successful and so powerful that he transformed the presidency and changed public attitudes about the institution. A "cult of the presidency" began to develop, wherein the office was elevated far beyond the intent of the Framers or the power resources given to the institution. The public began to expect, even demand, that the president solve problems. Power became more centralized, expectations focused on the presidency, and the road to power ran directly to the White House.

Roosevelt transformed the presidency. He created expectations of presidential power and leadership that would be imposed on his successors. The "heroic" model of the presidency was established as a result of FDR's leadership, and for the next thirty years, presidential scholars would promote the model as good and necessary. From that point on, all presidents would be in FDR's shadow.[11] Terry Moe explains what happened, after Roosevelt:

> All presidents would be held responsible for addressing every conceivable social problem—however gargantuan . . . intractable . . . far removed from the president's actual sphere of power—and they would be expected, through legislative leadership and executive control of the administrative apparatus of the government, to take action.[12]

And Roosevelt did not disappoint. Elected president four times, FDR was powerful, popular, and charismatic. He had a remarkable "power sense." He got the system moving. Increasingly, the presidency became more powerful, more personalized, and the United States was transformed into a presidency-centered system. It was during this era that what political scientist Thomas E. Cronin called the "Superman" or textbook image of the presidency took root.[13]

Roosevelt planted the seeds that would grow into a view of the institution of the presidency as the seat of power, benevolence, and wisdom. As Robert Spitzer notes, "Roosevelt would become the yardstick by which every future president would be measured."[14] High standards indeed. Roosevelt guided the nation through the Depression, led the nation to the eve of victory in World War II, and utterly transformed the presidency. Roosevelt was a great president, but the myth of FDR took on even greater stature. An inflated view of Roosevelt passed for fact in popular and scholarly conceptions of the presidency. He was never really as powerful as he is remembered. But if this FDR is the gold standard, the yardstick of measurement for presidential success, could any mere mortal be expected to live up to such Herculean standards?

Could this wisdom, virtue, and power extend beyond one man and be embodied in an institution? When FDR died in office toward the end of World War II, his vice president, the diminutive Harry S Truman, became president. How could Truman fill the shoes of FDR? How could this interloper presume to grasp and use the power of this grand institution?

Truman assumed the presidency in the final days of World War II. In an effort to hasten an end to the war, he ordered the atomic bomb(s) dropped in Japan. After the war, as the Cold War began, it was Truman who helped establish the United States as the world's leading power, who devised the "containment" policy toward the Soviet Union—a policy that each succeeding president would follow, more or less, until 1989 and the end of the Cold War. It was Truman who established the Marshall Plan, or European Recovery Program, the Truman Doctrine, helped establish the North Atlantic Treaty Organization (NATO), and led the United States back to a postwar domestic economic revival. It was also under Truman that the Korean War began.

To the surprise of most of his contemporaries, Truman became a very effective president (though his popularity could never match that of FDR, and it would be only after he left office that his contribution was fully appreciated). Truman created a sense often expressed in this way: "Surely if he can do the job, there must be something inherent in the office that brings out greatness in even the most common of men." Thus was born the "FDR halo," which could be passed down from president to president, a kind of magic that seemed to confer special powers on the occupant of the White House.

When Dwight D. Eisenhower (Ike), a Republican, became president in 1953, he lent a bipartisan air to the majesty of the office. While not an activist president, Ike did manage to exert a hidden-hand type of leadership in an era when the public seemed anxious to take a break from the hurly-burly world of politics [15] After all, the United States had been through a depression in the 1930s, a world war in the 1940s, and a nascent cold war in the late forties and early fifties. By the Eisenhower era, the American people wanted a rest. Ike, with a low key, almost apolitical style, gave them what they wanted. Ike was amazingly popular, especially for a president who seemed to do so little, and his popularity extended across the entire eight years of his tenure.

Eisenhower, the great military hero who had served as commander of U.S. forces in Europe, had a rather limited agenda as president. In general terms he sought peace abroad and prosperity at home. During his presidency, the Korean War ended and a massive interstate highway-building program began. While his substantive accomplishments may have been a bit thin, Eisenhower inspired trust and confidence and helped bring about stability and calm in the nation.

If the FDR halo seemed to be in limbo during the Eisenhower years, Ike's successor was determined to pull it out of mothballs. John F. Kennedy, the Camelot president, wanted an activist administration, and after eight years of Eisenhower, the public seemed ready for action. But try as he might, President Kennedy's legislative proposals often fell prey to unresponsive leaders in Congress. Stymied by an intransigent Congress, which took the system of checks and balances quite seriously, the Kennedy legislative record was at best mixed. The first Roman Catholic ever to be elected president, Kennedy won the presidency by a razor-thin margin in 1960. Kennedy presided over the Bay of Pigs fiasco in Cuba, placed military advisors in Vietnam, and successfully led the nation through the Cuban Missile Crisis. But his ambitious and progressive domestic initiatives often were blocked by a Congress controlled by conservatives in his own party. Kennedy did achieve tax cuts, which stimulated economic growth, started the Peace Corps, and placed civil rights reform on the presidential agenda, but overall he was stymied by a reluctant Congress.

This led to grumblings among the public and scholars. "How can the Congress stand in the way of progress?. . . There are too many checks on the presidency. . . . We need more power for the president" went the chants. If the presidency was good and just, it also deserved to be strong, and it was the Congress that stood in the way.

The untimely death of John Kennedy in 1963 left unattained the legislative agenda of the slain president. But his successor, Lyndon Johnson, was a legislative genius who, exploiting the opportunity, managed not only to pass most of the Kennedy proposals that lay dormant but even to expand Kennedy's activist program and promote a more ambitious social agenda, which he called the "Great Society." In 1964 and 1965, Johnson passed bill after bill, far surpassing anything his critics thought possible. It seemed the FDR halo and Camelot had merged to produce a protean presidency of power and purpose. We were a nation intoxicated by presidential power.

The FDR halo was truly revived. Lyndon Johnson brought the strong-presidency model back to life. The public could breathe easier knowing that a strong president—a Superman—was once again at the helm. Johnson's success confirmed the heroic-presidency model. It was proof positive that the strong presidency was a good presidency, that more presidential power meant greater public good. The public injected another dose of the drug of strong leadership, and it felt good. They placed their trust in the president, invested their hopes in the office, saw the president as powerful, good, and trustworthy. What political scientists have called a "Hallowed Be the President" (1932–1966) attitude consumed the public (see Table 1.1).[16]

But it would soon prove to be misplaced trust, because the seeds of the "Imperial Presidency" were planted in this period, and it would not be long before public trust turned to disdain. If the era of the cult of the presidency led to the public's and academics' (who probably should have known better) demanding more (unchecked)

Table 1.1   Modern Views of the Presidency

1932–1966: Hallowed Be the President
- FDR halo
- New Deal to JFK's Camelot, to LBJ's Great Society
- Cult of the presidency
- "Superman" image
- Seeds of Imperial Presidency

1967–1974: Deliver Us from Presidents
- Presidents above the law/president as king
- LBJ and Vietnam
- RMN and Watergate and Impeachment
- Imperial Presidency
- Era of cynicism spawned

1975–1980: Blessed Are the Meek
- Presidency-curbing period
- Ford and Carter, weak leaders
- Imperiled presidency
- Hangover from cult of the presidency

1981–1988: Search for a Savior
- Wizard of Oz in the White House
- Return of Imperial Presidency
- Reagan's Iran-Contra scandal
- U.S. as world's largest debtor nation

1988–2000: Where There Is No Vision, the People Perish
- Bush's visionless leadership
- "Wimpyman" image
- Bush as Clerk
- Clinton's "I feel your pain" leadership
- Zippergate and Impeachment

power for presidents and placing too much trust in the institution, the harsh lessons of political reality would soon haunt the all-too-trusting and unwary people in both camps.

If the public suspended its disbelief and almost blindly placed its faith in the strong-presidency model, why did academics so easily go along? Of course, there were voices in the wilderness, warning of the dangers of unchecked presidential power,[17] but in general, scholars and the public were equally intoxicated by the strong presidency. Richard Neustadt's seminal work, *Presidential Power*,[18] first published in 1960, is just one of many examples of a noted scholar encouraging presidents to maximize power and pursue the goal of presidency-centered politics.

Scholars were as captivated as anyone at the prospect of a strong president leading the fragmented system to new heights, overcoming the chains of the checks and balances, and achieving mighty and good ends. A sampling of quotes from the classic *The American Presidency* by Clinton Rossiter, first published in 1956, gives an indication of the status and esteem in which even the conservative Rossiter held the presidency.

> Few nations have solved so simply and yet grandly the problem of finding and maintaining an office or state that embodies their majesty and reflects their character. . . .
>
> There is virtually no limit to what the President can do if he does it for democratic ends and by democratic means. . . .
>
> He reigns, but he also rules; he symbolizes the people, but he also runs their government. . . .
>
> The president is not a Gulliver immobilized by ten thousand tiny cords, nor even a Prometheus chained to a rock of frustration. He is, rather, a kind of magnificent lion who can roam widely and do great deeds so long as he does not try to break loose from his broad reservation.[19]

Rossiter writes that the American presidency is "one of the few truly successful institutions created by men in their endless quest for the blessings of free government." He comes to this conclusion:

> It is, finally, an office of freedom. The Presidency is a standing reproach to those petty doctrinaires who insist that executive power is inherently undemocratic; for, to the exact contrary, it has been more responsive to the needs and dreams of giant democracy than any other office or institution in the whole mosaic of American life. It is no less a reproach to those easy generalizers who think that Lord Acton had the very last word on the corrupting effects of power, for, again, to the contrary, his doctrine finds small confirmation in the history of the Presidency. The vast power of this office has not been "poison," as Henry Adams wrote

in scorn; rather, it has elevated often and corrupted never, chiefly because those who held it recognized the true source of the power and were ennobled by the knowledge.[20]

Rossiter is not alone in his celebration of the presidency and presidential power. In 1960, Richard Neustadt published the influential *Presidential Power: The Politics of Leadership.* For Neustadt, a strong president was essential in order to overcome the natural lethargy of a system of "separated institutions sharing power." Neustadt writes:

> The contributions that a President can make to government are indispensable. Assuming that he knows what power is and wants it, those contributions cannot help but be forthcoming in some measure as byproducts of his search for personal influence. In a relative but real sense one can say of a President what Eisenhower's first Secretary of Defense once said of General Motors: what is good for the country is good for the President and vice versa.[21]

Gulliver goes to Washington

BOBDOLENAGIANS, I PRESUME?

We can thus see the intellectual origins of what Thomas E. Cronin would call the "textbook presidency," a Superman who was good, powerful, and essential.[22] After examining standard civics textbooks of the 1960s, Cronin discovered an idealized view of the presidency. This textbook version romanticized the office and heaped honor upon the president. The president was presented as Superman, able to leap tall separations of power in a single bound.

In 1960, Herman Finer presented this view in a combined religious and heroic vision of the presidency, not only as "the incarnation of the American people in a sacrament resembling that in which the wafer and the wine are seen to be the body and blood of Christ" but also as belonging "rightfully to the offspring of a titan and Minerva husbanded by Mars."[23] In 1965, James MacGregor Burns echoed this view in secular terms when he wrote in *Presidential Government* that "the stronger we make the Presidency, the more we strengthen democratic procedures."[24] And in 1967, Grant McConnell wrote that "to ask what is to become of the presidency is to ask what is to become of the entire American political order."[25]

This presidency-centered model, which came to dominate thinking, was more than an operating style of government; it was also a philosophy of governing. It was an operating style in that it promoted a system of government in which the president was to direct or lead the people and the other branches of government from a perch of great power. It was a philosophy of government in that it legitimized a stronger central government that took power away from the other branches, and perhaps even more important, took power from the people and vested responsibility in the hands of government (the president) to solve problems. Thus it diminished the democratic responsibility placed in the people (a Jeffersonian goal) and promoted responsibility and power in the leadership class (a Hamiltonian goal). It also failed to recognize the potential danger of the heroic-leadership model.

Lyndon Johnson's remarkable legislative achievements in the wake of John Kennedy's tragic assassination confirmed for many the wisdom of the strong-presidency model: the presidency was seen as the seat of wisdom, virtue, and effectiveness, and Lyndon Johnson looked like a Mount Rushmore type of leader. After all, was it not presidential leadership that brought about economic strength, international clout, expanding social services? More power to the presidency, it was argued, to do more good things.

Lyndon Johnson was a legislative genius. In 1965 and 1966, he and the 89th Congress passed an astounding array of bills: Medicare, Medicaid, the Civil Rights Act, the War on Poverty, the Air Pollution Control Act, the Elementary and Secondary Education Act; and they created the Departments of Transportation and of Housing and Urban Development.

At this point, a Marxist interpretation of politics seems appropriate: Groucho Marx once said that "Politics is the art of looking for trouble, finding it everywhere, diagnosing it incorrectly, and applying the wrong remedies." And that is precisely what seemed to be happening with the presidency.

Just when the public was lulled into a false sense of complacency and security concerning the benevolence of presidential power, things began to change. And they changed quickly and dramatically. It started with Vietnam.

U.S. involvement in Vietnam began quietly, escalated slowly, and eventually led to tragedy.[26] By 1966, the United States was engaged in a war that it could not win and from which it could not (honorably) withdraw. It was a "presidential war," and it brought the Johnson administration to its knees.[27]

As U.S. involvement escalated, and as victory seemed further and further away, blame was placed squarely on the shoulders of President Johnson. Although the Constitution gives the power to declare war to the Congress, in practice since the Truman administration and the "Korean Conflict," presidents have often acted unilaterally in this regard. By the time Johnson came to office, presidents had been setting policy in Vietnam for twenty years, unencumbered by the Congress. As U.S. involvement escalated, it was the president who was calling the shots. The tragedy of Lyndon Johnson is that after such a sterling start, after such great success, the blunder of Vietnam would overwhelm him and the nation. From such great heights the president fell to such tragic depths. The nation was torn apart. The glue that bound Americans together had lost its adhesiveness, and in its place, divisiveness and conflict overtook the nation. The strong presidency, so long seen as the savior of the American system, now seemed too powerful, too dangerous, too unchecked—in short, a threat. After years of hearing calls for "more power to the president," by the late 1960s the plea was to rein in the overly powerful "monster" in the White House.

It was a rude awakening. All the hopes, all the trust, all the expectations that had been invested in the presidency were being shattered. Johnson was compelled not to seek reelection in 1968 when faced with the near certainty of electoral defeat. But that was not the end of it. His successor was to degrade the nation's image of the presidency even further.

If the Vietnam War was tearing our nation apart, Johnson's successor, Richard M. Nixon, would continue to plunge the presidency and the nation toward the depths of division and degradation. Promising in the 1968 campaign to "bring us together," Nixon only brought the nation together in the collective shame of massive corruption and pettiness, when the president of the United States was named an "unindicted co-conspirator" by the federal grand jury during the crisis of Watergate.[28]

From the start of his administration, Richard Nixon faced "divided government"—a White House controlled by one party, the Republicans, but the Congress controlled by the Democrats. This made the already difficult task of governing even more problematic, and the divided government degenerated progressively into divisive government. Seeing little hope for working with a Congress controlled by his "enemies," Nixon attempted to govern by executive fiat and administrative discretion. It was a strategy doomed from the start.

Nixon extended, then ended the war in Vietnam, pursued detente with the Soviet Union, and opened doors to China. This led to a stunning reelection landslide victory in 1972. From then on it was all downhill. Nixon's administration was the most corrupt in U.S. history, and the president himself was deeply involved in the crimes of Watergate.[29] With the institution of the presidency already weakened by the tragedy of the Vietnam War, the revelations of corruption, referred to under the umbrella term "Watergate," led to a further diminution of presidential prestige.

In July 1972, during Nixon's campaign for a second term, agents for his reelection committee had been arrested for burglary at the Democratic party headquarters in the Washington, D.C., Watergate apartment building, after an attempt to wiretap telephones there. This precipitating event—which led almost a year later to the special Senate hearings called to investigate Watergate—proved to be only a minor part of the widespread corruption within the Nixon administration.

The revelations of Watergate stunned the nation. The president and a number of his top aides had been involved in a variety of crimes and dirty tricks (e.g., obstruction of justice, extortion, burglary, cover-ups, paying of hush money, etc.). What shocked the nation was the level of direct presidential involvement in many of these crimes.

Nixon, the only U.S. president forced to resign his office, did have several significant foreign policy achievements—the opening of relations with China, detente with the Soviet Union, drawing the war in Vietnam to a conclusion—and he was somewhat progressive in domestic affairs. But all of this is overshadowed by the crimes and corruption of Watergate. Nixon was forced to relinquish his office when faced with the certainty of impeachment by the House and conviction by the Senate.

A major transformation began to take place. As a result first of Vietnam, then of Watergate, our Superman became an Imperial President. Historian Arthur M. Schlesinger, Jr., in his influential book *The Imperial Presidency*,[30] argues that the abuse of power by presidents threatened the constitutional integrity of the U.S. system of government. With the rise of the president's war powers and the increased secrecy surrounding presidential initiatives, the president was usurping and abusing power and acting above the law. Cronin's Superman—savior of the people—became Schlesinger's enemy of the people. The presidency had become a danger to the republic, using its powers not for the public good but for self-aggrandizement. A new image of the presidency developed. Superman was no longer on the side of the people; the power of the institution, which we thought would be used for good, also granted the bearer of this power a capacity to do wrong. Historian Marcus Cunliffe was compelled to call the presidency a "Frankenstein monster."[31]

Watergate turned out to be the final nail in the coffin of the unambiguous acceptance of the strong-presidency model. The twin effects of Vietnam and Watergate led to an era of deep cynicism regarding politics and the presidency. Scholars and the public began to condemn the "excesses" of presidential power characterized as the Imperial Presidency,[32] and to call for a corralling of a presidency perceived as acting above the law. It was a presidency-curbing, if not presidency-bashing, period, an era of "Deliver Us from Presidents" (1967–1974).

As a reaction against the excesses of power (or should we say the "mistakes"?) in the Johnson and Nixon presidencies, the Congress attempted to reassert its power by taking a series of presidency-curbing steps, the most notable being the passage of the War Powers Act, which attempted (with little subsequent success) to curb the president's war powers. The presidency-curbing era also ushered in a period in which the public did an about-face regarding their trust in and support of presidents and the presidency. If blind faith had characterized the Hallowed Be the President era (1932–1966), blind distrust characterized the Deliver Us from Presidents period. Any and all presidential acts were suspect; virtually no support was given for presidential initiatives; and a weak-presidency model (though not a strong-Congress model) prevailed. In the midterm election of 1974, a new breed of activist Democrats was elected to the Congress. Weaned not on FDR's greatness but on Johnson's and Nixon's excesses, this new generation of legislators was less deferential to presidents, less willing to bow to claims of presidential prerogative, and more willing to directly challenge presidents. As a result, the legislative initiatives of Presidents Ford and Carter would fall victim to the Congress's revised, more suspicious attitude toward presidential power.

If the Johnson and Nixon years revealed an Imperial Presidency, the Ford and Carter years revealed an Imperiled Presidency. The cult of the presidency gave way to revulsion and distrust. It was a period characterized as "Blessed Are the Meek" (1975–1980). In 1980, Vice President Walter Mondale referred to the presidency as "the fire hydrant of the nation."[33]

After Vice President Spiro Agnew resigned the office in 1973 and pleaded nolo contendere to charges of tax evasion, Richard Nixon appointed Gerald Ford vice president. Following Nixon's resignation in August 1974, Ford became America's first "unelected" president. Shortly after taking office, Ford granted his predecessor a "full free and absolute pardon" for any crimes he may have committed as president. In Congress and among the public, suspicions persisted that Ford had pardoned Nixon for political or personal expediency. In this cynical atmosphere, President Ford's ability to govern foundered and he quickly became a caretaker president.

In his brief time as president, Gerald Ford did help restore the nation to a period of relative calm, and he helped slowly to restore the integrity of the presidency in a post-Watergate era. But the cynicism born of Vietnam and Watergate persisted, and Ford fell as one of its many victims.

In the aftermath of Watergate and the Nixon pardon, the public elected a relative unknown to the White House, Jimmy Carter. As president, Carter attempted to demythologize the presidency. He recognized that dramatic changes were taking place in the world and that America's power was declining relative to the robust hegemony the United States had enjoyed in the immediate aftermath of World War II. Carter tried to get the nation to adjust to these changing power circumstances, but he was unable to persuade a public hooked on consumerism that they had to settle for less.[34] When American hostages were taken in Iran, Carter seemed weak and paralyzed. The nation cried out for strong leadership, and Carter could not answer this call.

Like Gerald Ford, Jimmy Carter was a man of great decency but (again like Ford) limited political acumen. He faced a presidency-bashing age with great dignity but insufficient skill. He could not get the Congress controlled by his own party to pass his legislative agenda, and when events around the world came crashing down upon him, Carter seemed helpless and ineffective.[35]

President Carter's major success was the Camp David peace accords between Egypt and Israel. He also focused world attention on human rights and achieved civil service reform. But when double-digit inflation and soaring interest rates combined with Carter's seeming helplessness in the face of Iranian student radicals' taking hostage fifty-two Americans, Carter's presidency seemed doomed.

After a period of leaderless drift, the nation began to forget about the problems of presidential power, and a hunger for leadership reemerged. Problems accumulated, and the nation's "leaders" seemed powerless in the face of these hardships. The urge for the strong-presidency model reclaimed center stage, and a new era, the "Search for a Savior" (1980–1888), appeared.

The people wanted a strong leader, one who could solve problems, one who would flex America's muscles. Enter Ronald Reagan, a presidential knight in shining armor. Reagan seemed to be everything Ford and Carter weren't: strong, self-assured, a leader. He made grand promises, spoke in grand terms, built expectations high. He attempted to return to an era of American grandeur.

Reagan took Washington by storm. Claiming a bold mandate and focusing on several key economic items, Reagan managed to get most of his top agenda items enacted into law. But after an impressive start, Reagan faltered. Initial success in dealing with Congress gave way to frustration and defeat. The president could not overcome the system's roadblocks, and unwilling to accept the limits placed upon the office, he and members of his administration went beyond the law and abused power.[36]

Reagan was not what he seemed. He appeared strong, but was somewhat weak; looked like he was in control but was often manipulated by handlers or his wife; promised greatness but left the American economy and infrastructure in shambles. For Reagan, appearance did not match reality. He was a Wizard of Oz president. He gave the appearance of strength and power, but when the curtain was pulled away, a weak figure was revealed.[37] To compound matters, Reagan, like Nixon, displayed a distinct lack of respect for the law and attempted to impose a new Imperial Presidency,[38] and in the end his presidency was nearly destroyed by the Iran-Contra scandal.

Reagan's engaging personality and ready wit helped make him popular, and while his borrow-borrow, spend-spend approach to policy may have added to America's military might, it also left the nation on the brink of economic insolvency. The United States went from being the world's largest creditor/lender nation in 1980 to becoming the world's largest debtor/borrower nation in 1988. Thus, when opportunity presented itself, Reagan was unable to convert the collapse of Soviet communism to American advantage.[39] Reagan was successful at achieving early legislative victories, attaining the largest tax cuts in U.S. history, and he helped reduce the inflation rate. In foreign affairs his major accomplishment was signing the Intermediate-range Nuclear Forces (INF) treaty with the Soviet

Union. But his administration was marred by record budget deficits, scandal, and the Iran-Contra affair.

After Reagan, scholars and the public seemed once again thoroughly confused as to what limits to place on the presidency. The roller-coaster ride that alternated between strong and weak models of presidential power left the people feeling somewhat schizophrenic about it. (Anyone who wasn't schizophrenic just wasn't thinking clearly.) These dramatic shifts in attitudes about the presidency have led presidential scholar Michael Nelson to note that "the sheer velocity of the turnover in these models since the 1960s would seem to indicate that the best single-word description of how scholars evaluate the presidency is 'confusion.' "[40] The confusion led to another era, a "Where there is no vision, the people perish" period (1988–2000).

The presidency under George Bush was in a state of suspended animation. A man of uncompromising grayness, Bush was a manager at a time when the nation needed a leader. The end of the Cold War opened a window of opportunity to exert creative leadership. But Bush was shackled by a vastly depleted resource base (the legacy of Reagan's economic mismanagement) and an intellectual cupboard that was bare (no vision for a post–Cold War future). Bush often seemed a passive observer in a dramatically changing world. If the presidency of the Hallowed Be the President era could be classified as "Superman,"[41] the presidency in this era looked more like "Wimpyman."[42]

Bush was at his best when he had a clear goal to achieve (e.g., the Gulf War), a goal imposed upon him by events. But when it came time for him to choose, to set priorities, to decide upon direction, he floundered. As conservative columnist George Will commented, "When the weight of the [presidency] is put upon a figure as flimsy as George Bush, the presidency buckles. . . ."[43]

George Bush had the greatest resume in Washington, having served two terms in the House of Representatives, as ambassador to the United Nations, chairman of the Republican National Committee, chief of the U.S. Liaison Office in China, director of the CIA, and as vice president, but he served as a managerial president, not a leader. In the jobs he left few footprints. In a time that cried out for vision, Bush seemed paralyzed. He seemed to want to be president so as to add another impressive notch on his resume. There was no clear aspiration to accomplish any grand goals. Bush's successes include the Persian Gulf War and a winding down of the Cold War, but his failures—inability to build on the concept of a New World Order or to counter rising deficits, no domestic agenda to speak of, and a stand-pat attitude as the economy tumbled—opened the door to Bush's opponents in the 1992 election. When it came time for the public to render judgment on President Bush, it chose another relative unknown over George Bush.

In January 1993, Bill Clinton—who had been a successful governor of Arkansas but was an outsider to Washington politics and little known before the presidential campaign—began his administration with an ambitious set of campaign pledges and an economy creeping toward recovery. According to Lowi and Ginsberg, President Clinton was "haunted by two ghosts—the legacies of Ronald Reagan and James Madison."[44] The ghost of Reagan could be seen in the enormous deficit Reagan left to his successors; that of Madison could be seen in the system of checks and balances, of limited and shared powers—of a separation rather than a fusion of governmental power.

Bill Clinton and the Porn Starr

The Clinton presidency proved to be one of the most fascinating roller-coaster rides in history. Bill Clinton was a brilliant scalawag. He was a masterful politician, smart, resourceful, creative, energetic, with a deft touch and a rhetorical flair. He was also a man severely character challenged. His serial affairs and dishonesty about them led others to distrust him and resulted in the most extensive investigations ever launched into the conduct and sins of a president.

Bill Clinton was a president of extreme contradictions, possibly the most paradoxical president since Richard Nixon. Like Nixon, Clinton was a man of extremes: a deeply flawed character but a man of remarkable political skill; a man who produced huge blunders, but also great political successes; a man whom the people decidedly did not trust but on whom they showered high job approval ratings. And like Watergate, one is perplexed at the mystery of how so smart and politically astute a president could do such dumb things? His irresponsible personal behavior jeopardized his entire presidency and ended up greatly diminishing the office.

He was in Garry Wills words, "a virtuoso empathizer," but he was also a national seducer. He brought out the worst in his adversaries as he tried to bring out the best in the American people. In the end, he was saved by the enemies who so hated him that they overplayed their hand and ended up turning the public against the accusers. In 1995, after the Republican electoral landslide, Clinton looked like a lame if not a dead duck. But Newt Gingrich, in all his arrogant self-indulgence led by a slash-and-burn style of politics, stepped in to help orchestrate a governmental shutdown that made Clinton look good, and probably granted him victory in the 1996 presidential contest. And during the dark days of impeachment, when his adversaries had in their hands a credible case for impeachment, his enemies again stepped in and saved him. Independent Counsel Ken Starr (referred to by his critics as Porn Starr), Henry Hyde, and the House Republicans offered a dystopian alternative that forced the public into the president's corner, again saving him from himself. With enemies like this, who needs friends?

Clinton sparked strong emotions and intense ideological and generational conflict. The rancorous partisanship that had become part of Washington politics turned even uglier as the savage slash-and-burn politics of personal destruction polluted the political atmosphere. It was, as Clinton biographer Joe Klein told a *Daily Show* audience (March 14, 2002), a time more known "for the ferocity of its persecution than the severity of its crimes." And in the midst of all this, the Appealing Bill Clinton was at war with the Appalling Bill Clinton; his great political successes could not mask his deep personal failures.

Bill Clinton's accomplishments were many, especially given the nature and behavior of his political opponents who savagely (and often unfairly) attacked the president and Hillary Clinton, the controversial First Lady. In reaction to the Reagan years where the center of political gravity shifted the nation from a center-left to a center-right orientation, Clinton moved the Democratic Party to the political center. Clinton's "Third Way" (between the liberal left of the Democratic Party and the hard right of the Republicans) allowed him to "triangulate" himself between two political extremes, and offer voters a moderate alternative to the old style left-right models. Led by Republican and Independent Counsel investigations, the Clintons faced inquiries into an Arkansas land deal (Whitewater), the firing of travel office employees, accusations that they were responsible for the death of White House aide Vince Foster (who had committed suicide, two independent counsels concluded), as well as court proceedings related to accusations of sexual improprieties revealed by Paula Jones. Clinton also faced investigations into fundraising improprieties ("renting" out the Lincoln bedroom to fat-cat donors), and finally, Ken Starr's investigation of Monicagate, where the president had an improper sexual relationship with a White House intern (Monica Lewinsky), lied about it to the public, lied about it under oath, and sparked a move for impeachment.

Despite Clinton's job approval rating in the 60 percent range, the House of Representatives pressed for impeachment. The Judiciary Committee passed four articles of impeachment on a straight party vote. The grounds for impeachment included perjury, obstruction of justice, and abuse of power. For only the second time in history, the full House was asked to impeach a president.

When the House convened on December 19, 1998, to deal with the impeachment of William Jefferson Clinton, Speaker-designate Robert Livingstone shocked the nation by announcing his resignation. It seems Livingstone was about to be outed for having an extramarital affair. Then Henry Hyde, who headed the Judiciary Committee, admitted that the stories about his affair were true. Instead of resigning, Hyde led the charge against the president.

Eventually the House approved two articles of impeachment against the president: perjury and obstruction of justice. Impeachment cases are tried in the Senate with a two-thirds vote required for conviction. On January 7, 1999, the trial began. Members of the House Judiciary Committee made the case for impeachment, but in spite of the fact that the Republicans held control of the Senate, both articles of impeachment failed even to get a simple majority. Article 1 (perjury) failed 45–55, with ten

Republicans voting against the charge. Article 2 (obstruction of justice) ended in a 50–50 tie; with four Republicans voting against the article.

The Republicans failed to oust the president, but the Independent Counsel's office (which eventually spent over $60 million) continued to pursue Clinton. Shortly before leaving office, Clinton made a deal with the Counsel to end the inquiry. Clinton admitted that some of the answers he gave "were false," and agreed to a five-year suspension of his Arkansas law license and agreed to pay a $25,000 fine.

Bill Clinton emerged as the Roadrunner! Remember Wiley Coyote and how he would relentlessly pursue the Roadrunner, obsessed with catching him? He would paint a false opening on a mountain only to be shocked when Roadrunner would run right through. Wiley, in mad pursuit, would follow the Roadrunner into the cave, only to be flattened when he crashed into the side of the mountain. Bill Clinton could do this to his adversaries. As his accusers crumbled—Livingstone, Hyde, Starr, Gingrich—as their careers or reputations sank, Clinton survived.

What did Bill Clinton accomplish as president? Bill Clinton's record is mixed, but in political terms, generally positive. A list of his accomplishments must begin with the extraordinary success of the American economy on his watch. While many were responsible for this success, surely Clinton deserves high marks for his economic management. Under Clinton, Gross Domestic Product averaged over a 4 percent rise per year; productivity was up nearly 3 percent; inflation rose at only a 2.5% average; interest rates were down, taxes were made slightly more progressive; unemployment dropped to around 4 percent, the minimum wage rose, a free trade regime was strengthened internationally (NAFTA), the stock market rose dramatically, corporate profits soared, and not only did Clinton balance the federal budget (thought to be impossible before he became president), but he also left a huge surplus. Any way one measures it, the Clinton years were a time of economic boom in the United States. Likewise, most social indicators were headed in the right direction. Crime was down, teen pregnancy down, welfare rolls down, health care expanded (a bit).

In domestic policies, the Family Leave Bill was passed, environmental protection extended (against stiff Republican opposition), the Brady Bill (gun control) passed, health care, after initial failure, was extended, and a series of often small victories were accomplished. The *New York Times* called it "Progressivism Light."

In foreign policy, while Clinton was not able to chart a clear course for the post–Cold War world, he did stem the dangerous tide of isolationism in the United States, kept the country at the center of global leadership, and made international free trade and economic growth benchmarks for his administration. Having taken the first difficult steps toward recognizing "globalism" as the wave of the future, he also expanded the definition of national security to include facing threats to free trade, cyberterrorism, and economic as well as environmental threats to security.

Peace and prosperity were indeed impressive accomplishments during the Clinton era, and yet the gaping problems of character and the impeachment would always cast a dark shadow over his legacy. And while it may well be, as Clinton supporters hope, that history will regard the assault on his presidency in the same way most historians now regard the first presidential impeachment (overzealous Republicans were to blame!), Clinton can never escape the fact that he WAS impeached, a blemish that will hang over him forever. A man of enormous appetites and few personal restraints, he demeaned himself and diminished the office. He pressed his legal claims in the Lewinsky affair to their legal limits and thereby left the presidency weaker and more defenseless. Presidential immunity, privilege, and privacy have all been eroded due to Clinton's actions.

In the long run, history will probably put Clinton somewhere in the middle of the pack of presidents. Not great, not a failure. His many political successes will salvage something, but his personal faults will haunt him. He is indeed a complex and contradictory man, and his presidency reflected all his grand complexity.

He may have held the Republican (Gingrich) dogs at bay, but he was hounded by personal failures. He cheated political death often and leaves behind an impressive legacy of political accomplishments.[45]

This Is Guatemala[46]

The ballots made no results. The counters made the result.

—BOSS TWEED[47]

The 2000 presidential election in the United States is a cynic's paradise and a democrat's nightmare. With a plot seemingly taken from a baroque Graham Greene novel of colonial corruption and imperial arrogance, Election 2000 challenged many of the sacred assumptions Americans once held about the integrity of the electoral process and the legitimacy of their governmental system. Called into question were the core democratic values Americans previously took for granted.

Election 2000 was anything but ordinary. Indeed, it was an international embarrassment for the United States. After decades spent "monitoring" the elections of other countries to ensure democratic standards, the United States found itself trying to explain to others why the leader of the free world couldn't even get a vote count right!

In recent years, the Internet has served as a clearinghouse for instantaneous hyper communication. An e-mail that circulated in the aftermath of the November elections captured the hypocrisies of America's patronizing celebration of its premier status as an advanced, sophisticated democracy. Entitled, "Imagine," it reads as follows:

> A Zimbabwe politician was quoted as saying that children should study the U.S. election event closely because it shows that election fraud is not only a third world phenomena. To illustrate the point, he made the following comments:
>
> > Imagine that we read of an election occurring anywhere in the third world in which the self-declared winner was the son of the former prime minister and that former prime minister was himself the former head of that nation's secret intelligence agency.
> >
> > Imagine that the self-declared winner lost the popular vote but won based on some old colonial holdover from the nation's pre-democratic past (the electoral college).
> >
> > Imagine that the self-declared winner's "victory" turned on disputed votes cast in a province governed by his brother!

Imagine that the poorly drafted ballots of one district, a district heavily favoring the self-declared winner's opponent, led thousands of voters to vote for the wrong candidate.

Imagine that hundreds of members of that most-despised caste were intercepted on their way to the polls by state police operating under the authority of the self-declared winner's brother.

Imagine that six million people voted in the disputed province and that the self-declared winner's "lead" was only 327 votes. Fewer, certainly, than the voting counting machine's margin of error.

Imagine that the self-declared winner and his political party opposed a more careful by-hand inspection and recounting of the ballots in the disputed province or in its most hotly disputed district.

Imagine that the self-declared winner, himself a governor of a major province, had the worst human rights record of any province in his nation and actually led the nation in executions.

Imagine that a major campaign promise of the self-declared winner was to appoint likeminded human rights violators to lifetime positions on the high court of that nation.

None of us would deem such an election to be representative of anything other than the self-declared winner's will-to-power. All of us, I imagine, would wearily turn the page thinking that it was another sad tale of a third world country.

There exists, in the "world's most powerful democracy," the distinct possibility that the loser won the election—that, in effect, a democratic election may have been stolen. After 105 million citizens voted, it was a handful of justices who finally selected a president by a 5–4 vote largely along party lines.

The peculiar path from election to selection followed a series of macabre, bizarre, and unbelievable twists and turns that did indeed call into question the honesty, integrity, and viability of the American system of elections.

This contest—arguably the closest, certainly the longest, demonstrably the costliest presidential campaign in history—will be remembered for the strange 36-day election aftermath, in which five Supreme Court justices finally selected, from among their own party, the candidate who lost the popular vote and may have actually lost the electoral college vote. It wasn't supposed to be this way—not in America!

How are we to understand and put into proper perspective the peculiarities of campaign 2000? Ironically, the post-election swirl of events obscured rather than enlightened us. So many ups and downs, twists and turns, so many possible outcomes hanging on a single judge's decision or the interpretation of what to do about dangling, dimpled, or pregnant chads! It was, as Louis Menand described it, "the civics course from hell."[48]

Americans are accustomed to waking up on the day after a presidential election and knowing who would be at the helm. There was always a winner and a loser; no indecision here! But on November 8, 2000, the campaign had officially ended, but a new contest was just beginning and it would not be resolved for five weeks. As James Ceaser and Andrew Busch note, "There were two major questions at that moment that no one could answer: who would win, and who would decide who would win."[49] We know that Bush won; we also know that it was the U.S. Supreme Court that ultimately handed him the presidency.

In the end, George W. Bush became president in one of the closest elections in history. Not only was the presidential contest close — too close to call—but the Senate ended with a 50–50 tie (only to be broken a few months later when Vermont Republican Jim Jeffords left his party to become an Independent and vote with the Democrats), in the House of Representatives, the Republicans had a razor-thin majority (with the expectation they would lose majority control in 2002 midterm elections). At the state level, there was also a near even split in party control. In state legislatures, Democrats controlled 25 lower houses, the Republicans 24; Republicans controlled 24 state senates, the Democrats 21. Only among governors, where Republicans held a 29–19 advantage was there any measurable gap between the power of the parties. In big-city mayoral contests the Democrats had a lead over the Republicans.

In effect, George Bush became a president without a majority. Governing in the best of times is difficult enough. But governing without a majority when your legitimacy is in question is especially difficult. To his credit, Bush was able to assume office with few challenges to his legitimacy.

With no consensus or majority, American politics has flip-flopped dramatically in the past quarter century. From the

Democratic center left (Carter), the nation lurched to the Republican hard right (Reagan), then back to the Republican center-right (Bush), then—as a reaction to the impact of Reagan who had shifted the center of political gravity to the right, Democrat Clinton took his party from left to center and captured the White House. But two years later, with fears he was moving too far left, the voters lurched again to the hard right in 1994 with Newt Gingrich's Republican Revolution only to see that fizzle out and a centered Clinton easily win reelection in 1996. Then, impeachment fever hit the Republicans and they launched a new frontal assault on Clinton, only to be slapped down by the president's job approval ratings rise above 60 percent. This effort to subvert the public will and impeach a president with high job approval ratings led comedian Dennis Miller to "rant" that the Republicans were "more out of step with the rest of America than Joe Cocker in a line dance." This was of course followed by the close, indecisive election of 2000. Observers of the American political scene were more likely to emerge from their inquiries with whiplash than with insight. In this context of parity, no majorities, shifting political winds, and age of cynicism, the election of 2000 makes "some" sense.

Who Really Won? Or Chad Happens

> *I am not naive enough to think that the candidate with the*
> *most votes should win an election. That's the kind of uninformed,*
> *romantic, antediluvian belief that I clung to until about thirteen*
> *days ago. We now know that it is the candidate with the*
> *best lawyers who should win an election.*

> —JOEL ACHENBACH
> *It Looks Like a President Only Smaller,* p. 153

Who would have won Florida (and thus the presidency) if the U.S. Supreme Court had not halted the recount? Had time not been an issue, had the state officials in Florida been able to accurately count the vote, would Bush or Gore have emerged the victor?

Alas, we can never know the answer. So few votes separated the two candidates and depending on how votes—and which votes—were counted, each candidate could reasonably claim that he was the "real winner." If nothing else, the Florida fiasco revealed the fragile, complex, and dark underside of the electoral machinery. Most of the failures of Florida's vote counting system were errors of carelessness, confusion, and stupidity, not crimes or fraud. Confusing butterfly ballots may have been a mistake, but they were not the result of maliciousness. Dangling, dimpled, pregnant, and other chads were not an attempt to manipulate the vote outcome unfairly. They were the flawed outcomes of a flawed process.

The one truly disturbing charge to emerge from the Florida vote aftermath was found in the report of the U.S. Civil Rights Commission which concluded that Florida's election was marred by the "significant and distressing" barriers put in the way of African-Americans who were attempting to vote but prevented from doing so. Black voters (likely Gore votes) were, it seems, systematically prevented from voting.

The vast majority of those who were disenfranchised were African-Americans, and the Commission charged that the Florida election was marked by "injustice, ineptitude, and inefficiency" and urged the Justice Department to investigate whether laws were violated. The Commission maintained that this disenfranchisement was not "isolated or episodic" and that African-American voters were nearly ten times more likely than white voters to have their ballots rejected in Florida.

Bush vs. Gore vs. the Supreme Court—or Scalia Happens

*If I should need to name, O Western World, your powerfullest scene and
show, 'Twould not be you, Niagra; nor you, ye limitless prairies; nor your
huge rifts of canyons, Colorado;
Nor you, Yosemite. . .
I'd name—the still small voice vibrating-America's choosing day. . .
Texas to Maine-the prairies states-Vermont, Virginia, California
The final ballot-shower from East to West.*

—WALT WHITMAN,
"Election Day, November 1884"

As events in Florida unfolded at a bewildering pace, as each day seemed to bring a decision that favored one candidate, only to be reversed the next, as the outcome seemed as uncertain as the process seemed so confusing, both camps began to believe that the outcome would ultimately be decided in the courts: either Florida's or the U.S. Supreme Court.

There was a political time bomb ticking, but no one knew for sure who would ignite the final flame. As the days passed, time, or the shortness of time, would dictate events. The Supreme Court felt it had to cast the final deciding vote in the 2000 election; and while politically, no one should have been surprised that this very partisan Republican court sided with Bush, constitutional scholars had reason to feel surprise at the questionable ground on which this Court decided.

The Supreme Court that ultimately selected George W. Bush as president has been a highly partisan court. The majority, appointed by Republican presidents, has fairly actively embraced and promoted the Republican Party agenda. But in *Bush vs. Gore*, the Court had to violate its "constitutional principles" to satisfy its partisan goal. In order for the Court to side with Bush, it had to abandon its firm commitment to federalism, one of its pet conservative goals, and overturn the decision of the Supreme Court of Florida. The Court had to swallow its previous logic on the sanctity of states rights and undermine the very foundation on which its adherence to federalism was based. This Court had sided with states over the federal government in case after case after case. From striking down a federal law banning guns near schools as an infringement on state prerogative, to striking down on the same grounds a federal law allowing rape victims and battered spouses to sue their assailants in federal court, this Court has exalted state sovereignty. Not in *Bush vs. Gore*. It was a victory of politics over principle.

The decision of the majority in *Bush vs. Gore* was both confused and confusing. It is nearly impossible to find a respectable constitutional scholar who will defend it. The effect of their muddled decision was to effectively cut Gore off at the pass. He had no choice but to concede defeat.[50]

Are we to take the logic of the Court seriously, or must we merely consign their case to the laws of power politics? If the legal positions of Bush and Gore were reversed, could anyone imagine the Court making the decision it made?

In *Bush vs. Gore*, partisanship trumped law; politics trumped justice. The exit wound left by this case was eloquently noted in a dissent by Justice Stevens, who noted that damage was done to respect for the Court and law:

> The endorsement of that [Bush's] position by the majority of this Court can only lend credence to the most cynical appraisal of the work of judges throughout the land. It is confidence in the men and women who administer the judicial system that is the true backbone of the rule of law. Time will one day heal the wound to that confidence that will be inflicted by today's decision. One thing, however, is certain. Although we may never know with complete certainty the identity of the winner of this year's Presidential election, the identity of the loser is perfectly clear. It is the Nation's confidence in the judge as an impartial guardian of the rule of law.

A 9-1-1 Emergency Call

The Bush presidency began with the president facing formidable odds. The table was set for deadlock. But on September 11, 2001, everything changed. A terrorist attack destroyed the World Trade Center in New York City, and shook the nation's sense of self and security.

President Bush responded quickly, trying to reassure the nation. He declared war on the terrorists and those who harbored them. The nation faced a threat and rallied behind the president. In a crisis, the normal checks and balances neither check nor balance. Power gravitates to the president. Scholars who examine leadership argue that leadership is primarily contextual — that is, the situation, more than institutional structures or individual skills, determines power potential. Post–September 11 America is a strong argument in favor of this view.

On September 10, Bush faced a vast array of checks and balances; after September 11, he was handed extraordinary extraconstitutional power. George Bush did not become a political genius overnight. But the context did change and that dramatically added to his power. What he does with that power will determine his place in history. Crisis takes the measure of a leader. It gives him a relatively free hand to act. George Bush has the power to act. Time will tell the wisdom of his actions.

And Now, Back to Reality

The 1970s brought about the "dwarfing of the presidency," the early 1980s brought on a "they might be giants but turned out to be pygmies" period, the Bush years seemed to constitute a period of "stealth leadership" or presidential sclerosis, and the Clinton years were an era with no heroes. Following the public's repeated disappointments—with presidents who didn't or weren't able to keep their campaign promises and who time after time turned in substandard performances—its lowered perceptions of the presidency were combined with an equally reduced view of government's overall capacity to function. In effect, the people felt like Charlie Brown in the Peanuts cartoon that appears every fall. In it, Charlie Brown and Lucy are in a field, and Lucy, holding a football in place on the ground, insists that Charlie Brown run up and kick it. Charlie, who has gone through this every year, demurs, knowing that if the past is a prelude, Lucy will pull the ball away at the last minute and Charlie will fall flat on his rear. But Lucy insists, promising Charlie that she will not pull the ball away, and finally Charlie gives in. He runs up, goes to kick the ball, and—of course—at the last second Lucy pulls the ball away and Charlie falls flat on his butt. Every election, candidates promise salvation; every election, the public hesitates but eventually places its hopes and trust in one man; and every year, the football ends up getting pulled away and the public ends up flat on its collective butt. The end result is failed policies, voter cynicism, and a backlog of unsolved problems. Presidents just aren't up to the task of governing.

Presidential hopefuls will, during campaigns, promise much. Do they deliver? In a study of presidential promises kept and unkept, political scientist Jeff Fishel found that none of the modern presidents was able to fully keep half of his promises. The president who fully kept the highest percentage of campaign promises was Jimmy Carter at 47 percent, followed by Lyndon Johnson at 45 percent. If one includes promises fully and partially kept, the presidents rank as follows:

1. Kennedy　　71%
2. Carter　　　69
3. Johnson　　 69

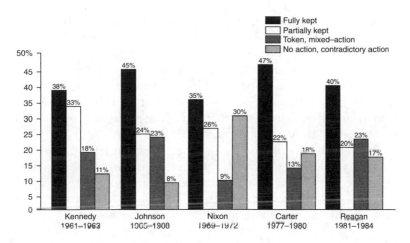

Figure 1.1　Percentage of Presidential Campaign Promises Kept, Kennedy to Reagan (*Source:* Adapted from Jeff Fishel, *Presidents and Promises* [Washington, DC: CQ Press, 1985].)

4. Nixon　　61
5. Reagan　　60

The president who acted least on promises or engaged most in contradictory action was Richard Nixon at 30 percent (see Figure 1.1 for full details).

Failing the Leadership Test

What does this all add up to? The history of the modern presidency (the presidents who have served for the past forty years) could, I argue, be seen as a period of disappointment. The United States alternated between weak leaders (Ford and Carter), corrupt or abusive leaders (Johnson, Nixon, Reagan, and Clinton), or lost and directionless leaders (Bush, Sr.). There is not one great leader, not one good leader, and barely an above average leader in the lot.

But is it fair to characterize the presidents of the past forty years as substandard leaders? Is that not a bit harsh? Couldn't we say "mediocre" instead? While in some respects it might be better to say that the modern presidents, taken as a group, have been mediocre, an unvarnished examination of their performance leads us to admit that they have been disappointing—that they have failed to live up to their own inflated promises, to our high expectations, or even to more modest standards of acceptability.

Not one of the presidents under examination left office under terms he would have preferred. Each of them departed under a cloud of shame or of bitter disappointment: Lyndon Johnson was compelled not to even seek reelection because of the problems of Vietnam; Richard Nixon resigned in disgrace because of the crimes of Watergate; Ford and Carter seemed totally overwhelmed by the job and were defeated at the polls; Ronald Reagan (popular but inept) left office with the Iran-Contra scandal damaging his image; George Bush was defeated at the polls, yet another one-term disappointment; Clinton left office under the cloud of impeachment. Not one had been a truly successful president.

In examining the administrations of the modern presidents (see Table 1.2), several patterns stand out. First, we note the absence of strongly ideological presidents. Of the twelve presidents listed in the table, only two have had strongly held ideological convictions (FDR and Reagan). Most of these presidents have been centrist in their political orientations. Second, in recent years we have seen the Republicanization of the White House—between 1969 and 1993, the Republicans have controlled the White House twenty of the twenty-four years—and the Democratization of the Congress. This institutionalizes divided government. Third, Democrats have tended to be more activist in domestic and economic policy, and Republicans more restrained (Reagan being the exception). Fourth, in foreign policy, all except Clinton and Bush II, have adopted, more or less, a Cold War approach to dealing with the world. Finally, as noted, recent presidents are not a highly regarded group of leaders. Of the last four presidents (Nixon through Reagan) who are ranked in the Murray-Blessing poll of U.S. historians, the combined average ranking of 28 (out of 37) would place them at the bottom of the below-average category among the presidents included in the poll.

Table 1.2 The Modern Presidency

President	Ideology	Background: Congress (C), Executive (E)	Party	Congressional Majority	Electoral Majority
F. Roosevelt	Liberal	E, Gov.	D	D	'32: 57.4–39.6 '36: 60.8–36.5 '40: 54.7–44.8 '44: 53.4–45.9
H. Truman	Pragmatic Liberal	C, E/VP	D	R/D	'48: 49.5–45.1
D. Eisenhower	Pragmatic Conservative	NA	R	R/D	'52: 55.5–44.4 '56: 57.4–42.0
J. Kennedy	Pragmatic Liberal	C	D	D	'60: 49.7–49.5
L. Johnson	Pragmatic Liberal	C, E/VP	D	D	'64: 61.1–38.5
R. Nixon	Pragmatic Conservative	C, E/VP	R	D	'68: 43.4–42.7 '72: 60.7–37.5
G. Ford	Pragmatic Conservative	C, E/VP	R	D	NA
J. Carter	Pragmatic Liberal	E, Gov.	D	D	'76: 50.1–48.0
R. Reagan	Conservative	E, Gov.	R	R/D	'80: 50.7–41.0 '84: 58.8–40.6

Continued

Table 1.2   The Modern Presidency   *Continued*

President	Ideology	Background: Congress (C) Executive (E)	Party	Congressional Majority	Electoral Majority
G. Bush	Pragmatic Conservative	C E/VP	R	D	'88: 53.4–45.6
W. Clinton	Pragmatic Liberal	E Gov.	D D	D: 2 yrs R: 6 yrs	'92: 43–38–19 '96: 49–41–8
G. W. Bush	Pragmatic Conservative	E Gov.	R	D/R	Minority Prss. Bush: 50,456,169 Gore: 50,996,116 Disputed Election

Table 1.2 The Modern Presidency *Continued*

President	Popular Support	Domestic Policy	Economic Policy	Foreign Policy	Management Style	Major Accomplishments	Rating
F. Roosevelt	Steady/High	Activist/New Deal	Activist/New Deal	WWII	High Involvement; Competitive Approach	New Deal Legislation; WWII Victory	#2; Great
H. Truman	Moderate to Low	Activist/Fair Deal	Activist/Fair Deal	WWII; Cold War Containment	Mixed/Mixed	Cold War Containment; Return to Postwar Economics; NATO	#8; Near Great
D. Eisenhower	Steady/High	Restraint	Restraint	Cold War	Mixed/Hierarchical	Ended Korean War; Return to Normality	#11; Above Average
J. Kennedy	Steady/High	Activist/New Frontier	Activist/Growth Policy	Cold War	High/Spokes-in-Wheel	Cuban Missile Crisis; Nuclear Test Ban Treaty; Peace Corps	#13; Above Average
L. Johnson	High to Low	Activist/Great Society	Activist/Growth Policy	Cold War; Vietnam	High/Spokes-in-Wheel	Great Society; Civil Rights	#10; Above Average

Continued

Table 1.2 The Modern Presidency *Continued*

President	Popular Support	Domestic Policy	Economic Policy	Foreign Policy	Management Style	Major Accomplishments	Rating
R. Nixon	Moderate to Low	Moderate	Restraint/ Wage and Price Controls	Cold War; Détente	High/ Hierarchical	Open Relations w/China; Détente w/Soviet Union; SALT I Treaty	#35; Failure
G. Ford	Moderate to Low	Restraint	Restraint/ Veto	Cold War	Mixed/ Spokes-in-Wheel	Return to Calm in Post-Watergate Age	#24; Low Average
J. Carter	Moderate to Low	Mixed	Mixed	Cold War; Human Rights	High/ Spokes-in-Wheel	Egypt-Israeli Treaty; Human Rights	#25; Low Average
R. Reagan	High to Moderate	Mixed/ Christian Crusade	Activist/ Supply Side	Cold War; Détente	Aloof/ Disengaged	End of Cold War; INF Treaty Tax Cuts	#28; Below Average
G. Bush	High to Moderate	Restraint	Restraint	Manage Decline/New World Order?	Mixed/ Spokes-in-Wheel	Gulf War; New World Order	NR
W. Clinton	Moderate to Low Post 96: high	Activist	Activist	Lack of Direction	High Involvement	NAFTA; Brady Act; Crime Bill; Haiti, High Economic Growth Debt Reduction Welfare Reform	NR
G. W. Bush	Post 9/11 very high	Moderate	Tax cuts	War on Terrorism	Somewhat Disengaged	War on Terrorism	NR

By contrast, the first four listed in the table (FDR through Kennedy) received a combined average ranking of 8.5, the near-great category.

One could conclude, then, that "the system" isn't working: The combined effects of gridlock, stalemate, voter desertion, excessive expectations, demand overload, widespread public cynicism, and ineffectual leadership have produced a clearly negative trend in the public's image of the presidency. Presidents now seem unable to navigate the choppy waters of America's brand of representative democracy. From both the political left and right, there is a general perception that something is wrong with the institution of the presidency—once seen as the instrument of political change in America—that it has not been able to accomplish the task of leadership. It was a short trip from Superman to Wimpyman.

Now, instead of being viewed as a powerful institution, the presidency is being portrayed as limited or weak. Instead of asking "Toward what ends should a president lead?" we begin to ask "*Can* a president lead?" From our view of Superman to that of the Imperial or Imperiled or Wimpyman presidency, we have made a complete turnabout. From the cult of the presidency we have shifted to the shackled presidency, from Superman to Nowhere Man.

Two decades ago, presidency scholar Harold M. Barger noted a trend that, if anything, is even more pronounced today:

> We live in a time of disposable presidents. Some might insist that this is not so unusual because our society is a disposable society. But presidents were not always so dispensable, and the reasons why the White House, which once symbolized stability and continuity, has lately become a revolving door for incumbents is only partly answered by our nation's tendency to consume and then discard. Americans dispose of one president after another because no recent incumbent has been able to measure up to the office. No incumbent measures up because an immense gulf has opened between what people have come to expect and what presidents can realistically deliver.[51]

Barger calls the presidency "impossible," arguing that, both at home and abroad, presidents are unable to deliver on promises or meet public expectations.

> The impossible presidency is the imperial presidency turned upside down. The imperial presidency was feared for what seemed to be unbridled powers over American military and foreign policy, as well as for a

frequently callous disregard for the will of Congress. The impossible presidency is a matter of concern because of its seeming inability to exert American power convincingly anywhere in the world, as well as for its incapacity to provide leadership in domestic policymaking.[52]

In less than thirty years, Superman—upon whom few checks seemed to exist—was replaced by presidents upon whom the system of checks and balances was resumed with a vengeance. Images of failure, limitation, and weakness dominate the new presidential literature. We can choose between Harold Barger's description of the "impossible presidency" and Theodore Sorensen's view of "political gridlock" or "all checks and no balances." James L. Sundquist writes of "failed presidents," James M. Burns of "deadlock," and Peter Smithers of "presidential paralysis." Hugo Heclo discusses the "illusion of presidential government," Thomas M. Franck the "tethered presidency," Paul Light the "no win" presidency, and Aaron Wildavsky "the beleaguered presidency." Thomas E. Cronin sees an "imperiled" presidency, and Godfrey Hodgson calls the modern presidency "impotent." As Hodgson states, "Never has so powerful a leader been so impotent to do what he wants to do, what he is pledged to do, what he is expected to do, and what he knows he must do."[53]

After "presidential" wars and scandals, after the resurgent Congress, after the public's withdrawal of support, presidential scholars became more sensitive to the weakness of presidential power and to the limitations, checks, and constraints placed on it: so many checks, so few balances; so many roadblocks, so few resources; so much separation, so little power. Institutional impotence, not power, has become part of the new textbook presidency.

We tend to judge presidents on the basis of four factors: (1) the scope of the *problems* they faced; (2) their *efforts* (actions) and *intentions* (vision) in dealing with these problems; (3) what they were able to *accomplish;* and (4) the long-term *results* of their actions. By these measures, the recent presidents have disappointed us.

If we compare our sample of presidents with the roster of earlier presidents, we find, according to professional judgments, that none of the modern presidents after LBJ is highly regarded. In the Murray and Blessing survey asking historians to rank the presidents, no modern president stands in the Great category (which includes Lincoln, FDR, Washington, and Jefferson).[54] No modern president ranks in the Near Great category (T. Roosevelt, Wilson, Jackson, and Truman). Three rank in the Above Average category (L. Johnson, at number 10, with Eisenhower and Kennedy at numbers 11 and 13, respectively). Two modern presidents are listed near the bottom of the Average category (Ford at number 24 and Carter at 25). One rates in the Below Average category (Reagan at 28). And one stands as a Failure (Nixon at number 35 of 37 presidents). Table 1.3 presents a list of all the presidents through Reagan.

Thus the average rating of the presidents under study would be 24.4, placing the composite near the bottom of the Average category. If Johnson is removed and we consider only presidents Nixon to

Table 1.3 Rating the U.S. Presidents: Murray and Blessing Poll

Great	Near Great	Above Average
Abraham Lincoln	Theodore Roosevelt	John Adams
Franklin D. Roosevelt	Woodrow Wilson	Lyndon B. Johnson
George Washington	Andrew Jackson	Dwight D. Eisenhower
Thomas Jefferson	Harry S Truman	James K. Polk
		John Kennedy
		James Madison
		James Monroe
		John Quincy Adams
		Grover Cleveland

Average	Below Average	Failure
William McKinley	Zachary Taylor	Andrew Johnson
William Taft	Ronald Reagan	James Buchanan
Martin Van Buren	John Tyler	Richard Nixon
Herbert Hoover	Millard Fillmore	Ulysses S. Grant
Rutherford B. Hayes	Calvin Coolidge	Warren G. Harding
Chester A. Arthur	Franklin Pierce	
Gerald Ford		
Jimmy Carter		
Benjamin Harrison		

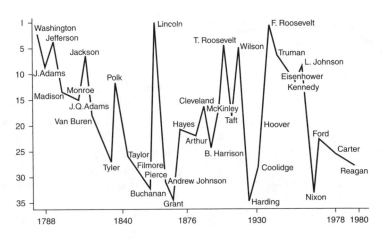

Figure 1.2   Historians Rate U.S. Presidents. (*Source:* Adapted from Murray and Blessing data, in Richard Rose, *The Postmodern President* [2nd ed., Chatham, NJ: Chatham House Publishers, 1991, p. 285].)

Reagan, the average plummets to a dismal 28, the Below Average category. Such ratings do not inspire admiration. (See Figure 1.2 for ratings of all presidents over time.)

Governing a Leaky Ship

Is the modern period unique? Was there at one time a magical period when great presidents abounded, when good presidents were numerous? Saying that the string of modern presidents performed poorly should not imply that there were extended periods of great leadership to which the recent years should be compared. True, there were times and conditions when individual presidents rose to greatness, overcame the constraints inherent in the office and governed successfully. But this is more the exception than the norm. If past is prelude, we should *expect* presidents to do poorly. Presidents are today in much the same position their presidential forefathers have been in: a fairly limited state of power, a fairly wide array of restraints. While there are differences between the modern and traditional periods of the presidency—the role of television, the propensity for presidents to "go public," the United States as a superpower, the rise of the national security state—there are also a number of historical continuities that stand out,[55] the most pronounced of which is the institutional design of the separation (and sharing) of power. Thus, the failure of leadership in the United States is not a phenomenon peculiar to the modern period. All presidents face enormous constraints, and most presidents are unable to overcome the multiple roadblocks built into the presidential condition.

Cries of "crisis" are not new. But there is an added urgency in the modern period. In the nineteenth century, presidential ineffectiveness and governmental gridlock were problems, but they were problems restricted primarily to the United States and its future. Today, with the end of the Cold War and with the United States as the world's only remaining superpower, the failure of U.S. leadership, both at home and abroad, can have dramatic (and possibly tragic) consequences. Scholars and practitioners (from Alexander Hamilton to Woodrow Wilson to Thomas Cronin) have been concerned about the dispersion of political power and the recurrent problem associated with giving direction to a fragmented government. The persistence or recurrence of crises in presidential leadership can be attributed to a variety of factors (which are discussed in Chapter 2), but it is clear that institutionally the presidency is a troubled and troubling office. From its inception, the presidency has confused and confounded those who wished to give energy to government while also maintaining democratic controls on officeholders. Confusion has reigned supreme because for the past two hundred years, we have never been certain what we really want of our president: powerful king or servant of the people, repository of government authority or constrained administrator? As Jimmy Breslin has noted, "The Office of President is such a bastardizing thing, half royalty and half democracy, that nobody knows whether to genuflect or spit."[56]

The office of the presidency has an enormous, larger-than-life quality. In spite of the dramatic ups and downs of the office in the past fifty years, it does seem to be, in Arthur Schlesinger's words, "the indestructible" institution.[57] It is at once the most powerful and weakest executive office in the world. The great opportunity to do good is matched by the equally strong capacity to do great harm. The constitutional design of the office was left vague enough to give presidents an opportunity to shape and mold the office to conform— in part—to the needs of the time, the level of political opportunity, and the skills of each incumbent. But it was also an office encumbered by obstacle after obstacle. As political scientist James David Barber reminds us:

> But the Presidency is much more than an institution. It is a focus of feelings. . . . The Presidency is the focus for the most intense and persistent emotions in the American polity. The President is a symbolic leader, the one figure who draws together the people's hopes and fears for the political future. On top of all his routine duties he has to carry that off—or fail.[58]

But if there were Washingtons, Jeffersons, Jacksons, Lincolns, and Roosevelts who stamped their imprints on the office, there were also—and more commonly—Buchanans, Grants, Hardings, Pierces, Coolidges, Fillmores, and Tylers, who were overwhelmed and defeated by the office. In fact, the office ends up defeating most presidents. When failures far outnumber successes, it is time to ask: Is something fundamentally wrong with the office itself?

The Finitude of Presidential Power

Management guru Peter Drucker presents a straightforward way of answering this question. "The rule," he writes, "is simple":

> Any job that has defeated two or three men in succession, even though each had performed well in his previous assignments, must be assumed unfit for human beings. It must be redesigned.[59]

By Drucker's measures, the American presidency must be considered a "dysfunctional institution." To those who would argue that, "Yes, the presidency gets the better of most occupants of the office, but there *are* several successes," I would caution you to remember that most of the great and near great presidents arose in times of crisis, times when the normal checks and balances which so frustrate presidents in "normal" times do not operate very effectively (e.g., Lincoln, FDR). It is precisely this failure of presidential leadership (along with other factors, of course) that helps to create crisis situations, which then centralize power and allow presidents to exercise leadership away from the constraints of the checks-and-balances straitjacket.

If presidents usually fail but sometimes succeed, we must try to understand under what conditions, with which skills, at which times, presidents are more or less likely to be successful. What factors lead to presidential success or failure? Why do so many leaders fail to govern well in the American political system? Having established the relative ineffectiveness of the modern presidents, we can now turn our attention to the reason why presidents so often fail.

For Discussion

1. The author attempts to make the case that the presidency, at least in the past forty years, has not lived up to our expectations or to the standards one many apply to a functional system of governance. Has the presidency really failed? Is the author being too harsh? Are you satisfied with the president's performance? Do you disagree with the author's conclusion about the modern presidency?
2. Are our expectations for the presidency too high? Are we being unrealistic in our hopes for presidential leadership?
3. Which president(s) do you most like? What is it about that president that makes him stand out in your eyes?
4. Growing up, what do you recall as your first memories of "the government"? Of the presidency?

Debate Questions

Divide the class into groups, of three to four people and use one class period to conduct a debate on one of the following questions:

I. *Resolved:* That the modern presidents should be considered failures.
II. *Resolved:* That questions of personal character and private behavior have no place in the presidential selection process.

CHAPTER 2
====

America's Leadership
Aversion System

It is no accident that in the United States, leaders usually can't lead. Presidents are often mere officeholders or clerks and only rarely leaders. In effect the deck is stacked against presidential leadership. The presidency is dealt a relatively weak power hand. How each president plays the hand he is dealt, how he uses his skills and opportunities, goes a long way in determining the success or failure of his administration. But *skill is not enough*. A variety of built-in roadblocks create an immunity system against leadership in all but the most extraordinary of times (i.e., crisis).

The power resources at a president's disposal, the ponderous and debilitating process of decision making, the obstructionist tendencies of the system, demand overload, and a host of other impediments make it especially difficult to galvanize the machinery of government into action. In terms of power resources, the presidency is rather anemic, and many initiatives get swallowed into the black hole of presidential weakness. And yet, the public expects, even *demands* that the president provide direction for the government. However, while demands are high, the powers to meet these expectations are very limited. Everywhere he turns (with the notable exceptions of crises and some areas of foreign policy), the president faces an array of obstacles in his path. If a president is to succeed, he must somehow find a way either to gain collaboration from the other elements of the separated government or else to try to impose his will on the system.

In the United States, the gap between the expectations and resources as well as the image and reality of power is enormous. In effect, there is a huge gap between what is expected of a president

47

and what he can realistically deliver. As a focus of national attention, the presidency truly is, in John Kennedy's words, the "vital center" of American government. But in *power* terms (the ability to get people to do something they wouldn't otherwise do), the presidency is only a *part* of the interconnected system of government; a part that must *share power* with other actors in the system.

This creates what Heclo and Salamon call "the illusion of presidential government." As Heclo writes, "Presidential government is an illusion—an illusion that misleads presidents no less than the media and the American public, an illusion that often brings about the destruction of the very men who hold the office."[1] Encasing the president is a web of restraints, a network of checks, which bind him and limit his power. Lyndon Johnson expressed the frustrations of office to his successor Richard Nixon thus:

> Before you get to be president you think you can do anything. You think you're the most powerful leader since God. But when you get in the tall chair, as you're gonna find out, Mr. President, you can't count on people. You'll find your hands tied and people cussin' you. The office is kinda like the little country boy who found the hoochie-koochie show at the carnival, once he'd paid his dime and got inside the tent: "It ain't exactly as it was advertised."[2]

Is the institution that seems so power*ful* really so power*less?* In some ways, yes. There are a number of obstacles that prevent presidents from being effective leaders. It should thus not be surprising that *most* presidents perform poorly most of the time. But why? What variables inhibit presidential performance? There are nine major factors that work against presidential power and effectiveness: (1) the Intent of the Framers; (2) the Structure of the American Government; (3) the Individual Skills of presidents; (4) America's Political Culture; (5) the Moods and Cycles of American Politics; (6) the Decline of Intermediaries; (7) Presidential Selection; (8) the "Market as Prison"; and (9) the Politics of Globalization. These factors can be reduced to three clusters of variables:

- *External* (1, Intent of Framers; 4, Political Culture; 5, Moods/Cycles; 8, Market as Prison; and 9, Politics of Globalization)

- *Process* (2, Structure of Government; 6, Decline of Intermediaries; and 7, Presidential Selection)
- *Individual* (3, Individual Skills of presidents)

These are the main barriers to presidential effectiveness, comprising an antileadership or leadership aversion system. They form the presidential fault line that can suddenly snap and leave the president buried in the earthquake. We now turn to an analysis of the elements along this fault line.

The Intent of the Framers

The Framers of the U.S. Constitution created—by design—an "antileadership" system of government. While on the surface this may sound bizarre, upon reflection, it is clear that their primary goal—rather than to provide for an especially efficient system—was to create a government that would not jeopardize liberty. Freedom was their goal: governmental power their nemesis. Thus the men who toiled on that hot summer of 1787 in Philadelphia created an executive institution, a presidency, that had *limited powers*.

Essentially, the Framers wanted to counteract two fears: the fear of the *mob* (democracy, or mobocracy) and the fear of the *monarchy* (centralized, tyrannical, executive power). In fact, the menacing image of England's King George III—against whom the colonists rebelled and whom Thomas Paine called "the Royal Brute of Britain"—served the Framers as a powerful reminder of the dangers of a strong executive. Thus, to contain power, they set up an executive office that was constitutionally rather *weak* (Congress had—on paper at least—most of the power), dependent on the *rule of law*, with a *separation of powers* in order to ensure a system of *checks and balances*.

For James Madison, the chief architect of the Constitution, a government with too much power was a dangerous government. Seeing himself as a keen student of history, he believed that human nature drove men—at this time, only men were allowed to enter the public arena—to pursue self-interest, and therefore a system of government designed to have "ambition checked by ambition" set within rather strict limits was the only hope to establish a stable government that did not endanger liberty. Realizing that "enlightened statesmen" would not always guide the nation, Madison embraced a check-and-balance system of separate but overlapping and shared powers. Madison's concern to have a government with controlled and limited powers is seen throughout his writings, but nowhere is it more vivid than when he wrote in *Federalist* 51, "You must first enable the government to control the governed; and in the next place, oblige it to control itself."[3]

Yes, government had to have enough power to govern, but no, it could not have enough power to overwhelm liberty. If one branch could check another, tyranny might be thwarted. In Madison's writings there is scant concern expressed for the needs of a *strong* government. Thus the Constitution became both an enabling *and* a disabling document.

To counter Madison, Alexander Hamilton emerged as the great defender of executive power. An advocate of strong central government, Hamilton promoted, especially in the *Federalist Papers*, a version of executive power quite different from Madison's dispersed and separate powers. Where Madison believed that the new government's powers should be "few and defined," Hamilton wanted to infuse the executive with "energy."[4] Hamilton advocated vigorous government and a strong presidency. As Hamilton wrote in *Federalist* 70, good government requires "energy," and he scornfully rejected the weak executive:

> A feeble executive implies a feeble execution of the government. A feeble execution is but another phrase for a bad execution; and a government ill executed, whatever it may be in theory, must be, in practice, a bad government.

Hamilton sought a strong president within a more centralized government. But such a system would undermine Madison's determination to check government power. The presidency, a unitary office headed by one man, would have no *internal* check. Thus, to Madison, there was the need for strong *external* checks—that is, a strong Congress. While Madison may have won the day at the Constitutional Convention, creating a presidency with fairly limited powers, history has been on the side of Hamilton, as the presidency has grown to resemble the Hamiltonian model more than was originally intended by the Framers.

'Okay, bring in the new guy ...'

Always looming in the background—quite literally, as he was in France at the time of the Philadelphia Constitutional Convention—was the enormous presence of Thomas Jefferson. An advocate of small government and democracy, Jefferson was very suspicious of power (his behavior as president aside). But Jefferson's vision of a decentralized government, an agrarian economy, and a robust democracy was given little attention at the Convention. It was a Madisonian model that emerged.

Madison, like most of the Founders, feared government in the hands of the people, but he likewise feared too much power in the hands of one man. Therefore, the Madisonian model called both for protections against mass democracy *and* limits on governmental power. This is not to say that the Founders wanted a weak and ineffective government; had that been their goal, they could have kept the Articles of Confederation. But they did want a government that could not easily act. The theory of government that the Madisonian design necessitates is one of consensus, coalition, and cooperation—on the one hand—and checks, vetoes, and balances on the other.

A rough balance was sought between governmental power and individual liberty. The government had to be strong enough to act but restrained enough so as not to threaten liberty. By separating powers, forcing institutions to share powers, and limiting powers via the rule of law, the Founders hoped both to allow power (ambition) to counter power and to decrease the opportunity for powers to be abused. Since the people could not be trusted to govern, and since as Madison wrote in *Federalist* 10, "Enlightened statesmen will not always be at the helm," power had to be fragmented and dispersed.

The result was that when left strictly to its own devices, the presidency became a rather weak institution. A dilemma was thus created, especially in the modern period: How could a president bring Hamiltonian energy, to this Madisonian system, for Jeffersonian ends? The Framers did not make it easy for the government to act or for presidents to lead—that was decidedly not their intent—and they left the powers and contours of the office somewhat vague, expecting George Washington to fill in the gaps. This created, in Edward S. Corwin's words, "an invitation to struggle" for control of government.[5] Looking at the Framers' design for government, a modern efficiency expert would likely conclude that the system could not work very well: too many limits, too many checks; not enough power, not enough leadership. But that is the way the Framers wanted it.

The Structure of American Government

What exactly did the Framers create? What structure or skeleton of power and government did the Founders of the U.S. system design? The chief mechanisms they established to control as well as to empower the executive (mentioned briefly in the previous section) are as follows: (1) *Limited Government*, a reaction against the arbitrary, expansive powers of the king or state, and a protection of personal liberty; (2) *Rule of Law*, so that only on the basis of legal or constitutional grounds could the government act; (3) *Separation of Powers*, so that the three branches of government each would have a defined sphere of power; and (4) *Checks and Balances*, so that each branch could limit or control the powers of the other branches of government.

In this structure, what powers and resources does the president have? Limited powers. Constitutionally, the United States faces a paradox: the Constitution both empowers and restrains government. In fact, the Constitution does not clearly spell out the power of the presidency. Article I is devoted to the Congress, the first and constitutionally the most powerful branch of government. Article 2, the executive article, deals with the presidency. The president's power cupboard is—compared to that of the Congress—nearly bare. Section 1 gives the "executive power" to the president but does not reveal whether this is a grant of tangible power or merely a title. Section 2 also gives the president absolute power to grant reprieves and pardons, power to make treaties (with the advice and consent of the Senate), and the power to nominate ambassadors, judges, and other public ministers (with the advice and consent of the Senate). Section 3 calls for the president to inform the Congress on the state of the Union and to recommend measures to Congress; grants the power to receive ambassadors; and imposes upon the president the duty to see that the laws are faithfully executed. These powers are significant, but in and of themselves they do not suggest a very strong or independent institution, and certainly not a national leadership position.

The Framers were clearly pulled in two different directions when inventing the president.[6] They wanted to give the executive enough "energy" to act and yet not enough to endanger liberty or promote tyranny. But, as political scientist Lyn Ragsdale notes, "Energy and safety are contradictory requirements."[7]

Thus the president has two types of power: *formal*, the ability to command, and *informal*, the ability to persuade. The president's formal powers are limited and (often) shared. The president's informal powers are a function of skill, situation, and political time (there is more about the president's power in Chapter 3). While the formal power of the president remains fairly constant over time, the president's informal powers are quite variable, dependent largely on the skill of each individual president. This is not to suggest that the president's formal powers are static—over time, presidential power has increased significantly—but the pace of change has been such that it was well over a hundred years before the presidency assumed primacy in the U.S. political system.

How much power does the president possess? Who governs in America? Political scientist Bert Rockman addresses this question:

Precisely where does this situate the presidency? The president is, after all, not the leader of "a government" but a leader who heads only a part of the government—a chief of state in a society whose culture resists the idea (but only the idea) of the state. The American form of government handicaps ambition in the White House, and presidential success in accomplishing objectives hinges upon support generated across other institutions. . . .The power to govern could never be assumed. It would always have to be struggled for in an environment of interdependence— the direct result of Madison's triumph, and the indirect result of Jefferson's conquest of the American political spirit.[8]

The president has few independent powers, many shared powers. Most are shared with a Congress that has greater enumerated constitutional powers but less of an institutional capacity to act. Sharing powers with a Congress that only occasionally responds to presidential initiatives makes leadership a hazardous minefield.

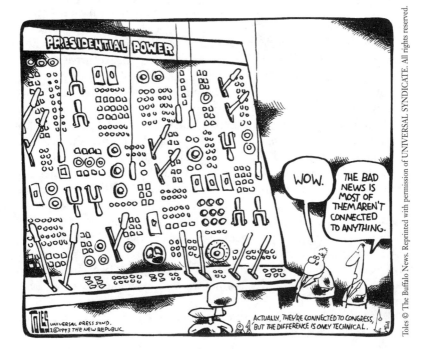

The constitutional structure of the government *disperses* or *fragments* power: with no recognized, authoritative vital center, power is fluid and floating; no one branch can very easily or freely act without the consent (formal or tacit) of another branch. Power was designed to counteract power; ambition to check ambition. This structure was developed by men whose memories of tyranny and the arbitrary exercise of power by the king of England was fresh in their minds. It was a structure designed to force a consensus before the government could act. The structure of government established by the Framers created not a single leadership institution but several— three separate, semiautonomous institutions that shared power. As James Pfiffner notes, "The Framers designed a system of shared powers within a system that is purposefully biased against change."[9] The forces of the status quo were given multiple veto opportunities; the forces of change were forced to go into battle nearly unarmed.

Because there are so many potential veto points, the American system generally alternates between stasis and crisis, paralysis and spasm. On occasion, the branches are able to cooperate and work together to promote change, but it is especially difficult for the president and Congress deliberately disconnected by the Framers—to forge a union. The resulting paralysis has many parents, but the separation of powers is clearly the most determinative.

The Framers purposely created uncertainty about who holds power in the United States. A system of baroque cross-powers and checked powers created a constitutional mechanism that prohibits one branch from exercising too much power on its own. Opportunities to check power abound; opportunities to exercise power are limited. Bert Rockman offers this reminder:

> The architect designed many doors, each seemingly with a different lock. In normal times there would be more locks than keys. Without the intervention of war (and, since Korea, even then) or the appearance of crisis, or the preponderance of like-minded majorities, the independence of institutions so greatly valued by Madison is conducive to the grinding, rather than the meshing, of gears. . . .What emerges is not "a government," but many, often competitive and sometimes cooperative, governments; not a decisive point of decision making at the center, but a diffusion of decisional points; and not a state presumably representing

a "common and durable interest," but a society whose abundant pluralism finds ready expression through the many conduits available in the polity.[10]

Again, this system of separation of powers was designated to thwart tyranny, not to promote efficiency. By its own standards, it has worked quite well. But the natural lethargy built into the system now threatens to grind it to a halt. The failure of government to govern, to act, to solve problems, now seems so overpowering that the fundamental legitimacy of the system is increasingly threatened.

Presidential leadership of Congress is further complicated by the persistence of divided government, in which, often, one party controls the White House while another party controls the Congress. As if presidents needed more reason to feel frustrated, the modern period has been one of divided government, with the "Republicanization of the presidency" and the "Democratization of the Congress," followed by gnawing splits in party control of Congress and the White House. It is no accident that, from 1968 to 1992, the persistence of divided government—the Carter presidency (1977–1981) being the exception—has corresponded with periods of failed leadership.[11] Divided government makes the already fragmented system of government divisive, and thus it is less likely to produce the cohesion and cooperation necessary for the branches to work together.

This fluidity and fragmentation of power creates a situation in which "the government" is controlled not by any single person or place or party but by different people in different places (if it exists at all) seeking different ends. Although noting that there is, in a technical sense, "a government," Rockman comes to this conclusion:

> There is no unified government, no government of the day in the modern sense of that term. Instead, the design of the separation of powers system is predicated on the view expressed by Madison in *Federalist* 51 that such a system is essential for the maintenance of liberty. . . .The result is a government founded on defensiveness. Each of its parts can be assertive, but the assertiveness of the parts makes for an unassertiveness of the whole. . . . In short, the system of separated powers was (and largely remains) an institutional design meant to frustrate the exercise of power. This is so because American institutions do not so much divide powers as they divide power. In Samuel Huntington's well-turned sentence,

"America perpetuated a fusion of functions and a division of power, while Europe developed a differentiation of functions and a centralization of power." Clearly, whatever the virtues of these antique institutions, their strong suit is not the efficient direction of an active government.[12]

The structure of government is thus stacked against presidential leadership. The result is that in all but the most unusual of circumstances, institutional impotence characterizes the American presidency. The amazing thing, then, is not that presidents usually fail—that is built into the very structure of American government—but that presidents sometimes succeed! (See Chapter 3.) With so much working against them, it should not surprise us when presidents stumble and fall.

Individual Skills

Politics is far more complicated than physics.

—ALBERT EINSTEIN

A number of presidential scholars argue that "if we could only get the *right person* in the White House, most of our problems would evaporate." Historian Arthur Schlesinger, Jr., challenges the structuralists, who argue that the separation of powers inhibits strong leadership, and insists that skilled presidents have been able to overcome structural roadblocks. He writes:

> Is the difficulty we encounter these days in meeting our problems really the consequence of defects in the structure of our government? After all, we have had the separation of powers from the beginning of the republic. This has not prevented competent presidents from acting with decision and dispatch. The separation of powers did not notably disable Jefferson or Jackson or Lincoln or Wilson or the Roosevelts. . . . The real difference is that the presidents who operated the system successfully knew what they thought should be done—and were able to persuade Congress and the nation to give their remedies a try. . . . Our problem is not at all that we know what to do and are impeded from doing it by some structural logjam in the system. Our problem—let us face it—is that we don't know what to do.[13]

While there is some merit to this argument—yes, skill does matter—it only tackles part of the problem of weak leadership. Skill is of great importance, but it is not enough. Getting better leaders would help, but it would not solve the leadership void in American government.

One would be hard-pressed to defend the job performance of individuals who have served as presidents in the modern period. As Chapter 1 suggests, the United States has had, for a third of a century, a series of presidents who simply were not up to the task of governing. Johnson, with flawed character; Nixon, with deeply flawed character; Ford, decent but inept; Carter, decent but politically naive; Reagan, amiable but limited; Bush, the visionless manager, and Clinton, with flawed character—all seemed to wrest political defeat from the jaws of victory.

The Search for a Savior as president overemphasizes the personal and underemphasizes the institutional. Much more is at work here than skill. As this study indicates, more is at fault than individual failings—as significant as they may be. True, recent presidents have not been an especially distinguished lot, but the fault is only partially theirs. Skilled leaders *could have* done better, but even with a greater reservoir of skill, there are roadblocks and hurdles that all presidents face, which make it very difficult to lead. When one combines limited skill with these other inhibitors, the result is failed leadership.

Presidential scholars agree that skill is important, but how important? Under what circumstances? No scholar is more identified with the skill argument than Richard Neustadt. His 1960 book *Presidential Power* is still considered one of the most important and useful books ever written about presidential politics.[14] Neustadt recognizes that the system or structure of the American system is designed to frustrate presidential leadership, and he argues that to overcome these roadblocks, presidents must make optimal use of their *informal* power resources: skill, prestige, reputation. Only then can presidents solve the "power problem" of the American system of government.

To have any hope of being successful in an antileadership system, presidents must employ a vast repertoire of skills and experiences: managerial skill, political skill, political experience, personal style, psychological traits, and so forth. Not all presidents have all the skills necessary to overcome the systemic roadblocks they face, but the wise presidents who lack skills *can* use their staffs and cabinet to compensate (there is more on the use of skill in Chapter 3).

If the presidency requires a leader with the skill level of an FDR, a crisis such as the Great Depression, and a huge legislative majority in order to govern, then the institution itself is deeply flawed. Even FDR, the very model of presidential skill, needed a crisis and vast congressional majority to lead. But not all presidents are FDR, and of late, the American voter seems intent on electing inexperienced outsiders to the White House (often with damaging consequences). Four of the past five presidents had *no* Washington experience, nor did they have any foreign policy experience. Is it any wonder that recent presidents have made a tough job all that much more difficult?

America's Political Culture

Are the citizens of the United States culturally inclined toward good citizenship/followership? The answer to this question is very much a mixed bag. What does it take to be a good citizen/follower?

The emergence of leaders within a group is both inevitable and necessary. However, leadership is but one side of the coin. For, if we are to have good leadership, we must also have good followership. Leadership matters, but what is leadership without followership? The general would be nothing without well-trained troops; the plant manager would be incapacitated without good workers; and, yes, the college president would be nothing without a highly professional faculty. As James M. Burns notes, "Great leaders require great followers."[15]

But what do we mean by followers? Lemmings following the leader off the cliff? Obedient, submissive, order-following conformists? Hardly. John Gardner notes that twentieth-century institutions have been caught in a savage crossfire between "uncritical lovers and unloving critics." Gardner goes on to remind us that love without criticism brings stagnation, and criticism without love brings destruction.[16] Today, as public outrage alternates with disgust and apathy, what can we expect of citizens?

What do we mean when we refer to good followership? There are five key tasks in followership: (1) *commitment:* support for the goals and values of the community; (2) *idea generation:* creative problem-solving and the percolation of ideas and pressure up to the top (what Tom Cronin calls Act 1 leadership); (3) *competence:* a degree of professionalism and skill; (4) *informed criticism:* knowledge matched with the ability to disagree agreeably; and (5) *self-management:* self-reliance, independence, and self-control.

How do leadership and followership fit together? What is needed? Equally—in government, business and the workplace, the university and the community—we need a shared commitment and shared responsibility to the shared destiny of the organization: a sense of *community.* Leadership is a collective enterprise, as is followership. Both must focus on developing a sense in which all rise and fall together.

Culturally, does the United States foster values and attitudes that promote a healthy sense of followership/citizenship for a democratic political system? By *culture* we mean those ideas and values, norms and symbols that comprise the American identity. The key components of America's political culture include a commitment to democracy (an open, egalitarian political system); liberty (get or keep the government off my back); and a competitive culture (which often sets citizen off against citizen) in a capitalist economic system (which is competitive) with an emphasis on materialism (in which accumulation and consumption loom large). These prevailing attitudes are set within a legalistic framework (which is adversarial in nature) with a strong commitment to the Judeo-Christian ethos (Americans have a comparatively high identification with organized religions) in a culture of individualism (in which the self is elevated over the group). The combination of these factors comprises what is often anti-authority in nature. The governing ethos in America thus imposes a series of restraints on the exercise of leadership. Clinton Rossiter clearly captures this dilemma:

> We have always been a nation obsessed with liberty. Liberty over authority, freedom over responsibility, rights over duties—these are our historical preferences. . . .Not the good man, but the free man has been the measure of all things in this "sweet land of liberty"; not national

glory, but individual liberty has been the object of political authority and the test of its worth.[17]

The combinations of these conflicting values often pull the public in different directions and are sometimes quite contradictory. For example, the commitments to individualism, competitiveness, and materialism make the average citizen ambitious, results-oriented, and productive. These same attributes also make the average citizen highly independent—which in turn works to make most Americans resistant to authority, suspicious of community, reluctant to solve problems as a group. Thus "politics" becomes a four-letter word, and followership becomes problematic: an antileadership culture.

How does this American Creed affect our attitudes toward leadership? While it creates a fundamentally antileadership disposition, the American propensity for individualism does generate a type of hero worship that feeds into the heroic model of the presidency. We thus honor the patriot Washington; the great democrats Jefferson and Jackson; the savior Lincoln; and the great leader FDR. But such hero worship masks, in some ways, the stronger cultural pull, which is antileadership and antiauthority. Thomas E. Cronin makes this observation:

> The paradoxes of the presidency do not lie in the White House but in the emotions, feelings, and expectations of us all. There exists some element in the American mind, and perhaps in the minds of people everywhere, that it is possible to find a savior-hero who will deliver us to an era of greener grass and a land of milk and honey. When this pseudomessiah fails, we inflict upon him the wrath of our vengeance. It is almost a ritual destruction; we venerate the presidency, but we destroy our presidents.[18]

In general, it is the antiauthority strain of the American Creed that has dominated in our culture. Max Lerner has written that "American thinkers have been at their best in their antiauthoritarianism."[19] From Jefferson and Madison to Calhoun and Thoreau, some of America's most profound and influential thinkers reflected deep strains of individualism and antiauthoritarianism. The implications of this for leadership were not lost on that thoughtful French observer of the American scene, Alexis de Tocqueville:

When it comes to the influence of one man's mind over another's, that is necessarily very restricted in a country where the citizens have all become more or less similar. . . .And since they do not recognize any signs of incontestable greatness or superiority in any of their fellows, are continually brought back to their own judgment as the mot apparent and accessible test of truth. So it is not only confidence in any particular man which is destroyed. There is a general distaste for accepting any man's word as proof of anything.[20]

It is very difficult (except in a crisis) for presidents to ask the people to make sacrifices for the common good, to move beyond self-interest. Indeed, in the post–September 11 period, President Bush was afraid to ask for sacrifices from the public and thus recklessly promoted an expensive war against terrorism *and* a huge tax cut! When Jimmy Carter asked citizens to turn their thermostats down to 68 degrees Fahrenheit (20 degrees Celsius) during the oil crisis, he was scorned. It should not be a surprise that when he ran for reelection he lost to a candidate with a spend-spend, buy-buy philosophy.

The United States lacks a coherent *public philosophy* of the role and purpose of government. Americans have always been a bit ambivalent regarding power and government, suspicious of authority (which is in many ways quite healthy in a democracy, but it also makes governing quite difficult).

A major shortcoming of this lack of a public philosophy is the lack of consensus as to what we as a people should do, where we as a nation need to move. As French sociologist Michael Crozier has written, we have "the land of consensus turned into the land of disorder and tumult."[21]

The sense of shared community, of a social contract, remains murky. We are not "one nation indivisible" but a collection of atomized individuals. Rarely do we pull together for the common good. Are we a "nation," a loose-knit collection of individuals, or a confederation of tribes?[22]

Effective leadership requires a supporting consensus behind governmental authority and presidential initiatives. Both are currently lacking. Disharmony and conflict characterize the American polity. A divided nation, a polarized nation, cannot be a well-governed nation. "Where did we go wrong?" asks leadership expert Warren Bennis. "America has always been at war with itself. We have always dreamt of community and democracy but always practiced individualism and capitalism. We have celebrated innocence but sought power. We are the world's leading sentimentalists, and it's a very short step from sentimentality to cynicism."[23]

While Americans demonstrate a high degree of patriotic fervor, as the aftermath of the 9/11 terrorist attack indicates, they do not demonstrate a deep sense of *community*, except in a crisis. From a strong commitment to community, one can elicit a *consensus* upon which to build *leadership*. Lacking a strong sense of community, leaders have a difficult time pulling the nation together (except in a crisis) to respond collectively, politically, as a nation. It is very hard to mobilize the people to pursue a public good. The major roadblock to building community is the powerful strain of *individualism* that dominates the attitudes of citizens of the United States. "We are," writes political scientist David F. Schuman, "a nation of Ones, and the political consequences are powerful."[24]

Samuel Huntington argues that American political culture is characterized by an "antipower ethic" dominated by belief in equality, liberty, individualism, and democracy, all of which are "antigovernment and antiauthority in character."[25] James Madison's vision—grounded in a pessimistic view of human nature—was that the problem of factions was "sown into the nature of man," and this necessitated limits and controls on power.[26] We could not be trusted to act together (democracy); we were too self-interested to be left entirely to our own devices. Thus was created a strictly limited government, which was designed to structure conflict, to set interest off against interest, and to embrace a strictly individualistic view. This view did not eliminate politics or collective action, but it did set as the premise of government, *individuals* acting out of their own self-interest, alone, not in concert. Thus being a leader in the United States is somewhat akin to trying to herd cats.

The Moods and Cycles of American Politics

Leadership does not occur in a time warp. There are different "seasons" of leadership, times when presidents are afforded more or less room for power.[27]

The most obvious cycle is the Normal vs. Crisis context. In normal or routine times, the separation of powers system sets a context for leadership that narrows or limits the president's range of power. In a crisis, such as a world war or the aftermath of the September 11 terrorist attacks, the expected checks and balances will for the most part dissolve, and the president assumes significant extraconstitutional powers. But there are other cycles as well. These cycles (what some might call a dialectic) take many forms: the business cycle of economic growth followed by recession; the political pendulum of liberalism followed by a conservative period; the mood swing of public confidence in government followed by a retreat into private interests and cynicism; the foreign policy shifts from isolationism to international involvement. These cycles are, for the most part, beyond the control of presidents, but they do have a great impact on presidential power. Bert Rockman, explains the situation this way:

> The culture of American politics and the structure of American government each predispose against the prospects for achieving and then sustaining coherent direction. To be sure, the obstacles for achieving direction are not all times equally severe. Opportunities for direction are not at all times equally severe. Opportunities for directive leadership ebb and flow, the product of cycles of longer and shorter duration. Within these cycles are phases during which some of the normal constraints on leadership are relaxed, and, of course, times during which these constraints become more inhibiting.[28]

There are times when (and conditions under which) presidents are afforded a great deal of leverage and power (e.g., crisis). There are also times when presidents are kept on a fairly short leash (a weak economy, low presidential popularity, etc.).

For example, in the aftermath of the war in Vietnam and Watergate, the public turned against the government and presidential power, and the United States entered a president-bashing mood. Presidents Ford and Carter were severely restricted in their opportunities to exercise leadership. The public was cynical and suspicious, the press was hostile, the Congress was reasserting its authority, and—if that weren't enough—the economy was in a free fall. Even if Ford and Carter had been highly skilled, gifted politicians (which they were not), their level of political opportunity was so low that there is almost no way they could have been very successful.

By contrast, FDR, a highly skilled politician, also benefited from a level of opportunity that was unusually high. He came to office in 1933, a time when the public *demanded* strong leadership, when the Congress was willing to accede power to the president. Thus the mixture of high skill and high opportunity granted FDR both power and success.

Political time is of importance.[29] During periods of regime change and social disruption, certain types of leadership will be more necessary, while during periods of normalcy, a different type of leadership may be required. Likewise, during periods of crisis,[30] a different sort of leadership is required. Clearly, there is not a leadership for all seasons. Effective leaders are able to adjust to these different seasons; they style-flex.

Several cycles are especially relevant to presidential leadership. One is the *succession cycle*. Valerie Bunce notes that major policy shifts are *most likely* when new leaders take over.[31] Thus leadership change is the key to policy change. There is also the cycle of *decreasing popularity*. In general, over time, presidents lose popular support, making it more difficult to put together political coalitions as time progresses. Yet another presidential cycle is the *cycle of growing effectiveness*.[32] The presidential *learning curve* is at its lowest at the beginning of a president's term and rises as time goes by. Thus presidents know more and more as time goes by. But their power is usually at its peak early in their terms, just when their knowledge is lowest. When presidents have the most power, they usually have the least knowledge.

In a broader sense, the cycle that seems most relevant to presidential leadership is the long-term ebb and flow, or pulse rate, of American politics. Historian Arthur M. Schlesinger, Jr., suggests that this cycle is like a pendulum swinging back and forth. The United States alternates between periods of "conservatism versus innovation" (Emerson); "diffusion versus centralization" (Henry Adams); "conservatism versus liberalism (Arthur Schlesinger, Jr.); "divergent goals of public and private happiness" (Herbert McClosky and John Zaller). Schlesinger describes these moods swings or cycles as "a continuing shift in national involvement, between *public purpose* and *private interest*."[33]

Schlesinger argues that the roots of this repeating cycle lie deep in human nature and the U.S. structure of government, and the pattern follows a life cycle of a thirty-year alternation between the pursuit of public purpose and private interest. In the twentieth century, there were three periods of high governmental activity in support of public purpose: (1) Theodore Roosevelt in 1901; (2) Franklin D. Roosevelt in 1933; and (3) John F. Kennedy in 1961. There have also been "high tides of conservative restoration—the 1920s, the 1950s, the 1980s."[34]

Thus the pulse of political change beats to an alternating, thirty-year pattern of high public purpose followed by high private interest. Erwin C. Hargrove adds to our understanding of leadership's impact on political change by focusing attention on the "cycles of the rise and fall of reform politics."[35] Hargrove sees a three-stage cycle of political reform: (1) "a period of preparation"; (2) "a burst of activism and reform"; and (3) "a time of reaction against the previous stage and therefore of consolidation and conservation."[36] Hargrove's three stages (Table 2.1) fit neatly into Schlesinger's cycles of change, giving a more coherent framework to the role of presidential leadership in these change cycles.

There is a certain logic to this pace of political activity. Rather than running at a steady pace, political change in the United States resembles a sprinter more than a distance runner. There is a short, quick burst of activity (Hargrove's stage 2), followed by a much needed rest (stage 3), at which time the reforms of the period of accelerated activism are consolidated into the system, and the public

Table 2.1   Twentieth-Century Presidential Cycles

1. Preparation	2. Activism and Reform	3. Consolidation
Theodore Roosevelt William Howard Taft	Woodrow Wilson	Warren Harding Calvin Coolidge Herbert Hoover
(Depression)	Franklin Roosevelt Harry Truman	Dwight Eisenhower
John F. Kennedy	Lyndon Johnson	Richard Nixon

Source: Erwin C. Hargrove, *The Power of the Modern Presidency* (New York: Knopf, 1974), p. 186.

has a chance to rest and recharge its batteries. But old problems persist, new ones emerge, and before long, there is a demand for change (stage 1). This leads to another burst of activity (stage 2), and the cycle repeats.

Thomas E. Cronin gives us a deeper insight into the connection between points in the cycle of change and the various types of leadership that are appropriate for different times and situations. Cronin sees leadership as evolving in three stages or acts, depending on the point in political time. These "acts" correspond to the Schlesinger and Hargrove cycles. In Act 1 (Hargrove's period of consolidation), because the public mood is more focused on private interest than public purpose (to use Schlesinger's terminology), "leaders are dreamers, visionaries, or creative catalysts."[37] In this stage, the down period of public activism, the "leader" is the (not so) average citizen who pushes, prods, creates new programs. Those to whom we conventionally look for leadership—officeholders—act as cautious consolidators, not creative risk-takers. Therefore, the responsibility to lead rests on the shoulders of the public.

Act 2 (Hargrove's period of preparation) finds an increased level of activity, but officeholders still display caution. As Cronin writes, "Act 2 leaders understand that no truly bold measure begins at the top. . . .Act 2 leaders willingly enlarge and amplify conflict. . . ."[38] Here, the public agenda shifts to a recognition of public problems and the public begins to demand a governmental response.

By the time the cycle shifts to Hargrove's reform period, officeholders become more active, the public demands reform, and in Act 3, the "mainstream establishment" embraces political change, and officeholders actively pursue a reform agenda. This is the height of Schlesinger's period of public purpose.

Cronin's work shifts attention away from the officeholder as leader to the citizen as leader, what might be called a "shared leadership model." By recognizing the important role played by the public in political leadership, and by discriminating between the different types of leadership in operation at different times in the political cycle of change, Cronin broadens our understanding of the connection between leadership, citizenship, political change, and political time.

Finally, James M. Burns provides us with the final piece of our puzzle of leadership, citizenship, and political change with his distinction between *transactional* and *transforming* leadership.[39] Burns sees transactional leadership as an exchange, a bargaining model. It is incremental in scope and narrow in range. Transforming leadership is more inspirational and nonincremental. It links leader and citizen together. This leadership taps something deep and fundamental in the people and is able to transform the political system. Transactional leadership generally corresponds to Schlesinger's down cycle, Hargrove's stage 1. Transforming leadership usually corresponds to the up stage of the cycle, Hargrove's achievement of reform. In the down period, a political leader's window of opportunity to act is fairly narrow. Thus transactional leadership usually fits this time frame. In an up cycle, the window of opportunity is fairly wide and the possibility of achieving transformational leadership exists.

How do all of these pieces fit together? In Figure 2.1, I attempt to display how each scholar's ideas fit into this framework of leadership, citizenship, and political change. Schlesinger depicts a rollercoaster ride of dramatic swings in political reform, with shifts between a public purpose and private interests. By adding Hargrove's three cycles, a certain logic emerges. Down periods allow for consolidation, absorption, conservation; the system can rest. But as

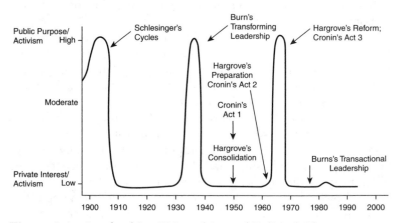

Figure 2.1   Leadership, Citizenship, and Political Change.

problems build, preparation for reform takes place. Then, in a dramatic burst of political energy, reforms are achieved. Burns sees this shift as the distinction between transactional leadership (the down cycle, a period of consolidation) and transforming leadership (sometimes achieved in the up cycle, a time of reform). Cronin draws our attention to the role played by the public in these cycles, with Cronin identifying the "leadership" role played by "followers" in the down period of the cycle (Act 1) and the leadership role played by officeholders in the up period of the cycle (Act 3).

By viewing political change as a symbiotic connection between leader (officeholder) and follower (citizen) at different points in time, we can broaden our horizons to the complex and interconnected nature of political change in a democracy. Leaders don't always lead; followers don't always follow. Different points in political time require different types of political leadership and a different set of political skills.

The Decline of Intermediaries

To move the machinery of government, presidents need help. They can only rarely act alone. Thus presidents need mechanisms to grease the governmental wheels.

In the past, presidents have occasionally been able to rely on such things as a consensus among leaders and the public regarding the direction in which the nation should go, or on strong congressional leaders to move the president's program At other times, presidents have been able to rely on party support to help get legislation through Congress. But consensus has degenerated into dissensus, congressional leadership has been disarmed, and the party system in the United States is relatively weak and nonideological (especially when compared with European counterparts). Even as party voting has become more pronounced and polarized in Congress, the roots of the political parties are severing. In recent years, the parties have further weakened, stripping presidents of a traditional tool in the struggle for power.[40]

When there is a general agreement on where the nation should go and how it should get there, when there is a consensus, it becomes easier to lead the government into action. But rarely can presidents rely on a consensus. Sometimes presidents can help create a consensus by focusing attention on particular issues, but even that is a relatively rare occurrence.

If presidents can only rarely rely on a consensus to aid in governing, can they at least rely on congressional leaders to guide their programs through congress? Stories of Lyndon Johnson's calling a few congressional leaders into the Oval Office for a late night chat and a few drinks—followed by Johnson's getting the congressional leaders to "deliver the votes" on a key issue—may be apocryphal, but they point to the potential (if not the ideal) of the president being able to use congressional leaders as intermediaries.

Congressional leaders can create a linkage between the separated president and Congress. But even when the president has a Congress controlled by his own party, he cannot rely on the leadership to deliver votes. This is because the leaders do not control the votes of the members. Members of Congress are more independent and entrepreneurial than in past years. The dramatic changes in Congress since the 1970s have opened up the process and have made it more democratic but less hierarchical and amenable to leadership. Thus presidents must work harder to get less from Congress.

The political party *can*, at its best, focus issues and public opinion, organize the masses, cue voters, offer candidates, develop programs, lend organization and unity to the dispersed power arena, and lubricate the machinery of government. And most political scientists continue to agree with James MacGregor Burns's assertion that parties are "indispensable to democratic leadership."[41] Though Thomas Jefferson once noted, "If I could not go to heaven with a party, I would not go there at all,"[42] in historical terms, parties have sometimes served as a great aid in a president's pursuit of policy goals.

But the modern parties, while making attempts to serve these functions, are often seen as weak and inadequate, unable to fulfill these roles. Political parties have become much less important in developing the coalitions necessary to organize power and move government.[43] Instead of having reliable party coalitions or strong congressional leadership from which to operate, presidents are forced to develop their own ad hoc coalitions, using the media and "going public,"[44] directly addressing the people in a game of plebiscitary politics.[45] As the bond of party has proved inadequate to meet presidential needs, presidents have developed adapting strategies, primarily using the media or administrative discretion but also acting on their own or acting in secret.

Thus, for presidents to govern, they must constantly campaign (a time-consuming and demanding task). To get elected, presidents must put together an *electoral coalition*, but to rule, presidents need a *governing coalition* (i.e., party support).[46] But without an adequate party system or strong leadership in Congress, presidents must perpetually "campaign," constantly play the popularity game, and always act like a candidate. This tends to trivialize politics and leaves precious little time for governing. In order to govern, presidents need help, and at various times in the past they could rely on intermediaries to provide it. Now they get less and less of this assistance and are thus left politically alone and vulnerable.

Presidential Selection

In many ways, the U.S. presidential selection process is proof that Darwin's theory about the survival of the fittest was wrong! Could it really be argued that the "fittest" candidates are to be found in the list of recent choices for president? (See Table 2.2)

Table 2.2   Recent Presidential Candidates

Year	Democrat	Republican
1964	Lyndon Johnson	Barry Goldwater
1968	Hubert Humphrey	Richard Nixon
1972	George McGovern	Richard Nixon
1976	Jimmy Carter	Gerald Ford
1980	Jimmy Carter	Ronald Reagan
1984	Walter Mondale	Ronald Reagan
1988	Michael Dukakis	George Bush
1992	Bill Clinton	George Bush
1996	Bill Clinton	Bob Dole
2000	Al Gore	George W. Bush

Burns calls the presidential selection process "the worst top leadership recruitment system in the democratic societies of the world."[47] Campaigns are long, lasting nearly three years (Rockman refers to the process as the "endless campaign"), costly, media driven, grueling, disruptive and intrusive on family life, trivial, overly personal, and often demeaning. Would anyone worthy of the office seek it?[48]

In the founding period, the nascent nation produced an array of leaders and statesmen of stunning quality: Washington, Jefferson, Madison, Hamilton, Franklin, Adams, and Paine, among others. In one generation, nearly a dozen truly outstanding men emerged. Today, the candidates seem like intellectual and moral dwarfs when compared to their forefathers. Is it that America has no great men or women left?

Rather than the assumption that the United States has no leaders capable of greatness, a more likely prospect is that the selection process tends to reward people with attributes that would generally be thought of as unwanted, and it tends to punish potential candidates who possess the qualities most desirable in a president.

Running for president is a three-year, full-time job. Shortly after the 2000 race ended, the 2004 presidential race began.[49] Who could, who would spend all that time running for president? Likewise, the need to attract campaign contributions serves as one of the keys to being pronounced—by the "Great Mentioner" (the opinion-making elite)—a viable candidate. Hubert Humphrey, no stranger to campaign financing, said the following concerning the need to beg for money during a campaign:

> Campaign financing is a curse. It's the most disgusting, demeaning, disenchanting, debilitating experience of a politician's life. It's stinky, it's lousy. I just can't tell you how much I hate it. I've had to break off in the middle of trying to make a decent, honorable campaign and go up to somebody's parlour or to a room and say, "Gentlemen, and ladies, I'm desperate. You gotta help me. . . ." And most likely one of them is in trouble and is somebody you shouldn't have had a contribution from.[50]

Finally, the hoops we make candidates jump through may not be functional, and they certainly aren't a very dignified way to select the leader of the free world. The selection process may appear to be a survival of the fittest contest, but it is really a personality and money-collecting contest, in which the skills needed to govern are rarely tested. Of course, the ultimate test of a selection process is the type of president who emerges from this system. In recent years the new president has tended to be inexperienced in, unprepared for, and incapable of governing at the top level.

The Market as a Prison

Presidential politics operates within an economic framework of corporate capitalism. How does this reality shape and influence presidential behavior?

Two major functions of the modern capitalist state are (1) the stimulation of material accumulation and (2) the legitimization of the social order. The first function derives from the fact that the state is ultimately held responsible for meeting the material needs of the society; thus, at least in some minimal terms, economic deterioration is blamed on the presidents. But in this regard the capitalist state is "weak," in that it does not own the means of production; they are privately held and will not be put in operation unless a return (profit) on investment is foreseen. Thus the capitalist state must use the carrot more than the stick, by helping the owning class in the accumulation of profit in order to promote production. Conversely, the owning class is in a strong position with presidents, who face the likelihood of an "investment strike" if policy is seen to hurt profits. This gives business a privileged position and places the president in a position of some dependency on what is referred to as "business confidence." In order to govern effectively, presidents must please the business community, lest they face a decline in business confidence and a deterioration of the overall economy, thus leading to a decline in presidential popularity and power.

It is just this situation that Charles Lindblom—though not referring specifically to the presidency—discusses in his article "The Market as Prison."[51] Lindblom argues that political regimes with market systems have built-in defense systems that automatically trigger punishment whenever there is an attempt to tamper with or alter the basic structures of such systems. This built-in punishing mechanism makes market systems resilient and highly resistant to change because attempts at change bring quick and sure punishment. As Lindblom writes, "Many kinds of market reform automatically trigger punishments in the form of unemployment or a sluggish economy."[52] This punishment is not the result of any conspiracy on the part of business; it is simply a built-in by-product of market-oriented systems. Lindblom writes:

> Business people do not have to debate whether or not to impose the penalty. They need do no more. . . . than tend to their own business, which means that, without thought of effecting a punishment on us, they restrict investment and jobs simply in the course of being prudent managers of their enterprises.[53]

While Lindblom does not focus on the presidency in this context, he does discuss the notion that the economic system is highly resistant to change by political leaders. He describes the situation thus:

> What about governmental officials? It is critical to the efficiency of automatic punishment that it be visited on them. For it is they who immediately or proximately decide to persist in policy changes or to withdraw from such initiatives. The penalty visited on them by business disincentives caused by proposed policies is that declining business activity is a threat to the party and the officials in power. When a decline in prosperity and employment is brought about by decisions of corporate and other business executives, it is not they but government officials who consequently are retired from their offices.
>
> That result, then, is why the market might be characterized as a prison. For a broad category of political/economic affairs, it imprisons policy making, and imprisons our attempts to improve our institutions. It greatly cripples our attempts to improve the social world because it afflicts us with sluggish economic performance and unemployment simply because we begin to debate or undertake reform.[54]

Thus, with policymaking being "imprisoned" in market-oriented systems, the leverage of presidents for reform is severely restricted by this self-regulating, self-punishing mechanism built into the system.

The other function, legitimization of the social order, derives from the need for the state to be seen as ruling in the interest of all, not in the interest of a dominant class. Welfare programs for the nonowning classes and entitlement programs for the middle class are examples of policies to satisfy this task. But when profits are squeezed, the revenues to support such programs become tight, and a crisis for the state can occur because it cannot reach an adequate balance between these contradictory goals.[55]

Edward S. Greenberg develops the notion of the privileged position of business in policymaking in these words:

> Presidents must act in such a way that they maintain the confidence of business leaders and ensure an economic environment conducive to profitable investment. The president's popularity and thus much of his ability to effect a domestic program and foreign policy objectives is dependent on the state of the economy and the sense of well-being felt by the American people.
>
> Since business people cannot be forced to make productive, job-creating investments in the American economy, government must induce them to do so. They are induced, in the main, by public policies that encourage and ensure profitability, especially among the most powerful economic actors and enterprises in the system. Thus, while no president can afford to respond to every whim of important business leaders, all his actions are bounded by the need to maintain "business confidence."[56]

There is no active conspiracy on the part of business to "capture" the presidency. Rather, presidential success is intimately connected with business success. As presidential popularity rises and falls, in part due to economic conditions, presidents quickly learn that what is good for business is usually good for presidential popularity.[57] When corporate capitalism gains, the president usually gains. Conversely, a sluggish economy is blamed on an administration's activities or lack thereof. Thus the fate of the president is closely connected to fluctuations in the economy. Presidents help themselves by helping business.[58]

In this way, presidents who do not have the confidence of business find themselves at a distinct political and economic disadvantage. As John Kennedy noted:

> I understand better every day why Roosevelt, who started out such a mild fellow, ended up so ferociously antibusiness. It is hard as hell to be friendly with people who keep trying to cut your legs off. . . .There are about ten thousand people in this country involved in this—bankers, industrialists, lawyers, publishers, politicians—a small group, but doing

everything they can to say we are going into a depression because business has no confidence in the administration. They are starting to call me the Democratic Hoover. Well, we're not going to take that.[59]

But Kennedy recognized the other side of the business confidence coin as well, as he attempted to act as economic cheerleader:

> This country cannot prosper unless business prospers. This country cannot meet its obligations and tax obligations and all the rest unless business is doing well. Business will not do well and we will not have full employment unless there is a chance to make a profit. So there is no long-run hostility between business and government. There cannot be. We cannot succeed unless they succeed.[60]

Similarly, presidents who wish to pursue a reform agenda find themselves in a bind: "Do I sacrifice economic reforms for economic performance and personal popularity, or, do I play it safe and hope for incremental changes?" Which president would want to stir the embers of the market's self-punishing mechanism? Shortly after his election, Bill Clinton met with his top economic advisors to devise an economic stimulus package. After a lengthy discussion, a consensus was reluctantly arrived at that determined the first priority of the president: to rescue the bond market. Angry and frustrated that his reform agenda was being hijacked by the bond market, an exasperated Clinton threw his arms up in the air and said, "We've all become Eisenhower Republicans!" Which president could afford to stir the beast that will likely produce a sluggish economy and lower presidential popularity? Thus presidential leverage in economic reform is severely limited by the invisible prison of the market.

Thomas Cronin, probably the most highly regarded of today's presidential scholars, begins to suggest a structural impediment in presidential choice vis-à-vis the business community when, in a lengthy reexamination of Richard Neustadt's *Presidential Power,* he chides Neustadt for failing "to take into account the degree to which presidents are almost invariably stabilizers or protectors of the status quo rather than agents of redistribution or progressive change." Cronin adds that "all our presidents have had to prove their political orthodoxy and their acceptability to a wide array of established powers, especially to corporate leaders."[61]

Political scientist Bruce Miroff notes that presidential scholars remain firmly committed to a "progressive" interpretation of the presidency. But as Miroff writes, "The Presidency, even (perhaps especially) in liberal hands, is best understood as the chief stabilizer—and not the leading force for change—in American politics."[62] No president has "sought to question, much less assault, corporate power and its extraordinary skewing of resources and rewards. The present structure of the American economy has been accepted by modern Presidents as a given of American life."[63] In line with Charles Lindblom's concerns, Miroff writes:

> Because of their acceptance of the prevailing social and economic order, even the more liberal of recent Presidents have had little novel or profound that they really wanted to achieve in domestic affairs. Their most controversial domestic proposals have envisioned only modest reforms. Basically, these Presidents have sought to patch up remaining holes in the New Deal, and to stabilize and rationalize the corporate economy. None have acknowledged more fundamental problems in American society; none have proposed anything that resembles a program of social and economic reconstruction. Contrary to the conventional view, it has not been an obstructionist Congress or an apathetic public that has kept Presidents since FDR from major domestic accomplishments as it has been the orthodoxy of their own domestic vision.[64]

Presidents are thus constrained by the needs of corporate capitalism. They are in part imprisoned, limited in what they can do, by the requirements of accumulation and legitimization.

The Politics of Globalization

The United States is the world's only superpower. In fact, it is a hyper-power. With military might second to none, a massive economy, and cultural penetration to all parts of the globe (I defy you to go to any large city in any country in the world and not find a McDonalds, Starbucks, or a local kid wearing a New York Yankee baseball cap or a "23" basketball jersey), the United States is the hegemonic power, or "big kid on the block." But if we are so strong, why do we seem so weak? Why, at a time when there are no rivals to power, is our grip on international events so fragile and tenuous?

When the Soviet Union imploded—marking the end of the Cold War—analysts wondered what international regime would replace the old order. For a time policymakers groped for an answer. George Bush (the first), in response to the invasion of Kuwait by Iraq, developed a multinationalist coalition based on a "new world order." But as the Gulf War ended, Bush abandoned this promising approach to international order and stability.

It was not until the Clinton years that the parameters of the new regime would come into view. Called "globalization," it encompassed an international acceptance of global capitalism—market economies, open markets, free trade, and integration and interdependence. Building on the institutions designed to oversee, coordinate, and stabilize the international economy—the International Monetary Fund (IMF), the World Bank, and the General Agreement on Tariffs and Trade (GATT), now the World Trade Organization (WTO)—these institutions have helped create a more integrated international economy.

The promise of globalism is political (countries that are connected by common bonds will better cooperate) and economic (a rising tide lifts all boats, although critics might argue that the rising tide lifts all yachts!) Those opposing the rise of globalism fear the widening gap between rich and poor nations, environmental degradation, and a decline in worker's rights.

In this age of globalization, what role and power would be assumed by the United States? And what role and power would be assumed by the presidency? Globalism takes power out of the hands of nations and places it in the hands of the market and corporations. National sovereignty is diminished as the requirements of the global economy drive policy.[65] Globalism demands that market forces shape policy. Thus governments must please the international market or decline.

The United States is the most powerful actor in this system, and draws benefits from its leadership position. But this new system inhibits the freedom of a president to choose. Bound by the demands of a global economy, and the need to develop multinational responses to a variety of problems, the president is less free to pursue policies he chooses and increasingly compelled to succumb to the demands of the market.

Globalism is a two-edged sword. It brings some economic benefits but imposes further limits on choice. Non-Governmental Organizations (NGOs), international institutions, central banks, and market forces gain in power. Nations—and the U.S. president—lose power.

Conclusion

There are, one can see, a variety of good reasons why presidents rarely perform up to public expectation. Some of the blame rests with individual presidents who lack sufficient political skill. Part of the blame rests with the structural design of the American constitutional system that separates and fragments power. And as this chapter points out, there are a variety of other permanent and temporal roadblocks that inhibit presidential leadership.

The American presidency, public misperceptions to the contrary, is in many ways a very limited office with limited powers. The president faces heavy responsibilities and high public expectations with limited political resources. For presidents, the presidency is not a very user-friendly institution. It should not surprise us that disappointment in the presidential performance is commonplace.

The result is (usually) presidential paralysis, political gridlock, and public cynicism. Historically, this problem is not new. In other eras, other presidents have faced gridlock and political fragmentation. But in recent years, this paralysis has taken on a new tone of urgency. With the demise of the Soviet empire, the dramatic changes taking place in the post-1989 world, the rise of globalism, the evaporation of political consensus at home, and the demands of the war on terrorism, the need for creative political leadership is high.

But some presidents do lead, do move the machinery of government, do succeed. Why? How are we to explain presidential success? What magic do those few great leaders work on the lethargic American system? We now turn our attention to the strategies presidents can employ to heighten their chances of political success.

For Discussion

1. Were the Founders right? In creating the American system of government and in inventing the presidency, were they correct about (a) human nature; (b) the need to control power; (c) the utility of a separation of powers systems; (d) the rule of law and limited government; and (e) the amount of power given to the president in the Constitution?
2. The Founders wanted to prevent tyranny and limit governmental power. Today, we need more efficiency, we need to run the government like a business. Discuss.
3. How might globalism affect U.S. policy? What role should the United States play in this emerging world?
4. Is America's political culture really antileadership and antiauthority? Isn't most of the nation conformist and obedient to their rules? Is American culture too individualistic and consumer oriented?
5. Does capitalism imprison the president, or does America's great wealth liberate a president, free him to do great things?
6. What tests of character and competence should our presidential selection system impose on candidates? Are "private/personal" issues (such as a candidate's sex life) relevant to presidential selection?

Debate Questions

I. *Resolved:* That the presidency is too big a job for one person to handle.
II. *Resolved:* That the public expects and demands too much of its presidents.

CHAPTER 3

Presidential
Power-Maximizing Strategies

And now for something completely different.

—MONTY PYTHON

If "successful presidents" seem to be an endangered species, it is for good reason: Most presidents do not succeed, are not able to overcome the lethargy built into the system, cannot bring sufficient skill to bear on the limited opportunities they face. But some presidents do succeed. Why? What makes successful presidents successful? What do they do that other presidents don't do or can't do?

To be successful, a president must be a jack-of-all-trades *and* a master of all. It *is* rocket science. Since power floats in the United States,[1] since it is so elusive, a power vacuum is the natural order, and someone or something fills it. Usually, the vacuum is filled by those who wish to protect the status quo: As the protectors of what is, they have most of the advantages over the advocates of change. In the United States, there is a great deal of *negative power*, multiple veto points, but there are few opportunities to promote change.

Many rivals attempt to fill the power void, but no one is better situated to do so than the president. In effect, the presidency is the only "modern" institution of government. The Congress acts slowly, the Court must wait for a case to arrive. But the presidency is a modern institution in the sense that it can move quickly, react with speed and dispatch; it can decide. In this sense, the Congress adapts poorly, while the presidency can adapt quickly. As the world becomes smaller, as communication becomes almost instantaneous, as travel speeds up, as technology progresses, the perceived need to

81

move quickly, adapt, and adjust heightens. The presidency, with a single hand at the helm, can move, can fill the power vacuum.

By what means can a president fill that power vacuum? By the creative force of presidential leadership. As used here, presidential leadership refers to more than mere office holding. Leadership is a complex phenomenon revolving around *influence*—the ability to move others in desired directions. Successful leaders are those who can take full advantage of their *opportunities, resources,* and *skills*. A president's level of political *opportunity* is the context of power.[2] It is measured by such factors as the margin of victory in the last election; the issues the president ran on in the election; number of the president's party in Congress; ripeness of issues; and public mood and the level of their demand for action. *Resources* reflect the power granted to the president. As mentioned, constitutionally the president has limited power. Further, the structure of government, the separation of powers, also reflects limited presidential powers. *Skill* is what each individual president brings to the job. A successful leader converts resources to power, but it is not automatic. To convert resources to power requires skill.

The leader's skills—his style, political acumen, experience, political strategy, management skill, vision, ability to mobilize political support, character traits, and personal attributes—provide a behavioral repertoire, a set of competencies. Opportunities, resources, and skills interact to determine the potential for success or failure in attempts to lead and influence.[3]

A president who can play to the optimum the cards of opportunity, resources, and skill has a chance of succeeding. Such a leader can resemble Superman or Leviathan rather than Gulliver tied down by thousands of lesser figures. But unusual is the president who maximizes power. More often, the president resembles the helpless giant.

The presidency, as popularly understood, can't work. Our expectations are too high and the president's powers are too thin: so many roadblocks, so few useful road maps: so many veto points, so few avenues to power. As Thomas E. Cronin has written, "Their [presidents'] responsibilities exceed their meager powers."[4] The surprise shouldn't be that most presidents can't lead effectively; the surprise is that some do lead. We cling to the romantic myth of FDR and ask, why can't they all do what he did?

But few presidents are FDR, and few face the opportunities for leadership that FDR enjoyed. Power is dispersed; it "exists only as a potential. Leadership is the means by which the president can exploit that potential. This is no easy task."[5]

The president has vast responsibilities, with overwhelmingly high public expectations but limited power resources. But as an institution, the presidency has proved to be somewhat elastic; it stretches to accommodate skilled leaders in situations of high opportunity, but it also contracts to hem in less skilled leaders.[6] Noting the variable nature of the power potential in the presidency, Robert Dahl has written: "The Presidency is like a family dwelling that each new generation alters and enlarges. Confronted by some new need, a President adds on a new room, a new wing; what began as a modest dwelling has become a mansion; every President may not use every room, but the rooms are available in case of the need."[7]

The variable nature of presidential power has left presidency scholars somewhat schizophrenic regarding the proper scope and limits of presidential power. As presidents performed credibly (1930s to early 1960s), scholars called for an enlarged institution. But as presidents faltered (1960s to 1980s), they called for restrictions on presidential power. In the 1990s, confusion reigned. This variability is reactive; it is based on the subjective judgments derived from the political performance of presidents. But such evaluations miss the key point: the *normal* state of the presidency is one of constrained power. To be successful, presidents much overcome nature, or at least, the nature of power built into the system. Thus, for our purposes, it is better to look at the requirements for leadership generically—at the preconditions necessary for the exercise of political leadership—than merely to react to the current temporary occupant of the White House. By doing this we can see not only how well a particular president performed but also which threads, or common factors, run through the presidency.

Generically the presidency is a relatively weak institution. The president is especially vulnerable (to outside veto points) and dependent (on others to go along with him). His independent powers are quite limited. It is an office of enormous responsibility, extravagant expectations, but limited power. How do presidents make up for this power shortage? How do they lead?

It should be noted that while the Founders sought a governing structure that was slow, deliberative, and multifaceted, they also wanted a government of energy, but a specific type of energy— energy that resulted from *consensus* and *cooperation*. What model or type of leadership is required to move such a system? A model based on *consensus*, not fait accompli; *influence*, not command; *agreement*, not independence; *cooperation*, not unilateralism. Such a model of power requires presidents to think strategically, to play a complex game.[8]

If the model of leadership built into the presidency is one of cooperation and consensus, what paths are open for presidents to lead? Under what conditions can a skilled president take a relatively limited office and exert leadership? What are the fuels that ignite presidential power? What are the preconditions of successful presidential leadership?

Presidential Leadership

The President is at liberty, both in law and in conscience,
to be as big a man as he can. . . . His capacity will set the limit.
—Woodrow Wilson

I claim not to have controlled events, but confess plainly
that these events have controlled me.
—Abraham Lincoln

In the social sciences, the word *leadership* and *power* are often used interchangeably. This is a mistake. Leadership suggests *influence;* power is *command*. Leaders inspire and persuade; power-wielders order compliance. Leaders induce followership; power-holders compel or force acceptance. Officeholders have (to some degree at least) power merely by virtue of occupying an office. Leaders, on the other hand, *earn* followership. The officeholder uses the powers granted to his official position. The leader tries to reshape the political environment; "he seeks to change the constellation of political forces about him in a direction closer to his own conception of the political good."[9]

On occasion, a president can act on his own authority, "independent" of other political actors. President Bush's 1989 decision to overthrow the government of Manuel Noriega in Panama is an example of this form of power. But such unilateral acts as this are the exception, not the rule. In most cases, presidents share power. Therefore, leadership, the informal "powers" so eloquently elaborated upon by Richard Neustadt, becomes important to presidents who wish to promote political change.

All presidents have some power, some ability to command. But such power is short-term and limited. It ceases to exist when the president leaves office. Its effects can often be undone by a new president.

A president's formal power—for so long the focal point of presidential studies[10]—includes constitutional authority, statutes, delegated powers, and those areas in which others follow a president's command. But with the publication of Richard Neustadt's influential *Presidential Power* in 1960,[11] the more informal power to persuade took center stage in presidential studies. Rather than take an either-or approach to the debate over formal versus informal powers, we should see these two potential sources of strength as complementary, as presidential options in the pursuit of their goals. While presidents derive some of their powers from constitutional sources, they derive others from political and personal sources. Effective presidents use *all* the resources available to them. They assess the situation and determine where are their best chances for success, and they are flexible enough to make the adjustments necessary to optimize their power. In short, effective presidents are able to adjust their dance to fit whatever music is played.

True leadership occurs when presidents are able to exploit the multifaceted nature of opportunities both to command *and* to influence. In his classic study, *Leadership*, Burns suggests that leadership takes place when

> persons with certain motives and purposes mobilize, in competition or conflict with others, institutional, political, psychological, and other

resources so as to arouse, engage, and satisfy the motives of followers. . . .
Leadership is exercised in a condition of conflict or competition in
which leaders contend in appealing to the motive bases of potential followers.[12]

For better or worse, only presidential leadership can regularly
overcome the lethargy built into the American system and give focus
and direction to government. Congress can, on rare occasion, take
the lead on a policy, as was the case when the Congress overcame
presidential opposition from Ronald Reagan and imposed economic
sanctions on the white minority government of South Africa or in
the early days of Newt Gingrich's time as Speaker of the House during the Clinton presidency. But such cases are infrequent. Congress
simply is not institutionally well designed enough to provide consistent national leadership over extended periods of time. In the second
half of the twentieth century, the citizens have most often looked to
the White House for leadership and direction. If the president does-
n't lead, gridlock usually results. In this sense, John F. Kennedy's
view that "The presidential office is the vortex into which all the elements of national decision are irresistibly drawn"[13] rings true.
Presidential leadership remains the key for moving the machinery of
government. But, given all that is arrayed against presidents, how
can they lead rather than merely preside?

The Building Blocks of Presidential Leadership

Out of the multitude of factors affecting any president's ability to
lead, only two are really within his personal purview: the president's
vision and skill. These two elements provide the foundation upon
which the president's potential for leadership largely rests. Given the
limits established for the institution of the presidency, vision and
skill—all the possible power that generates from the president himself—are also the starting points of our attempt to answer this question: How, then, must the president—for better or worse—act to
direct *and* lead the way against the plethora of demands pressing
downward upon his center of power?

Vision

Beyond question, the most important "power" a president can have is the ability to present to the public a clear and compelling vision. A well-articulated, meaningful, positive vision that builds upon the building blocks of the past, addresses needs and hopes of the present, and portrays a hopeful, optimistic image of a possible future opens more doors to presidential leadership than all the skills and other resources combined. A moving vision can transform a political system, can recreate the regime of power, can chart a course for change. Vision energizes and empowers, inspires and moves people and organizations. A president with a compelling vision can be a powerful president.

Few presidents use what Theodore Roosevelt referred to as "the bully pulpit" to develop a public philosophy for governing. Rather than attempting to educate and lead the public, most presidents seem content to serve as managers of public business. But if presidents wish to craft change, and not merely preside, they must use the bully pulpit to promote a moral and political vision in support of change.

A visionary leader, akin to what James M. Burns calls a transforming leader,[14] gives direction to an organization, gives purpose to action. Visionary leadership charts a course for action. Such leaders are both instrumental for change and catalysts of change.[15]

When asked how he worked, Albert Einstein replied, "I grope." Groping may be acceptable for a genius of Einstein's caliber, but presidents must do more than grope; they must lead. Of course, the reality is that most presidents merely grope and are thus mere officeholders. But groping is not enough; holding office is not enough. And one of the essential differences between a leader and a mere officeholder is that leaders have a vision, communicate that vision, and animate the public and Congress through expressions of that vision. As leadership expert Burt Nanus of the University of Southern California writes, "There is no more powerful engine driving an organization toward excellence and long-range success than an attractive, worthwhile, achievable vision of the future, widely shared."[16]

Effective leaders, in government, business, and public organizations, share a common trait: they are visionaries. Nanus writes:

There is no mystery about this. Effective leaders have agendas; they are totally results oriented. They adopt challenging new visions of what is both possible and desirable, communicate their visions, and persuade others to become so committed to these new directions that they are eager to lend their resources and energies to make them happen. In this way, effective leaders build lasting institutions that change the world.[17]

Visions do not spring full blown from the belly of the leader. Developing a vision involves the ability to consider "existing realities as transformed possibilities."[18] Visions are enabling and empowering. They are derived from the core values of a community, flow from the past, are about the future. Visions inspire, give meaning and direction to a community, are road maps. Visions are about achieving excellence.

A vision is an idea, a dream of the future, a dream that is realistic enough to appear attainable, different enough to inspire, attractive enough to gain consent and commitment. It is about hope: this is what tomorrow can be, this is what it looks like, this is how we can get there, this is the cost, and this is our ultimate reward. A vision grabs our attention, stirs our imagination, and appeals to what is best in us.

Bennis and Nanus offer this description of leaders:

> Leaders articulate and define what has previously remained implicit or unsaid; then they invent images, metaphors, and models that provide a focus for new attention. By so doing they consolidate, or challenge prevailing wisdom. In short, an essential factor in leadership is the capacity to influence and organize meaning for members of the organization. . . . Communication creates meaning for people. Or should. It's the only way any group, small or large, can become aligned behind the overarching goals of an organization.[19]

Visionary leaders are remembered and continue to have an impact long after they leave office. For example, it has been over forty years since John Kennedy was killed, and over thirty-five since the death of Martin Luther King, Jr., and yet the memories of their leadership—the power of their ideas and the impact of their words— remain influential forces in the contemporary political arena.

On a smaller and decidedly opposite political scale, Ronald Reagan was able to mobilize and inspire his followers because he was skilled at presenting his vision to the public. In contrast, George H. Bush, who admitted he wasn't big on "that vision thing," was a singularly uninspiring officeholder, and weeks after his leaving office, he had all but faded from political memory. Why is Reagan's presence still felt while Bush has become invisible? Vision.

No other actor on the political scene is better positioned to present a vision to the public than a president. Already the focus of much media and public attention, presidents can become "highlighters" of important issues to be addressed as a part of the president's vision. While presenting a somewhat more limited role, political scientist Lester Salamon has written that presidents need to develop

> a more strategic approach to the office, one that conceives of the president not as the ultimate decision maker but as the preeminent "national highlighter," whose most important task is not to settle all issues, but to identify a handful of issues of truly national importance and focus on them the attention, visibility, and support that only a president can provide. Such a role is far more consistent with the unique advantages of the office. . . . And far more compatible with the capabilities of the institution and the demands of the job.[20]

Skill

The general public seems to assume that skill is all that is necessary for a president to be successful. If only we could get another FDR— so the belief goes—we could make things work. Wrong.

Skill is important but skill is not enough. Even the most skilled individuals face formidable roadblocks. Skill helps determine the extent to which a president takes advantage of or is buried by circumstances, but circumstances, or the political environment, set the parameters of what is possible regarding leadership. President Reagan used to refer to the "window of opportunity," his way of talking about how open or closed were the circumstances for exercising presidential leadership. For example, a skilled president who faces a closed window—such as the opposition party's controlling the Congress during a period of economic troubles in which the president's popularity is low—will be very limited in what he can accomplish. In contrast, a president of limited skill who has an open window of opportunity will have much greater political leverage, even though his skill base is smaller. President George W. Bush was an object of media ridicule before September 11, but after that tragedy his window of opportunity—and his power—increased dramatically. It was not that Bush became more skilled overnight; it was a change of circumstances that opened a window to power. It is thus entirely possible for a president with limited skill to be more successful than a president with great skill. If one is dealt a weak hand, there is only so much that skill can do. But if one is dealt four aces, *fortuna*—not skill—determines power.

Again, this is not to say that skill is unimportant. It does make a difference. But in the constellation of factors that contribute to success or failure, skill is but one, and it is probably not the most important element.

At election time one often hears political cynics whine, "It doesn't matter who gets elected; they all end up doing the same thing anyway." Social science lends *some* support to this cynical view. After all, we social scientists widely believe that the institution, role, expectations, and other conditions play a significant part in determining behavior. But while the cynic has a point, it should not be taken too far. Individuals are constrained, but to an extent, individuals *do* matter.[21]

Another way of looking at the skill versus opportunity dilemma is to focus on what is referred to as a president's "political capital." Is a president's capital like a bank account, in which a one-time deposit is made at the beginning of his term, and must he then invest carefully and draw on that account prudently, lest he run out of resources? Or, can a president add to his bank account from time to time, renewing his resources?

George Bush, Sr., seemed to think that his capital was a fixed sum, and in spending it, he dissipated his capital. Bill Clinton, on the other hand, did not view his political capital as a fixed asset. He regularly spent, then tried to replenish his assets. As President Clinton has noted,

> even a President without a majority mandate coming in, if the President has a disciplined, aggressive agenda that is clearly in the interest of the majority of the American people—I think you can create new political

capital all the time, because you have access to the people through the communications network. If you have energy and sort of an inner determination that keeps you at the task, I think you can re-create political capital continuously throughout the Presidency. I have always believed that.[22]

Princeton political scientist Fred Greenstein sees the presence of the following factors as making a situation especially bendable to individual variations: (1) ambiguity; (2) an absence of standardized "mental sets" or roles; (3) a lack of sanctions attached to an action; (4) a presence of high intensity of personal feelings or beliefs; and (5) an involvement of high-skill-based actions.[23]

There are thus certain situations where the individual, not the institution, dominates. Do leaders make a difference? Yes, sometimes. As Erwin C. Hargrove writes, "Surely the issue is not, Do individuals make a difference? but Under what conditions do they make a difference? The relative importance of leaders varies across institutions and across time and place. The task of scholarship is to integrate the study of individuals with the social and institutional forces that move them and that they, in turn, may influence."[24]

When do individuals matter? When is skill an important variable in presidential success? While it may sound obvious, it is nonetheless important to note, as Hargrove does, that "effectiveness in achieving goals was enhanced if skill and task were congruent."[25] To that I would add a third element: opportunity level. Skill matched to task when the window of political opportunity is open usually leads to goal attainment. Hargrove himself recognizes the importance of opportunity when he writes, "The impact of individual leaders on events and institutions is greater or lesser depending upon the historical situation and the opportunities available to them."[26]

The stamp of individual presidents who made a difference in specific policy areas is unmistakable: Lyndon Johnson and the war on poverty, Richard Nixon and China, Jimmy Carter and human rights, Bill Clinton and gun control, George W. Bush and the war against terrorism, and so on. These presidents had choices, moved in new directions, made a difference. Their options were limited, but they were able in these areas to overcome the natural lethargy of the system and succeed in selected policy arenas. The fact that presidential behavior in most areas and on most issues appears more similar than dissimilar should not obscure the fact that—on some issues at some times—some presidents *can* make a difference.

The attempt to determine what role skill has played in these events remains a slippery task. Could any president have opened doors to China? Probably not. Could any president emphasize human rights in his foreign policy? Probably. So where are we? When does skill matter? How can we recognize or measure political skill? Lamentably, it is probably too elusive a concept to wrestle to the ground. Suffice it to say that high levels of skill, task congruence, and opportunity usually lead to presidential success, and low levels of the aforementioned usually lead to disappointment.[27]

Begging the question: If skill is of *some* (unmeasureable) importance, it might be useful to ask, what skills are most useful to a president? *Political experience* is often touted as a requirement for effective leadership, and while this sounds like good common sense, the correlation between experience and achievement is not strong.[28] After all, some of our most experienced leaders were our biggest disappointments (Nixon and Johnson). But overall one could argue that more experience is better than less experience, although it is by no means a guarantee of successful performance. While Washington, D.C., "amateurs" (Carter, Reagan, Clinton, and Bush II) have made serious blunders in part due to their lack of experience, experienced political hands (George Bush, Sr., had the best resume in Washington) have often done poorly despite their backgrounds. This suggests that while experiences *can be* very helpful, there are other factors that to a great degree determine the success or failure of a president.

Both the Reagan and Clinton presidencies serve as excellent examples of D.C. amateurs behaving amateurishly in the White House. Reagan in Beirut, and Clinton in Somalia, placed American military personnel in harm's way, without sufficient support or protection and against the recommendations of many experienced advisers. In both cases, Americans were ambushed, leading to the death of over 220 marines in Beirut and a dozen in Somalia before changes in policy led to increased safety precautions. In both cases, leaders with no foreign policy experience made tragic blunders leading to the loss of American lives that could have been and should have been avoided. More experienced hands probably would have known better.

Political skills are always in short supply, and the president who has a high level of political acumen can sometimes gain the upper hand. By political skills we mean a good sense of *timing* (to know when an issue is "ripe"—when to move, when to hold back); *task competence; a power sense, situational skills* (crisis versus routine-decision skills); *policy skills* (to develop sound workable programs); and *political savvy* (to love playing politics, as FDR did, not hate politics as Nixon did). Of FDR's love for politics, James M. Burns has written the following:

> If other leaders bent under the burdens of power, Roosevelt shouldered his with zest and gaiety. He loved being President; he almost always gave the impression of being on top of his job. Cheerfully, exuberantly, he swung through the varied presidential tasks. . . . The variegated facets of the presidential job called for a multitude of different roles, and Roosevelt moved from part to part with ease and confidence.[29]

To be successful, presidents also need people skills. Presidents must know how to persuade, bargain, cajole, and co-opt. They must be masters of self-presentation. They must be able to motivate and inspire, to gain trust and influence. Charisma helps. In short, occupants of the White House must master the art of "presidential schmoozing."

Personality skills also loom large in the arsenal of presidential requirements.[30] All presidents have a drive for power. For some, it is held within healthy bounds; for others—Nixon, for example—it destroys a president. To be effective, presidents should be self-confident, secure, flexible, and open. Presidents who are consumed by self-doubt, insecurity, rigidity, and a closed personality (Barber's "negative" characters) are often dangerous and apt to abuse power.

Related to this, presidents also need *self-knowledge*. We all have our weaknesses, but we do not all let our weaknesses consume us. By recognizing his or her strengths *and* weaknesses, a good leader can attempt to deal constructively with weakness, come to grips with failings, offset the negative. For example, a president who is inexperienced in foreign policy may need to compensate by surrounding himself with very experienced foreign policy insiders.

Managerial skills, sometimes referred to as process skills, are also extremely important if a president is to succeed.[31] This set of skills is dealt with separately and is merely mentioned here.

Finally, a president must have *personal style skills*. By this I mean he must be disciplined, have great stamina, intelligence, sound judgment, and maturity. Good presidents are creative, empathetic, and expressive. They have a sense of optimism that gives people reason to hope. And they have a sense of humor. Ronald Reagan's self-effacing sense of humor served him well as president; it disarmed opponents and won over much of the public.

Political Timing

The "when" of politics matters greatly: when major legislation is introduced, when the public is ready to accept change, when the Congress can be pressured to act, when the president leads and when he follows, when he pushes and when he pauses. A sense of political timing, part of the overall "power sense" all great leaders have, helps a president know when to move, when to retreat; when to push, when to compromise. Primarily, there are two elements of political time most germane to the leadership dilemma of a president: the *transition* and the *honeymoon* period.

The Transition

Getting a good start is a key element of political success, and during the transition—the eleven-week period between the November election and the January inauguration—some of the most important work of an administration is done.[32] In this preparation stage before taking office, the president-elect lays the groundwork for much that is to follow, and he sets the tone that shapes the way others see the new administration. During the transition, the president-elect must, in essence, make all of the following key decisions: who will be the top advisers, who will fill important cabinet positions, and how will the staff be structured; what decision-making (management) style will he employ; will he pursue a partisan strategy or try to woo the opposition; how will he mobilize the public; and what issues will the administration push during the first year. Much like the journalist's key questions, these five *w*'s (*who, what, when, where,* and *why*) and an *h* (*how*) of politics set the stage not only for how the administration will operate but also for the way the public, Congress, and media will view and respond to the new administration. The Clinton transition—slow, awkward, drifting—was seen as an opening by the Republicans and the press to jump on the new president earlier than is customary. Thus Senator Bob Dole (R., Kansas) led a highly orchestrated series of early attacks on the new president, designed to undermine his leadership. Likewise the press, sensing disarray (and wishing to show bipartisanship after Republican attacks on the media), jumped all over themselves in an effort to find negative things to say about Clinton.[33]

The transition is thus important because, as James P. Pfiffner points out, "power is not automatically transferred, but must be seized. Only the *authority* of the presidency is transferred on January 20; the *power* of the presidency—in terms of effective control of the policy agenda—must be consciously developed."[34] Thus Pfiffner suggests that in order to seize power, presidents must adopt a strategic approach to the transition, one that leaves little to chance and that deals self-consciously with seizing and using power.

Of Honeymoons and (Un) Happy Marriages

Gerald Ford, upon taking office in the midst of the Watergate scandal, said he wanted a happy marriage, not just a honeymoon. He got neither. The marriage between a president and Congress is a mixed marriage that rarely turns out to be a happy one over the long haul. Therefore, presidents need to get all they can as early as they can before the marriage slips into bickering and sniping. To do this, a strategic president does all he can to take advantage of the honeymoon period. The honeymoon is a brief period of time, lasting anywhere from roughly three to ten months (or, for Clinton, three to ten minutes), immediately following a presidential election, when the public, press, Congress, and others begin to give the president the benefit of the doubt, go soft on him, refrain somewhat from criticism, and are most likely to vote for measures proposed by the president. The president "claims" an electoral mandate; the opposition, uncertain of how strong the new president will be, usually goes easy on him; and everyone is waiting to see if indeed the new guy will seize power. In short, the vultures are not yet circling the president's carcass. Thus the president is often at the peak of his power in his honeymoon period.

As Lyndon Johnson said, "You've got to give it all you can, that first year. Doesn't matter what kind of a majority you come in with. You've got just one year when they treat you right."[35] And the best way to get as much as you can, early, is to have a short disciplined agenda, focus exclusively on that agenda, and push, push, push.

Presidents are more likely to propose new programs in their first year in office than at any other time. Their success rate with Congress in the first year is usually the highest of their term. The irony here, as Paul Light points out, is that presidents are at their strongest when they are least knowledgeable.[36]

To take advantage of this potential to exercise power during the honeymoon, a president must strategically approach his transition and early weeks of the new administration with a clear game plan, a focused mode of presentation, a short, disciplined agenda, and an unceasing sense of political pressure on the system.

It is considered wise to select a few big issues in the early going and to focus all attention on attaining those goals. The difference here, between Ronald Reagan on the one hand, and Jimmy Carter and Bill Clinton on the other, is striking. When Reagan took office, his administration very self-consciously chose to focus on a select few big-ticket items: a tax cut, for example. All other issues, including important foreign policy matters, were put on the back burner (which infuriated Alexander Haig, the new and short-lived secretary of state).[37] This allowed the Reagan administration to devote all its energies to hitting a select few legislative home runs, and it also conveyed an image that this president could succeed, could get his way, could win. He appeared to be, and for a time was, powerful.

By contrast, both Carter and Clinton had large, unyielding legislative agendas. What did they want? Everything, it seemed, and nothing. They could not decide what was most and what was least important. President Clinton, when he should have been focusing attention on his economic stimulus package in early 1993, instead got sidetracked by the issue of gay rights in the military. This issue may have been important, but in the big scheme, it ranked well behind the economic stimulus package. When Carter and Clinton seemed sprawling and unfocused, Reagan maintained a short, disciplined issue focus.

Overall, Clinton had a very shaky start. In the early going he suffered defeat on his economic stimulus package, fumbled the Haitian refugee issue, backed away from his middle-class tax pledge, blundered on several early cabinet appointees, and was indecisive on Bosnia-Herzegovina and Somalia. At the time when Clinton was supposed to be at his strongest, he kept shooting himself in the foot. And the Democrats in Congress, unaccustomed to having a compatriot in the White House, at the first smell of presidential blood seemed instinctively to form a circle for a firing squad. It was not a pretty sight. It is amazing that, in spite of his shaky start, President Clinton was able, time and again, to recover and even to snare a few wins. While he missed opportunities in the honeymoon, he recovered and was able to win significant victories later.

In the honeymoon period, a president must "hit the ground running"[38] by concentrating on a few key policy issues, working hard to cooperate with (even co-opt) Congress, focusing public attention on his agenda, promoting himself and his program, seizing center stage, controling the agenda, and setting the terms of debate. That's all. But that is the time when the president's window of political opportunity is often open fairly wide, and a skilled president can drive his legislative program through the system. In the United States, and in other systems, the early part of a new leader's term often finds the most significant political changes occurring.[39]

In some ways, the honeymoon comes at the best of times: following an election, with a promise and hope for change, an air of optimism. In other ways, however, it comes at the worst of times. Under normal circumstances the president is at his peak of power when he is least able to cope with the demands of office: He is new, inexperienced, learning the ropes, most prone to error or misjudgment. Paul Light recognizes this when he writes of how a president's power is high during the early stages of his term but, due to what he calls "the cycle of decreasing influence," will erode over time. Though the president's "cycle of increasing effectiveness" makes him more skilled or adept later, over time his power declines.[40] When a president is most capable, he is least powerful, and when he is least capable, he is most powerful. The dilemma was recognized by President Reagan's first Office of Management and Budget Director David Stockman, who feared a "GOP Economic Dunkirk" if quick action wasn't taken:

> Things could go very badly during the first year, resulting in incalculable erosion of GOP momentum, unity and public confidence. If bold policies are not swiftly, deftly and courageously implemented in the first six months, Washington will quickly become engulfed in political disorder commensurate with the surrounding economic disarray. A golden opportunity for permanent conservative policy revision and political realignment could be thoroughly dissipated before the Reagan administration is even up to speed.[41]

The problem, of course, is that Reagan did pass dramatic tax reduction legislation and increased defense spending dramatically, thus driving the federal budget to the brink of economic insolvency. Presidents are thus most prone to make mistakes when the system is most likely to follow their lead.

But Presidents are in some ways prisoners of time and must make the best of what they are handed. They are usually handed (apart from a crisis) the most power when they are least adept. Thus, to hit the ground running becomes an essential ingredient for presidential success, just as that same success in those early days can often lead to major blunders.

Scholars point to the Reagan honeymoon as an example of how to make the most out of early opportunities. Reagan combined an attractive personality with a compelling television presence and a vision that he articulated masterfully, and he focused on only a few key issues. But he was a poor planner and weak manager. During his transition, his key advisors put together—with little involvement from the president-elect—a narrow, focused agenda and initiated a public relations and legislative blitzkrieg that ended in the president's gaining almost all of his early legislative agenda. This in turn added to the aura of power surrounding Reagan and made it easier for him to win subsequent contests because the Congress "feared" Reagan.[42]

A key factor in adding to a president's power during the honeymoon is the nature of the previous presidential election: Can the president claim an "electoral mandate"? If so, he will have an easier time getting his program passed by Congress. Therefore, the nature of the presidential campaign is very important. A mandate is based on three features: (1) the size of a president's electoral victory; (2) the type of election (issue oriented or personal); and (3) the number of the president's party elected to Congress (the president's coattails and the aggregate numbers). Ronald Reagan serves again as an excellent example of both the benefits of a mandate and the absence of such.

In 1980, Reagan ran a campaign in which he discussed big issues. He laid out a clear vision, discussed his proposed changes, and paved the way for his agenda. After the election he claimed a mandate and was able to convince the public and some wavering Democrats in Congress that his way was the way the nation had to move. During his early months in office, Reagan focused attention on a few select issues, pushed hard, and won some big victories. He was successful because the conditions were right and the strategy appropriate.

But during his 1984 reelection bid, Reagan ran a purely personal, issueless campaign. He ran on personality, not policies. Thus in spite of his winning a huge electoral landslide, it was widely seen as a victory for the man—not the ideas—and when, during his second term, Reagan went to the public and Congress with his proposals, he was soundly rebuked.

Finally, where timing is concerned, Machiavelli reminds us that *fortuna* also guides our fates. Luck, good and bad, plays a role in presidential leadership. For example, Jimmy Carter had the bad luck of being president at a time when the oil-producing nations (OPEC) clamped a stranglehold on the West by sending the price of oil through the roof. This caused the economies of the developed nations to plunge into a tailspin of low productivity and high inflation.

By contrast, Ronald Reagan had the good fortune to become president at a time when OPEC was breaking up and oil prices shot downward. This picked up the economies of the developed nations and cooled inflationary pressures. Thus, through no effort of his own, Carter's popularity suffered (Carter reminded us of the old blues song, "If it wasn't for bad luck, I wouldn't have no luck at all") and Reagan's was aided by events beyond his control.

Controlling the Agenda

The president's top job, as stated earlier, is to articulate and promote a vision for the nation's future. Presidents must identify the national purpose, then move the machinery of government in support of that vision.

Goal-oriented presidents sometimes control the political agenda; they take charge, are masters and not victims of their fate. To have a chance to control the agenda, a president must (1) develop and articulate a compelling vision; (2) present a series of policy proposals designed to achieve that vision; (3) sell it to the public and Congress; and (4) place emphasis on the presentation of self and programs. If accomplished with skill and timing, this program *may* allow the president to control the political agenda and thereby make the rest of the political system dance to his music.

While opportunity often shapes the parameters of permissible presidential actions, presidents do have some control over their fates. But in setting the agenda, every president must remember that other officials and interest groups have their own priorities, and that they compete with the president for control of the agenda. While the president may be the center of attention, he is only one of many actors vying for attention.

Think of the presidents who had an impact, who dominated the political landscape. They may not have been the "best" presidents (e.g., Reagan), but they were the ones who mattered, who won, who got their way. Of course, one thinks of FDR and Reagan. Both dominated the issue agenda, refashioned the debate, forced the rest of the system to respond to their initiatives.

Reagan presents an interesting case in agenda control because he was probably the most ideological president of the last century. And

Reagan's extreme conservatism helped him develop a clear vision, a policy agenda, and an action program. There is a good and bad side to being an ideologue. It can be good in that a strong ideology can simplify complex problems; on the bad side, some problems (most problems) do not lend themselves to simple solutions. On the good side, ideology gets the administration marching in the same direction; on the bad side, they may be marching like lemmings, over a cliff. Ideology highlights certain variables in problem solving; at the same time, it hides or obscures other equally important variables. Finally, ideology gives passion to purpose; it can also degenerate into crusading extremism.

In contrast with the ideologues, Bill Clinton, a political moderate, attempted to re-create himself on every issue. Being more moderate and pragmatic helped him avoid the mistakes of either extreme, but it created problems of its own. It is difficult to develop a vision and generate a committed following around a moderate position. While it way be easier for political moderates to *get* elected, it may be harder for them to set visions and govern.

Because power in the American system is floating, a policy entrepreneur can, on certain issues, capture control of the policy agenda. If this can be done, a president may be able to force an otherwise reluctant Congress to at least meet him partway on his policy goals. And no one is better positioned to attract attention than the president. If he is to lead and not merely preside, the president must control the agenda. If the agenda escapes him—as it did after the 1994 midterm election for Clinton—a president appears weak and distracted, which may force him into a reactive, not a proactive, mode.

Coalition *and* Consensus Building

The model on which the American system of government was founded is based on consensus and coalition building. Consensus means agreements about *ends;* coalitions are the *means* by which the ends are achieved. Since power in our system is fragmented and dispersed by design, *something* (usually a crisis) or *someone* (usually the president) has to pull the disparate parts of the system together.

In other words, power can be formed *if* the president has a clear, focused agenda and can forcefully and compellingly articulate a vision, and *if* the public is ready to embrace that vision. If a president can develop a consensus around his vision, he can then muster the power to form the coalitions necessary to bring that vision to fruition.

Simply placing a legislative package at the doorstep of Congress is not enough, as President Carter so painfully learned: presidents must work to build support within and outside Congress. As Thomas E. Cronin notes,

> The office does not guarantee political leadership; it merely offers incumbents an invitation to lead politically. It is in this sense that those best suited to the job are those who can creatively shape their political environment and savor the rough-and-tumble give-and-take of political life.[43]

To govern in the United States is to build coalitions, to form alliances and power networks. There are relatively few areas in which a president can act unilaterally and not face at least a few challengers to his authority. Custom and the design of the U.S. system necessitate coalition building by political leaders.

Of course, this is easier said than done. The centrifugal force of American politics pulls the system apart, encourages independent entrepreneurship. Power is not fused as it is in parliamentary democracies; instead, the president and the Congress are elected in campaigns that are relatively independent of one another, and political parties do not develop a great deal of cohesion among the branches. Political scientists Benjamin Ginsberg and Martin Shefter agree that since elections fail to provide clear governing coalitions, the president and Congress end up resorting to "politics by other means" in order to influence policy.[44] Institutional combat, not power sharing, characterizes this relationship because both branches attempt to usurp power and govern autonomously. Of course, this usually leads to conflict and/or gridlock.

This dilemma highlights the essential difference between what it takes to get elected and what it takes to govern. Getting elected requires the development of an "electoral coalition"; governing requires the development of a "governing coalition." These may be very different, even contradictory things.

This difference between electoral and governing coalitions was noted by James M. Burns, who has written that "there's an increasing disparity between the test for winning office and what's required in governing. The kinds of quick, dexterous ploys, mainly public relations ploys, that are called for in public campaigning are a very far cry from the very solid coalition building that is needed to make this system of ours work."[45]

To get elected, Bill Clinton made appeals to a wide variety of traditionally Democratic interest groups, hoping to pull a sufficient number of these groups together to ensure his election. It was a successful electoral strategy. But was it good for governing? As soon as the election was over, all these groups approached Clinton, *demanding* that he keep his promises and deliver the goods. Clinton tried to deliver on his promises and, for example, broadened federal support for abortion rights (which garnered some backlash); he also attempted to allow openly gay persons to serve in the military. These two issues generated a tremendous backlash as opposition from the military and fundamentalist religious groups all but paralyzed the new administration in the honeymoon period, and these early and highly publicized controversies did significant political damage to the new president precisely at the time he should have been at his power peak. In effect, Clinton's honeymoon was in part sacrificed at the altar of his electoral coalition.

By contrast, George W. Bush had the luxury of not being forced to pander too much to traditional Republican constituencies. So anxious were Republicans to wrest control of the White House from the Democrats, that usually demanding groups such as the fundamentalist religious right gave Bush a "free pass" in the election. This allowed Bush to run as a centrist and attract more votes from independents. To pay the religious fundamentalists back for this, Bush selected John Ashcroft to serve as his attorney general. This pleased the fundamentalists but backfired when Ashcroft performed so poorly in the aftermath of September 11.

To govern, presidents must play the politics of the Beltway, that defining area surrounding Washington, D.C., which is sometimes seen (usually by political losers) as an alien culture. Governing requires the skills of "presidential schmoozing": pressing the political flesh, deal making, cajoling, trading, bargaining, persuasion, negotiation. It involves being feared and loved, playing what James M. Burns calls the lion and the fox; it involves being a politician. And all good politicians are coalition builders. It is the difference, journalist Hedrick Smith notes, between "outside politics" and "inside politics."[46] Smith writes further on the topic:

> In the campaign game, the winning presidential candidate builds a personal organization, but the successful president must work effectively with other organizations. He must work with other factions in his party, his party's national structure, the leadership in Congress, sometimes the opposition. Indeed, several recent presidents failed because of their inability to deal effectively with rival power centers: Kennedy and Carter, unable to forge durable governing coalitions in Congress; Nixon, Johnson, and Reagan, overreaching for power, usually in disregard of Congress because they did not want to deal with organized opposition or modify their positions to gain wider support. The contrast between campaigning and governing is, ultimately, the difference between stagecraft and statecraft.[47]

The political party can serve as an aid in coalition building. In 1981, Ronald Reagan relied on a unified Republican party to help push his program through Congress. President Clinton spent a good deal of time lobbying congressional Democrats on behalf of his agenda, but the Democrats were a fractured and combative lot (they wouldn't be Democrats if it were otherwise), and Clinton had a very difficult time keeping his majority together in Congress.[48]

Popularity

Leading the public is believed to be one of the key sources of power for a president. But the ability to move the nation and generate public support takes time and effort; it is not automatically conferred at the inauguration, nor is it always translated into political clout. Presidents spend a great deal of time and effort trying to build popular support both for themselves and their programs. Usually their efforts come to very little.[49]

A president with popular support (and other skills to complement popularity) can exert a great deal of pressure on Congress and is more likely to get his program passed.[50] As a result, presidents are keenly aware of fluctuations in popularity, and they routinely engage in efforts aimed at dramatizing themselves in the hope of increasing their ratings.

Popularity as a Source of Power

It is widely believed that popularity is a very convertible source of power, that presidents can convert popularity into congressional votes, better treatment by the media, and less criticism by political opponents. While hard evidence to support these claims is scarce, one must remember that, in politics, *perception* counts more than *reality*. If a president can convince the Congress that he is popular and therefore powerful, and that to defy him is politically dangerous, the battle is half won. In his first two years in office, this is precisely what Ronald Reagan was able to do. Democrats in Congress were afraid that Reagan's popularity might really have been as wide and as deep as Reagan claimed, and they therefore were more likely to vote for his legislative proposals and less likely to take him on frontally. The perception of power thus gave Reagan more power. In the aftermath of the 9/11 attack, President Bush's popularity soared to the 90 percent range. This led Democrats to be very cautious in their criticism of the president, and softened their opposition to some of his policies.

Can presidents convert popularity into power? Political scientist George Edwards is skeptical. After a statistical study of the relationship of popularity to power, Edwards concluded that while popularity may help, there is no certainty that presidents who are popular will get their legislative programs through Congress.[51]

But in *Presidential Power,* Richard Neustadt puts a great deal of emphasis on public support as a source of potential power, seeing the absence of support as a great weakening agent:

> The weaker his apparent popular support, the more his cause in Congress may depend on negatives at his disposal, like the veto, or "impounding." He may not be left helpless, but his options are reduced,

his opportunities diminished, his freedom for maneuver checked in the degree that Washington conceives him to be unimpressive to the public.[52]

Public support may empower presidents but is not an easy thing to attain. Abraham Lincoln knew well the potential power that rested in the hands of the public when he said, "Public sentiment is everything. With public sentiment nothing can fail, without it nothing can succeed."[53] And that is the challenge for presidents, to gain public support *and* convert it into political power. But as noted, public support is not always easy to attain nor is it always fungible. As Edwards and Wayne note, "The President is rarely in a position to command others to comply with his wishes. Instead he must rely on persuasion. A principal source of influence for the president is public approval of his performance and his policies."[54]

But how can presidents *lead* public opinion? Franklin Roosevelt asserted that "all our great Presidents were *leaders* of thought at times when certain historic ideas in the life of the nation had to be clarified," and his cousin Theodore Roosevelt observed, "People used to say of me that I . . . divined what the people were going to think. I did not 'divine' . . . I simply made up my mind what they ought to think, and then did my best to get them to think it."[55] But how?

The more active and policy-oriented presidents are not content to let popularity settle at its natural waterline; they actively pursue popular support and thereby hope to add to their political capital. Presidents invest a great deal of time and energy in self-dramatization, information control, image management, media events, generating "pretty pictures" for television, giving carefully crafted speeches, relying on symbolism and ceremony, to the point that the "public relations presidency" has in many ways eclipsed the policy presidency in time and attention.

Of course, there is only so much a president can do. Even Ronald Reagan, the "great communicator," had his limits. While he had the ability to put the best possible light on a given situation, he could not reshape reality at will. As Jody Powell, President Carter's press secretary, noted:

[With] communications and the management of them, the impact is marginal. The substance of what you do and what happens to you over the long haul is more important, particularly on the big things like the economy. . . . Poor communications comes up after a problem is already there, if an economic program doesn't work, if it is ill-conceived, or if circumstances change. . . . The ability to turn a sow's ear into silk purses is limited. You can make it into a silver sow's ear, that's all.[56]

The Public and the President

The president serves a variety of functions for the American public. Political scientist Fred Greenstein summarizes the psychological connection between the president and the people, noting that to the people, the president serves (1) as a symbol of national unity, stability, and the American way of life; (2) as an outlet for affect, for feeling good about America; (3) as a cognitive aid, simplifying complexity into a single symbol; and (4) as a means of vicarious participation in the political world.[57]

Because the president serves both as head of government (the nation's chief politician) and head of state (the symbolic representation of the nation), he is the chief divider of the nation as well as its chief unifier. Ronald Reagan was a masterful head of state, as evidenced in the aftermath of the Challenger disaster, when Reagan took on the role of high priest and national healer for a nation devastated by tragedy. This role, played so well by Reagan, added to his prestige and enabled him at once to reinforce his role as shaman, and to rise above politics and become a symbol for the whole nation. Likewise, a beleaguered Bill Clinton, facing a wide range of accusations and investigations, was able, in response to the terrorist attack in Oklahoma City, to serve as national healer and shaman for a grieving nation. This has also been a role played with mixed success by George W. Bush in the aftermath of the 9/11 attacks.

Thus invested in the office of the presidency is not only high respect but also high expectations (added to by presidential campaign promises). And yet, as noted in Chapter 2, the president's powers are not commensurate with his responsibilities or the public's expectations. This often leads presidents to frustration and also to declines in their popularity. In addition, if the public continues to demand that the government deliver on contradictory expectations (e.g., lower taxes *and* more government services), presidents are put in no-win situations. Given this dilemma, what's a president to do?

Theodore Lowi argues that presidents resolve this dilemma by resorting to rule by political manipulation. Impression management replaces policy achievement. Appearances are everything.[58] It is the president as the Wizard of Oz. The handlers of Ronald Reagan were the masters of the art of image manipulation. True, they had an excellent product to manage, but they masterfully played the media game, offering "pretty pictures" and staged events all designed to put the right spin on the situation. Brace and Hinckley maintain that this excessive reliance on appearances has led to the development of a "public-relations presidency . . . concerned primarily with maintaining and increasing public support."[59] In *The Personal President*, Lowi describes this development as "a plebiscitary republic with a personal presidency."

The President, the Public, and Democratic Theory

What is the proper function of the president as leader in our democratic system? Should he follow the public's wishes? Should he attempt to educate the public? Or should he attempt to *act*, to move the government in the direction he feels is best? Should the president find out what the people want and merely attempt to give it to them? Or should he speak truth (however unpleasant) to power?

The role of leader in a democratic society unveils a web of paradoxes and contradictions that can never be wholly resolved. And while the Founders feared a president who might fan the embers of popular passions,[60] it is clear that the "democratization"[61] of the presidency has led to the president's becoming the embodiment of the nation's government, making the president serve as a modern "interpreter in chief."[62]

Bruce Miroff writes eloquently of the "tension between leadership and democracy," arguing that for leadership to be democratic, the leader must have

> a respect for followers, rooted in a recognition of what Herman Melville called the "democratic dignity" of every individual. . . . Democratic leaders want for followers what they want for themselves; their goals are egalitarian rather than exclusionary. Committed to the democratic belief in self-government, they understand that leadership must aim at engagement with followers rather than mastery. Yet engagement is a far cry

from pandering; to nurture the democratic possibilities of citizenship, democratic leaders must be willing to question, challenge, even defy common conventions. In the face of the conventional antithesis between power and education, democratic leadership raises the possibility that dialogue between leaders and followers can be mutually empowering.[63]

In essence, democratic leadership encompasses a moral vision with egalitarian goals. Democratic leaders question, challenge, and empower citizens. They engage in a dialogue with the people. They are educators.[64]

During his presidency, Jimmy Carter often attempted to educate the people on the limits of America's power, thereby treating the American public with the respect due an educated citizenry in a democracy. But Carter was unable to convince the public that it had to settle for less, make sacrifices, and accept limits. Or perhaps the public refused to listen, refused to believe, and blamed the messenger. This opened the door for Ronald Reagan, who mocked limits, scoffed at sacrifice. He promised the public easy, quick solutions to complex problems. He flattered the public and told them to buy, buy, spend, spend. They did. And at the end of the eight years of the Reagan presidency, the United States went from being the world's largest creditor nation to the world's largest debtor nation. Carter spoke of a tough reality; Reagan offered the public candy. Carter gave the public stagflation; Reagan offered a new approach. Carter lost; Reagan won. In the absence of war, calling for sacrifice seems to be a no-win proposition.[65]

The Vagaries of Presidential Popularity

If popularity is a potential power resource,[66] and if presidents spend a great deal of time and effort attempting to boost their popularity, one can fairly ask, how malleable is opinion to efforts at presidential manipulation?

Between 1953 and 1965 (excluding only 1958), the average yearly presidential Gallup poll approval rating hovered at 60 percent or better. But starting in 1966, roughly the time when the most recent era of "failed presidents" begins, the level of popular support declines dramatically. Presidents who attained a 50 percent support

Table 3.1   Percentage of Public Expressing Approval of
President's Performance

President	Years in Office	Average During Presidency	First Year Average	Final Year Average
Harry Truman	1945–1952	41%	63%	35%
Dwight Eisenhower	1953–1960	64	74	62
John Kennedy	1961–1963	70	76	62
Lyndon Johnson	1963–1968	55	78	40
Richard Nixon	1969–1974	49	63	24
Gerald Ford	1974–1976	46	75	48
Jimmy Carter	1977–1980	47	68	46
Ronald Reagan	1981–1989	53	58	57
George Bush	1989–1992	61	65	40
Bill Clinton	1993–2000	57	50	60

Source: Averages compiled from Gallup polls, 1945–2000.

level were unusual (see Table 3.1). In the age of failed leaders, the average yearly popularity of presidents has dropped roughly 10 percent. As public expectations for the heroic model of the presidency soared, a gap between what was expected and what was delivered helped create what might be called a "delivery gap." Greater expectations led to greater disappointments—no matter what presidents do, it isn't enough (e.g., Clinton's September 1994 agreement on Haiti met with as much criticism as praise). No wonder these presidents have a hard time leading.[67]

While public approval is the result of many factors, and while presidents can get a short-term boost in popularity during what are called "rally events" (e.g., international threats), it is also clear that over the long haul, popularity is the product of public judgments both over the way things are going generally and how the president is doing his job.[68]

Popularity or, more broadly, "prestige"—to use Neustadt's term—is shaped by a complex web of factors, but overall, the most important is the public's perception of the state of the economy.[69] The public will praise or blame the sitting president for the state of the economy, regardless of what a president does or does not do. Thus, when the economy is booming, presidential popularity rises; when the economy is in a bust, the president's popularity drops. Students of presidential popularity would do well to remember the advice posted on the wall of the Clinton campaign headquarters during the 1992 election: "It's the economy, stupid!" Candidate Clinton persistently focused attention on the sour state of the economy, knowing that George H. Bush (whether he deserved it or not) would be blamed for the slow economy.

If popularity equals (to an extent) power, and if efforts to manipulate levels of popular support are limited, presidents are caught between a rock and a hard place (the Bermuda Triangle of presidential politics). They must constantly be concerned (obsessed) with their popularity, and yet their ability to generate support is often out of their control. Gone are the days when Harry S Truman could publicly show his disdain for approval ratings:

> I wonder how far Moses would have gone if he'd taken a poll in Egypt? What would Jesus Christ have preached if he'd taken a poll in Israel?. . . It isn't polls or public opinion of the moment that counts. It is right and wrong and leadership . . . that makes epochs in the history of the world.[70]

Polls and popularity ratings "have altered the time frame of democratic government, from quadrennial election to monthly review."[71] They force the president to dance to a different and much faster tune. With one eye always focused on popularity, presidents may be less likely to make the tough choices, the hard decisions.[72] Flattering the public has a greater short-term benefit than speaking the painful truth.

The relationship between the president and the public he is to simultaneously serve and lead is a complex one. In order to govern, a president must have a fairly high level of popular support. But the avenues open to a president for attaining that support are limited. Public demands and expectations are high and often contradictory. The public wants presidents to deliver good news, not hard reality. (It is no accident that candidates with a message of hope and optimism are more successful than candidates of gloom and doom.) In order to lead, presidents must juggle twenty different balls at once. It is no wonder that so few are up to the job.

The Media

Politically, the president is the nation's center of attention. But rarely can a president reach out and touch "real people." The media serves as the president's conduit for reaching the public. Through the media, especially television, the public sees the president, hears about his ideas, gets interpretations of how well or poorly he is doing his job. In this way, the media are, as Edwards and Wayne note, "the principal intermediary between the president and the public, and relations with the press are an important aspect of the president's efforts to lead public opinion."[73] Harold M. Barger puts it another way: "Presidents cannot succeed without the media, but they have difficulty surviving because of the media."[74]

Because the president is the nation's center of political attention, public expectations are fueled and the impression is created that the president is more powerful than he is. The media's fascination with presidents, their families, and their pets has led to increased attention lavished upon the president, who serves as the nation's "celebrity in chief." The gravitational pull of the presidency gives the president a ready-made bully pulpit, but it also has a down side. In an era of hypercritical investigative reporting, everything and any-

Reprinted with permission of Paul Conrad.

thing a president does is fodder for tabloid journalists. With TV talk shows such as Larry King and radio call-in shows with slash-and-burn DJs, we have an abundance of information but a shortage of knowledge. The micro coverage of the president trivializes the office, the man, and politics itself. Washington has become Hollywood-on-the-Potomac, and the president becomes one more pop cultural icon.

Presidents are too politically attractive to ignore. John Orman's study of periodical literature shows that Franklin D. Roosevelt averaged 109.5 stories per year of his presidency, John Kennedy averaged about 200, and Jimmy Carter averaged 407 per year. Ronald Reagan averaged over 500 stories per year.[75] By contrast, network news coverage of Congress has declined by roughly 50 percent between 1975 and 1985.[76]

This trend has both positive and negative consequences. But one thing is clear: It places the president at the center of media attention and elevates the president in the minds of the public. Hedrick Smith comes to this conclusion:

> As a nation, we focus obsessively on the president, out of proportion with other power centers. This happens largely because the president is one person whom it is easy for television to portray and whom the public feels it can come to know. Other power centers are harder to depict: The Supreme Court is an aloof and anonymous body; Congress is a confusing gaggle of 535 people; the bureaucracy is vast and faceless. It is almost as if the president, most politicians, and the press, especially television, have fallen into an unconscious conspiracy to create a cartoon caricature of the real system of power. There is a strong urge for simplicity in the American psyche, a compulsion to focus on the single dramatic figure at the summit, to reduce the intricacy of a hundred power-plays to the simple equation of whether the president is up or down, winning or losing on any given day or week.[77]

Since the media serve as the president's conduit to to the public, and because so much is riding on good press coverage, no president can afford to ignore, or even leave to chance, his relations with the media. Presidents must devise and implement strategies for attaining good press, and efforts at media manipulations are quite common. This has led to the creation of what Thomas E. Cronin has called the "theatrical presidency,"[78] in which public relations specialists take precedence over policy people and style rules over substance. Reagan handler Michael Deaver (dubbed the "Vicar of Visuals") went so far as to admit that "image is sometimes as useful as substance."[79]

With the rise of the theatrical presidency has come an increase in efforts at presidential self-dramatization, at using public relations techniques and image management as a replacement for policy, at staging media events and framing the president in "pretty pictures" for the evening news. (During the 1988 presidential race it seemed impossible to turn on a television set and *not* see George Bush wrapped—literally and figuratively—in an American flag.)

Given that presidents are limited in what they can accomplish, and given that the public expects presidents to deliver the goods, sometimes, when faced with an inability to achieve policy results, presidents will resort to political grandstanding to give the impression that they are doing something. No administration used image management more often or better than the Reagan team. It is no overstatement to say that they were obsessed with image, and style was often used as a replacement for substance.[80]

In a perverse example of the tail wagging the dog, policy is often used for the public relations advantage it might deliver. And presidents can use selected pictures and images to erase political reality. At the time President Reagan proposed a cut in funds to assist the handicapped, the president went to a Special Olympics event and the pictures on the evening news showed a caring, concerned Ronald Reagan while the reality was that the president wanted to slash funding. And when polls revealed that the public disapproved of Reagan's civil rights policies, the president paid a very public (and media-filled) visit to a black family that had had a cross burned on its front lawn. (The cross burning occurred five years before Reagan's visit, but when one needs good visuals, what's a few years?) Reagan *appeared* to be concerned and caring. If his policies revealed an attempted reversal in civil rights reinforcement, then his pictures had to supplant reality. It was the Wizard of Oz *before* Toto pulled back the curtain. If carefully managed, one picture truly can be worth a thousand words.

This obsession with image has in effect forced presidents to campaign 365 days a year—and to attempt to govern in a campaign mode and constantly paint pretty pictures for public consumption. As Hedrick Smith notes:

> In the image game, the essence is not words, but pictures. The Reagan imagemakers followed the rule framed by Bob Haldeman, the advertising man who was Nixon's chief of staff, the governing principle for politics in the television era: The visual wins over the verbal; the eye predominates over the ear; sight beats sound. As one Reagan official laughingly said to me, "What are you going to believe, the facts or your eyes?"[81]

Going Public

The image-management strategy of presidential power in the media age is called "going public." Samuel Kernell sees an unending political campaign in which presidents go public in an effort to increase political clout within the Washington community.[82]

In this, the United States has come a long way from what the creators of the presidency envisioned. The inventors of the presidency, as Jeffrey Tulis reminded us, feared a president who was too closely linked to the public because it might "manifest demagoguery, impede deliberation, and subvert the routines of republican government."[83] Such fears reflected the opposition to democracy shared by many of the Founders. Over time, such concerns gave way to the unstoppable logic of the electronic media and the need to use whatever levers a president could find to increase power.

Today, presidents go public because they have few other options. In a political landscape cluttered with the carcasses of failed presidents, an incumbent must use whatever resources are available, and governing by appearance, when governing by accomplishment fails, is something to which presidents often resort.

Managing the News

Upon entering office, presidents feel compelled to announce their intention of having an "open presidency." Such efforts are always short-lived. As James Davis notes, "News management follows on the heels of the so-called open presidency as the fall follows summer."[84] Presidents soon become concerned with the release of bad news, or leaked information, and begin to engage in news (or information) management.

Presidents can wield a carrot or a stick in dealing with the press, and some presidents revert to a "blame the messenger" strategy and attack the media. During the Nixon years, Vice President Spiro Agnew was used as the pointman in media attacks designed to (1) soften press coverage, (2) put the media on the defensive, and (3) plant seeds of doubt in the minds of the public so they would be less likely to believe press criticism of the president.[85]

While press harassment can have an effect, most presidents mix strategic approaches. In attempting to positively influence press coverage, presidents used a mix of strategies ranging from co-optation (Kennedy) to condemnation (Nixon).

It is important to link the media strategy to a president's political agenda. To do this, the president must coordinate the media strategy to the policy. In this, presidents would be advised to follow the Haldeman rule. As Richard Nixon's chief of staff, Bob Haldeman insisted that before something went on the president's agenda, or schedule, the staff member who proposed it had to tell (1) what the expected headline would be; (2) what the photo accompanying the headline would be; and (3) how the first paragraph of the story would read. The Reagan administration followed a variant of this model. Key aides met at 8:15 every morning to decide what the story of the day would be. They also developed long-term strategies for shaping the agenda.

By thinking strategically with a media focus, a president may be able to command media attention and shape the coverage of his agenda. The president must choreograph every step, "wallpaper" stories with attractive visuals, and when things sour, send the spin doctors out to do damage control.

Walter Mondale may be partially correct when he says that the electronic media are largely to blame for turning the presidency into the nation's "fire hydrant,"[86] but the media are also a source of presidential power. There are times when the media are the lapdog for the president,[87] and at other times, the media check presidential power. If a president does not actively use the media, he may become their victim.

Whether the media are lapdog or power drain to a president depends on a variety of factors: the president's performance, his management of the news, events, the president's "charisma," and so on. But no president can casually approach the media. A clear strategy or game plan is needed if presidents are to dominate in this relationship.

Are the media biased? If so, are they biased in favor of the left or right of the political spectrum? During the twelve years of Republican presidents from 1980 to 1992, conservatives insisted that the press was out to get first Ronald Reagan and then George Bush. But was this charge accurate? The media do a strange mating dance when the president is the subject, and one may be inclined to level the charge of bias when one's preferred president is being criticized in the press. In point of fact, George Bush did get rough treatment form the media in 1992. If that is the point at which one measures bias, it might appear that indeed the press was out to get Bush. But if you choose a different point of time to measure bias, say, the first six months of the Clinton presidency, an entirely different picture emerges. Clinton was pummeled in the media during his presidency (to a degree, deservedly).[88] Less than two weeks into the Clinton presidency, ABC News's Sam Donaldson said, "This week we can talk about 'Is the [Clinton] presidency over?" No president in recent years was treated as roughly as Bill Clinton. So relentless were the media attacks on Clinton that the Oval Office began to resemble an Oval Bunker. After the Clinton years, accusations that the media were biased in favor of liberals rang hollow.

Rather than look upon the media in a left-right fashion, it is probably more accurate to see the media as a herd. Generally, the media follow a herd mentality. When the president is up, they lay off (Reagan in 1984, Nixon in 1972, Bush post–9/11); when the president is down, they gang up (Nixon in 1974, Bush in 1992, Clinton in early 1993).[89]

Overall, presidents dislike the press because it quotes them. But, in order to govern, presidents must work with and through the media, and presidents must think and act strategically where media are concerned. Good press makes governing a bit easier; bad press makes governing all but impossible. The easiest way to get good press is to do a good job. Failing that (and almost all presidents do), presidents often degenerate into efforts to control and manipulate the media.

Congress

Major Pierre L'Enfant, principal designer of the nation's capital, had more than space in mind when he located the president and Congress at opposite ends of the avenue. The Congress would be housed atop Jenkins Hill, giving it the high ground. The President would find his home about one mile away, at the end of a long street that would serve as a threadlike link connecting these two institutions. Not only did the Constitution separate the executive and legislative branches, but geography as well would keep these two branches apart.[90]

But for the U.S. system to work, both branches must find ways to bridge the gap, to join what is separated. The Founders saw the separation of powers not as a weakness (as we tend to see it today), but as a strength, as a way to ensure deliberation and thoughtfulness, as a way to prevent tyranny. But how does a president develop the syncopation of the branches necessary to make the system of separate institutions sharing power work? How can a president couple what the Founders decoupled?

Beyond question, the relationship between the president and Congress is the most important one in the American system of government, and while the president spends a great deal of time and energy courting the media and appealing to the public, he does so in order to gain leverage with Congress. For, in the long run, presidents must get Congress to formally or tacitly accept their proposals, lest they run the risk of deadlock, delay, or failure. After all, only Congress can allocate resources, and presidents who consistently attempt to go around the Congress cannot long succeed. The president may not like it, but he can't live without Congress.

While there are a select few areas in which presidents may act semi-independently of the Congress, most of the president's goals require a partnership with Congress. This is no easy matter. As one longtime presidential adviser has noted, "I suspect that there may be nothing about the White House less generally understood than the ease with which a Congress can drive a President quite out of his mind and up the wall."[91]

In matters requiring legislative authorization, the Congress ultimately has the upper hand. Though the president may be seen as leader of the nation, agenda setter, vision builder, or legislator in chief, it is often the Congress that has the final say. And since there are multiple veto points in Congress, any of which may block a president's proposal, the forces wishing to prevent change almost always have the upper hand. The American system has many negative veto points but few avenues for positive change.

In the expectations game, the president is supposed to dominate Congress. But public expectations notwithstanding, the president's legislative powers are constitutionally (Article 2, Section 3) quite thin. He has the veto power,[92] reports on the state of the Union, and extraconstitutionally may suggest legislation, lobby Congress, set the agenda, and build coalitions, but overall his *powers over* Congress are very limited.

In this sense, the Constitution sets up what Edward S. Corwin refers to as an "invitation to struggle" over political control of the Constitution (the power of the government). Another way to look at it is to see the Constitution as creating a situation in which "guerilla warfare" between the president and the Congress is almost inevitable.[93] Since Congress has "all legislative powers" and the president has limited legislative powers, conflict is built into the system.

Originally (constitutionally) the Congress was established as the dominant branch of government, and the first few presidents were only minimally involved in the legislative process. But the Founders' vision soon gave way to political reality, and slowly presidents began to pull power into the White House, and generally the Congress was a willing participant in giving more and more power to the presidency. Today, as Robert Spitzer describes it, "What was designed as a congressionally centered system has evolved into a presidentially centered, or 'executive hegemonic', system."[94] Still, the Congress has a way of frustrating even the most skilled of presidents.[95]

While the image or expectation of the president is as "chief legislator" who "guides Congress in much of its lawmaking activity,"[96] the reality is quite different. The decentralized nature of the Congress, the multiple access and veto points within the congressional process, the loosely organized party system, the independent-entrepreneurial mode of the legislators, and the weakness of the legislative leadership all conspire against presidential direction and leadership.[97] As Edwards points out, this means that presidents impact Congress only "at the margins" and are more "facilitators" than leaders.[98]

Lest the system break down into hopeless gridlock, the president and Congress must find ways to work together. The theory upon which the U.S. government is based hinges on some cooperation between these two branches. As Justice Robert Jackson wrote in 1952, "While the Constitution diffuses power the better to secure liberty, it also contemplates that practice will integrate the dispersed powers into a workable government."[99]

Dealing with Congress

Under what conditions is a president most likely to establish his agenda and get congressional support? Put another way, when is Congress most likely to follow a president's lead?

Several factors lead to presidential success when dealing with Congress. First, in a crisis, the president is accorded a great deal of deference, and the Congress usually backs up the president. Second, when a president has a clear electoral mandate (when the campaign was issue-oriented, the president wins by a wide margin, and the president's party has a sizable majority in Congress), the Congress sometimes will follow. Third, the president can exert pressure on members of Congress when he, the president, wins the election by a landslide *and* runs ahead of the members in his or her own district (this is usually referred to as "presidential coattails"). Part of President Clinton's problems with Congress can be traced to the fact that he ran behind most members in their districts, didn't have a clear electoral mandate, and did not face a crisis. Fourth, high levels of presidential popularity are often said to be a source of power over Congress. But how easily can presidents translate popularity into power? Many social scientists are suspicious, believing that popularity has only a marginal impact on presidential success within Congress.[100] But others argue that popularity does translate into power.[101] Richard Neustadt places a great deal of emphasis on presidential prestige as a source of power and influence, and his view is echoed by Stanford's Richard A. Brody:

> Presidential poll ratings are important because they are thought to be important. They are thought to be important because political leaders look for indications of when it is safe or dangerous to oppose their policy interests or career ambitions to those of the president and because indications of political support—which in other political context might be preferred—are too limited in scope to be relied upon in this context.[102]

Fifth, skill does make a difference, but how much of a difference? As is the case with popularity, scholars disagree about the importance of skill in legislative success, with some arguing that skill is of little importance,[103] while others see skill as very important.[104] Presidency scholar George Edwards warns that

> it is important to depersonalize somewhat the study of presidential leadership and examine it from a broader perspective. In this way there are fewer risks of attributing to various aspects of presidential leadership consequences of factors largely beyond the president's control. Similarly, one is less likely to attribute incorrectly the failure of a president to achieve his goals to his failure to lead properly. Things are rarely so simple.[105]

High skill levels can give a president greater leverage to win in the congressional process. A variety of skills—knowledge of the congressional process and needs; good timing, bargaining, deal making, persuasion, and coalition-building skill; moving the public, setting the agenda, self-dramatization, arm twisting, trading, consultation and co-optation, and even threats—can all be used to advance the president's goals.

Lyndon Johnson, arguably the most skilled of the modern presidents vis-à-vis Congress—who also came into office on the heels of the martyred President Kennedy, won election by a huge landslide,

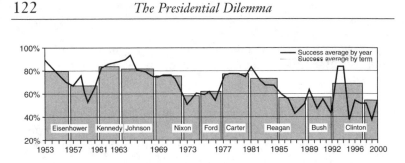

Figure 3.1   Presidential Success in Congress.
Source: Adapted From Congressional Quarterly Weekly Reports, December 19, 1992, p. 2896; updated.

and had a huge partisan majority and a shattered opposition in Congress—explained that there was only one way to deal with Congress

> and that is continuously, incessantly, and without interruption. If it's really going to work, the relationship between the president and Congress has got to be almost incestuous. He's got to know them even better than they know themselves. And then, on the basis of this knowledge, he's got to build a system that stretches from the cradle to the grave, from the moment a bill is introduced to the moment it is officially enrolled as the law of the land.[106]

President Johnson perfected what came to be know as "the Johnson Treatment." Journalists Evans and Novak describe it as follows:

> Its tone could be supplication, accusation, cajolery, exuberance, scorn, tears, complaint, the hint of threat. It was all of these together. It ran the gamut of human emotions. Its velocity was breathtaking, and it was all in one direction. Interjections from the target were rare. Johnson anticipated them before they could be spoken. He moved in close, his face a scant millimeter from his target, his eyes widening and narrowing, his eyebrows rising and falling. From his pockets poured slips, memos, statistics. Mimicry, humor, and the genius of analogy made The Treatment an almost hypnotic experience and rendered the target stunned and helpless.[107]

Lyndon Johnson could be a presidential pit bull, but he was afforded that luxury only partly due to personal skills. LBJ had, as mentioned earlier, other significant advantages that made his power more robust and his threats more credible (compare the resources Johnson had to the more meager power resources of Bush or Clinton). One of the most important of these power resources is party support.

Partisan support in Congress is the sixth major factor shaping presidential success in Congress. Lyndon Johnson had such a large majority in Congress that, even if several dozen Democrats abandoned the president, he could still get his majority in Congress. George H. Bush, on the other hand, faced a Congress in the control of the opposition, and he was thus stymied in Congress. Bill Clinton had a paper-thin majority, and any defections undermined his legislative hopes. This forced Clinton to do a great deal of vote trading and deal making with congressional Democrats in order to get his 1993 deficit-reduction bill passed by Congress as not one Republican voted for the president's proposal. In fact, deal making is a very common form of presidential leverage in attempting to extract votes from a recalcitrant Congress. Reagan Budget Director David Stockman noted that "the last 10 or 20 percentage of the votes needed for a majority of both houses on the 1981 tax cut had to be bought, period. . . . The hogs were really feeding."[108]

Related to this is the seventh factor: the nature of the opposition in Congress. How many votes do they have? How ideologically driven are they? How willing are they to work with the president? In 1981, President Reagan faced a Senate controlled by his own party but a House controlled by the Democrats. Reagan was able—via skill, luck, and circumstance—to win over enough Democrats (referred to as the "Boll Weevils") to win several significant legislative battles. By contrast, while President Clinton had majorities in both houses, the Republican opposition was so ornery (Senator Dole of Kansas, in the first six months of Clinton's term, seemed determined to bring the Clinton presidency down) and so unified (on Clinton's 1993 economic package, not one Republican senator supported the president) that Clinton had an amazingly difficult time getting a win.[109]

Because of the nature of partisan politics, the eighth factor that shapes presidential success or failure in Congress is the nature of consultation between the two branches. One of the lessons President Clinton learned is that a president must consult not only with his own partisans but with the opposition as well. There are so many veto points in the legislative process that attempting to gain cooperation and agreement must be the first step. If a president sets up an effective legislative liaison office and he can co-opt the Congress, he can often gain support.

Finally, the type of agenda a president pursues has a significant impact. George H. Bush had a very "thin" legislative agenda, and he pursued it only half-heartedly. Bill Clinton had a very ambitious agenda, making it more difficult to get the Congress to go along.

In recent years, presidents have spent less time "going Washington" and more time "going public." The inside bargaining skills necessary to cut deals have been replaced by or supported by efforts at self-dramatization. In the loose bargaining regime of the Congress, presidents feel their time is better spent appealing directly to the public for support (which may translate into clout in Congress). But ultimately presidents must cut deals in Congress.

Initially, President Clinton's style of dealing with Congress was to use the "soft sell." Rarely did he twist arms or pressure legislators for a vote. This was partly a function of Clinton's preferred personal style of operating, but it also reflected his tenuous political position. Whereas Lyndon Johnson liked to and had the power to bully legislators, Clinton neither liked to nor did he have the power to get away with playing the role of presidential pit bull.[110]

But as the first year of Clinton's presidency drew to a close, the president changed form and as the vote on the North American Free Trade Agreement (NAFTA) drew close, Clinton showed a great dexterity in dealing with Congress. With some he cajoled, with others he traded, with still others he applied pressure.[111] President Clinton demonstrated that, unlike most presidents, he could learn from his mistakes, develop a flexible style of "going Washington," and win major come-from-behind legislative victories.

Riding high in the aftermath of the NAFTA victory, Clinton was able to push a major crime bill through Congress, got the House to pass the controversial Brady Bill (a modest gun-control proposal), and began his push for health-care reform. Overall, Clinton had a very good (early blunders not withstanding) first year in Congress, winning legislative support for his proposals roughly 90 percent of the time. By this measure, President Clinton had one of the more successful first years in modern history.[112]

Can presidents lead Congress? Yes, but not often and not for long. A mix of skill, circumstances, luck, popularity, party support, timing, and resources need to converge if the syncopation of the branches is to occur.

Management

Political leadership is more than "great men" (persons) charting new territory and inspiring the masses to change. Leadership, in fact, rarely if ever follows the "great man/person" theory. True leadership does involve the promotion of vision. But it involves much more than this. Good management is also necessary if the leader is to succeed.

This raises the question: which dominates, the president or the presidency, the individual or the institution?[113] And how bendable are institutions to the will of individual presidents?[114]

The presidency is not just one man; it is also an institution. With the growth of the positive role of the federal government in solving the nation's problems, and with the growth of presidential responsibilities to accomplish these problem-solving tasks, the Institutional Presidency was born. So vast is the modern executive structure that most people see the presidency as unmanageable. The administrative duties of the presidency have risen enormously since the days of FDR, to the point that today the president is the unmasterful master of an enormous amalgamation that includes the White House staff, the Cabinet, the Executive Office of the President (EOP), and the bureaucracy.

The modern presidency is a collection of people in an institutional framework. How a president organizes his administration goes a long way in indicating what his interests, goals, and priorities are. But there are a number of potential pitfalls in presidential administration. Problems of sheer size and unmanageability, complicated issues and problems, competing demands for scarce resources, clientele demands, congressional controls, interagency competition, and a host of other problems await the president as Chief Administrator.[115]

There is a difference between leadership and management. Management is a subset of good leadership. Generally, good leaders are (must be) good managers, but not all good managers are good leaders. Many institutions are well managed but poorly led.[116] Doing the wrong thing well is no bargain. Success at accomplishing bad things is not the goal of government. Warren Bennis sees the difference between leadership and management in the following manner:

- The manager administers; the leader innovates.
- The manager is a copy; the leader is an original.
- The manager maintains; the leader develops.
- The manager focuses on systems and structure; the leader focuses on people.
- The manager relies on control; the leader inspires trust.
- The manager has a short-range view; the leader has a long-range perspective.
- The manager asks how and when; the leader asks what and why.
- The manager has his eye always on the bottom line; the leader has his eye on the horizon.
- The manager imitates; the leader originates.
- The manager accepts the status quo; the leader challenges it.
- The manager is the classic good soldier; the leader is his own person.
- The manager does things right; the leader does the right thing.[117]

It behooves presidents to pay close attention to management. If a president wishes to see his policies and directives implemented, he will have to rely upon government agencies to faithfully execute his wishes. And as we know, presidential orders *are not* self-executing. One could trace almost all of the major scandals and presidential blunders to failures of management.

One of the first questions a president must decide when putting together his administration is, How strong a chief of staff will he have? James P. Pfiffner, the leading academic voice of presidential management, argues that there are "two firm lessons of White House organizations that can be ignored by Presidents only at their own peril: No. 1, a chief of staff is essential in the modern White House; No. 2, A domineering chief of staff will almost certainly lead to trouble." (Note, for example, the troubled tenures of Sherman Adams under Eisenhower, H. R. Haldeman for Nixon, Donald Regan for Reagan, and John Sununu for Bush.) Pfiffner concludes that "the preferred role for a chief of staff is that of a facilitator, coordinator, and neutral broker."[118]

Apart from his selection of a chief of staff, a president must also decide how to organize that staff. There are a variety of different models one could follow: FDR's competitive approach, which set staff members off against other staff members in a dynamic tension; JFK's collegial style, which sought a cooperative, bonding approach; Nixon's hierarchical model, with a closed, rigid pyramid of access and line of authority; and Reagan's delegating style, which transferred power and authority to the underlings.[119] Presidents tend to select a staff system based on (1) previous experience (Eisenhower chose a hierarchical model because he was accustomed to operating in a military structure) and (2) personality needs and preferred operating style (Nixon wanted a hierarchical system to protect him and keep him out of staff discussions).

There is no ideal organizational model. Each style of staff organization has costs and benefits. The key for the president is to know himself—his strengths and weaknesses—and to model his staff in a way that takes advantage of his strengths but also prevents his weaknesses from leading to serious mistakes. (Box 3.1 presents a list of management skills needed.)

Walt Williams's list is an excellent starting point that catalogues the key skills necessary for effective White House staffing. But it is the president's job to ensure that the administration is both well led and well managed. In this the president has a number of options from which to choose.

While there is no "correct" staffing model, there are several things presidents must be aware of lest they risk managerial (which translates into political) failure: (1) presidents need to spend time on managing; (2) presidents need to spend political capital managing;

BOX 3.1

Staffing Knowledge and Skills in a White House Policy Unit

1. **Integration capacity:** the ability to synthesize across policies and between policy and politics.

2. **Strategic thinking:** the ability to develop broad (macro) objectives, to analyze these objectives and the underlying assumptions as to consistency with other states objectives and as to feasibility of implementation, and to refine and integrate these objectives.

3. **Process management leadership:** the ability to manage for the president (or his inner-circle designee) policy formulation or problem resolution in the executive branch.

4. **Policy analysis and quantitative techniques:** a mastery of the various policy analysis approaches and techniques and statistical techniques used by peer analysts inside and outside the government.

5. **Substantive (policy area) knowledge:** an in-depth understanding of particular policy areas, including relevant scholarly work, program and policy information, and analyses.

6. **Political knowledge:** an in-depth understanding of the political process, including the politics of particular substantive areas as manifested in the EOP, Congress, and federal agencies.

7. **Organizational knowledge:** an in-depth understanding of the organizational structure and bureaucratic politics of the agencies responsible for particular substantive areas.

8. **Monitoring:** the capacity to engage in efforts to ascertain how well policies and programs in the analyst's policy area are being implemented or managed.

Source: Walter Williams, *Mismanaging America: The Rise of the Anti-Analytic Presidency* (Lawrence: University Press of Kansas, 1990), p. 134.

(3) presidents need a mix of old experienced White House staffers *and* some new fresh thinkers from the outside; (4) presidents need a devil's advocate close to the center of power whose job it is to poke holes in the ideas and programs that are proposed (all presidents need someone who can tell them to their face that they are screwing up); and (5) presidents need to be somewhat flexible in style.

The Rise of the Administrative Presidency

As presidents fail to get Congress to respond favorably to their legislative proposals, ways are sometimes found to "get around" Congress. Frustrated by the Congress' nay-saying, presidents look for ways to achieve their policy goals without going through the difficult and cumbersome legislative arena. One strategic approach popularized by recent presidents is to devise an administrative agenda for governing.[120]

When Congress fails to legislate, presidents sometimes try to administrate. That is, they employ managerial or administrative means to policy ends. Durant and Warber identify three facets of the administrative presidency:

> First, congressional opposition to presidential legislative initiatives is the rule rather than the exception. Second, federal agencies make policy as they exercise bureaucratic discretion when implementing statutes. Consequently, presidents have another opportunity to "legislate" that does not require them to mobilize legislative majorities or supermajorites in Congress. Third, and premised on conventional notions of hierarchical control, presidents indirectly can influence policy by naming political appointees to agencies who either substantively or ideologically share their policy agendas. These appointees, in turn, can change agency rules, budgets, structures, and personnel requirements to suit presidential policy goals. In contrast to this more "indirect" (or "contextual") approach of acting through agents, presidents can take a more direct (or "unilateral") approach. They do so when issuing executive orders, proclamations, presidential signing statements, national security directives, and presidential memoranda.[121]

Increasingly presidents use these administrative devices to make policy. Richard Nixon is credited with "inventing" this strategy, but it did not fully blossom until the Reagan presidency. Reagan aggressively employed a strategy that politicized the managerial side of the presidency in an effort to circumvent Congress and govern on his own terms. President Clinton, learning the lesson well, continued using an administrative strategy to govern, especially after 1995 and the Republican takeover in Congress.[122]

Using executive orders, memoranda, signing statements, and a variety of other administrative devices, presidents have been able to make policy without and sometimes against the will of Congress. This form of unilateral power gives the president the ability to impose his will in the absence of congressional approval and, with the support of the Supreme Court, which has held that Executive Orders have, under most circumstances, the full force of the law.[123]

An "executive order" is a directive issued by the president to assist him in his capacity as chief executive of the nation. Originally, the executive order was intended for rather minor administrative and rule-making functions, to help the nation's chief administrative officer administer the laws of the nation more efficiently and effectively. However, over time, the executive order has become an important and sometimes controversial tool enabling the president to make policy without the consent of Congress as required by the Constitution.[124]

As the nation's chief executive, the president bears significant administrative and managerial responsibilities. In order to do his job, a president needs the power and authority to issue administrative orders and instructions. The executive order is an "implied" power, not specifically mentioned in the Constitution but deemed essential for the functioning of government. Thus presidents rely on executive orders to better fulfill their constitutional duties as chief executive.

George Washington issued the first executive order on June 8, 1789. It instructed heads of departments (cabinet officers) to make a "clear account" of matters in their departments. Under the National Administration Procedure Act of 1946, all executive orders must be published in the *Federal Register.* Congress, if it wishes, can overturn an executive order. Executive orders can also be challenged in court on grounds that they may violate the Constitution.

Over time, presidents have gone beyond the use of executive orders for merely administrative matters and have begun to use orders to "make law" on more substantive and controversial matters.

Increasingly, presidents have turned to administrative techniques such as executive orders in an effort to bypass the slow and frustrating process of going through Congress to pass legislation. Thus presidents use executive orders along with proclamations, memoranda, findings, directives, and signing statements to boost their administrative reach over policy. Such efforts to bypass Congress sometimes overstep the bounds of what is an appropriate use of administrative tools of the office. Presidents have been accused, with some justification, of "going around" Congress and "legislating" independently of Congress.

Presidents have used executive orders to implement some very controversial policies. In 1942, during World War II, Franklin Roosevelt interned Japanese-American citizens in detention centers. In 1948, Harry S Truman integrated the military. In 1952, Truman attempted to seize control of steel mills. And in 1992, Bill Clinton directed the Coast Guard to return Haitian refugees found at sea to Haiti. In 2001, President Bush issued a series of orders aimed at undermining terrorist organizations in the United States and abroad. All these acts were done through executive orders.

Many of these presidential efforts have been challenged in the courts. And while in general the courts have recognized the legitimacy and legality of executive orders, not all orders pass the test of constitutionality. In 1952, for example, during the Korean War, President Truman seized the nation's steel mills to prevent a work stoppage that might have negatively affected the war effort. The Supreme Court, in *Youngstown Sheet and Tube Co. v. Sawyer*, decided that the president's actions were unconstitutional. Truman was forced to back down. But such limitations are the exception. Overall, presidents have been able to take control of a variety of significant policy areas through the use of administrative tools such as the executive order. They have become an important weapon in the president's arsenal and are likely to remain so into the future.

Politicizing the Bureaucracy

Over time, presidents have a tendency to get suspicious, even paranoid, about the bureaucracy. The fear that members of his administration would, in Nixon aide John Ehrlichman's words, "go native" and represent the interest of the agency—and not the president—permeated the Nixon White House, and it is a view shared by many presidents.

As the nation's chief executive officer, the president is supposed to sit at the top of the bureaucracy and control its actions. But his control is incomplete at best. A president operates under a four-year time restraint; the bureaucracy has no such time constraint. The old saying "Presidents come and go but bureaucrats stay and stay" speaks volumes to the different time frames under which the president and bureaucracy operate. The president is the temporary occupant of the White House; the bureaucracy is part of the permanent government. Notorious Clinton political consultant Dick Morris describes the bureaucratic essence:

> The permanent bureaucracy of the executive branch of a democratic government is dedicated to a single mission: to change nothing. Left or right matters little. they are neither liberal nor conservative. They are in favor of things as they are. In pursuit of that mission they are canny, shrewd, ruthless, and conspiratorial. They infiltrate the ranks of those who want change with the goal of destroying them. They use delay and details to overwhelm new ideas and to force a continuation of the status quo.[125]

What approach should the president take in the management of the bureaucracy? Should he seek "neutral competence"—a non-politicized collection of experts? Or should he seek to politicize the levers of the administration—that is, to develop "responsive competence" so as to promote responsiveness to his partisan and policy objectives? This latter approach is characterized by Richard Nathan as the "administrative presidency strategy."[126] In this case the president, frustrated by the roadblocks Congress places before him, concentrates on an administrative strategy for accomplishing political goals. Given that Congress is unusually unresponsive, this method allows the president to bypass Congress and achieve through management and regulatory techniques what he could not get in the legislative arena.[127]

The model for a politicized bureaucracy was the Reagan administration. Facing a Congress controlled by the opposition, and wanting to implement a clear ideological agenda, Reagan was not content to rely upon the legislature to accomplish his goals. He employed an

administrative strategy characterized by the self-conscious recruitment of ideological loyalists (Reaganauts, or "Reagan-nuts" as their
critics charged); a focused ideological agenda, using administrative
rule-making instead of legislative authorization; and, where necessary, a disregard for the law (exemplified by the Iran-Contra scandal). The results were mixed.

While Reagan was able to accomplish some of his goals via an
administrative strategy, the downside included a very high level of
corruption (Iran-Contra, the HUD scandal, the sleaze factor); some
ideologically sound but incompetent appointments (James Watt at
Interior); and the creation of a backlash when Reagan's political end-
run strategy came to light.

Good management requires time and effort. There is no administrative quick fix. The temptation of presidents to overly politicize
the bureaucracy may seem to hold great promise, but it is fraught
with dangers. Rather than settle for neutral competence or seek to
overly politicize the bureaucracy, a strategy of responsive (but not
politicized) competence seems the wisest course.

Policy Arenas: Foreign Versus Domestic

Most scholars believe that there are significant differences in the
institutional balance of power when one compares the realms of
domestic and foreign policy. It is widely believed that presidents have
greater power in the foreign policy arena than they do in domestic
and economic policy.

In the mid-1960s, political scientist Aaron Wildavsky argued that
since the end of the World War II, presidents have been more successful at attaining their policy goals from Congress in foreign policy than in the domestic arena. Thus, Wildavsky concluded, there
may be one president, but there are "two presidencies": one, a fairly
powerful foreign policy presidency; the other, a fairly constrained
domestic presidency. Commenting on the power of the presidency in
the international arena, Wildavsky asserted that "there has not been
a single major issue on which Presidents, when they were serious and
determined, have failed."[128]

Initially, Wildavsky's thesis became holy writ. But recently, challenges have emerged.[129] Wildavsky's data, so convincing when they were drawn from the 1950s and 1960s, were not as convincing in the post–Vietnam War era. After Vietnam, the Congress became more assertive and intrusive, and presidential leadership became more problematic. Even Wildavsky, by the late 1980s, had backed away from his two-presidencies thesis, writing that "'The Two Presidencies' is time and culture bound" and also admitting that in his initial formulation, the thesis was very narrowly defined, with congressional voting patterns as *the* measure of proof.[130]

Indeed, by its narrowest measure, the two-presidencies thesis does appear less plausible in the post-Vietnam era. But merely looking at congressional voting patterns does a disservice to the broader, richer opportunities of which presidents take advantage to get their way in foreign policy. Congressional voting is but one—and not the most important—measure of power in foreign affairs. Presidents can act, make policy, be proactive, leaving the Congress behind. Congressional voting only measures a president's success *in* Congress. But so much is done *without* the Congress that in foreign affairs, presidents maintain considerable leverage over the legislature.[131] Indeed, there *are* two presidencies, and the foreign policy presidency, while not in absolute control of foreign affairs, does have a great deal of latitude in determining policy.

Even in the post-Vietnam era of political contention, divided government, and ideological division, presidents *usually* got their way in foreign affairs. For example, during the Reagan years, even though the Congress expressly voted to prevent Reagan from aiding the rebels (Contras) in Nicaragua, Reagan violated the law and ended up doing what he wanted anyway. This was possible because presidents have a variety of ways of accomplishing their foreign policy goals, apart from congressional enabling legislation. Presidents can merely act. "I make foreign policy," Harry Truman said, and indeed presidents are widely seen (the Constitution notwithstanding) as being the primary directors of foreign policy for the nation.

While Wildavsky's two-presidencies thesis may be a bit oversimplified, it does capture a certain element of truth. In foreign affairs, presidents can assert their will, act, and by being proactive, force the Congress to be reactive. By setting policy, the president sets in motion events of his choosing. If Congress wishes to intercede, it does so in response to acts already taken. The *initiative* usually belongs to the president.

Constitutionally, the president may be on shaky ground, but in practical terms, it is very difficult to stop an assertive president in foreign affairs. While all presidents claim that their use of foreign policy power is grounded in the Constitution, such claims of independent authority are generally flimsy. It is the Congress—even in foreign affairs—that has the broadest and clearest constitutional mandate, but its power has atrophied due to lack of use. Even the power to declare war, which is expressly granted to the Congress, has slipped through the hands of the legislature. The War Powers Act notwithstanding, it is the president who holds primacy in war and foreign affairs.

The presumption of presidential leadership in foreign affairs gives the president a wide range of opportunities to take the initiative and act. It is less likely that Congress will challenge the president's authority in foreign than in domestic affairs (though it may be difficult to convince the president of this), and while the Congress is more intrusive today than in the 1950s and 1960s, the fact remains that presidents still can set the agenda, act, and lead in foreign affairs with much greater likelihood of success than in domestic matters.

A great deal of foreign policy involves diplomatic activities that are generally under the purview of the executive, and in most areas, presidents simply presume authority to act. Likewise, much activity in foreign affairs does not require legislation,[132] and to make matters worse (or better if one is president), during a crisis the president acts with almost unlimited authority and few checks.[133]

Perhaps the greatest power a president has is the presumption that he speaks for and represents the nation to the world. This allows the president the opportunity to act, to make decisions, and to announce policies, thereby preemptively eliminating many potential challengers. The president presents a fait accompli, which thus may tie the hands of potential rivals on the congressional side. To defy the president on a matter of national security *may* appear unpatriotic, especially in moments of international tension. Thereby, the president can both silence (or muffle) potential critics and force the Congress to submit to his will. There are many examples: Teddy

Roosevelt's sending the U.S. fleet halfway around the world in defiance of congressional budget restrictions, then saying, "I sent the fleet. . . . will they leave them there?"; George Bush's sending U.S. troops to the Middle East following the 1991 Iraqi invasion of Kuwait, preparing for war, building public support, then challenging Congress to issue a vote of support; and Clinton's sending U.S. troops to Haiti in 1993. All of these actions show how presidents, by forcing the hand of Congress, can get their way.[134]

Over time, presidents spend more and more time dealing with foreign affairs precisely because they get frustrated after being rebuffed in domestic and economic policy but can feel a greater sense of power and accomplishment in foreign policy. Since a president needs to be seen as accomplishing great things in order to maintain his reputation as a leader, he almost naturally gravitates to the area in which his power is greatest. The irony here, of course, is that the president has the greatest power in the area where he is potentially most dangerous and most in need of controls or checks and balances; conversely, he is most controlled in the least dangerous area, which is most in need of his leadership.

Although an ongoing theme in this book involves presidential weakness and the limits of power, the position shifts in the area of foreign policy, where the president more closely resembles Superman, not Wimpyman. It is only in the domestic and economic policy arena that the president has the most trouble getting his way.

One reason why modern presidents so often appear to fail is our tendency to judge them primarily on the basis of the success of the economy, something over which presidents have very little control. Yet, if their power is at its lowest ebb in economic policy—the area in which their reputation is most susceptible—and at its peak in the area with much less political reward, then our standards of judgment are out of whack.

This dilemma (curse?) was visited first upon George H. Bush, who inherited an economic mess from Ronald Reagan, and then upon Bill Clinton, whose resources and options were severely limited due to the irresponsible economic policies of the Reagan years.[135]

The Supreme Court

Historically, the Court has not been a very effective check on presidential power.[136] In general, the Court has supported presidential power claims and been very hesitant to restrict the power of the president.

Under the doctrine of judicial review, the Court can exercise some control over the president. But in practice the Court has been very reluctant to get involved, and when it has, its decisions have usually expended presidential powers, not restricted them. Especially in the areas of foreign and defense policy, the Court has been extremely reluctant to rein in the powers of the presidency.

Of course, Court decisions are like the Bible: You can find a case to support almost any conceivable position. But overall, presidency-curbing decisions by the Court have been few and far between. Can the Court serve as protector of the rule of law against presidential usurpation of power? Glendon Schubert writes that

> they [American citizens] undoubtedly expect that, should the occasion ever arise, the Supreme Court would uphold the majesty of the law against the pretensions of a usurper. History warns us, however, that this assumption may be false: in every major constitutional crisis between the executive and the judiciary, the President has emerged the victor.[137]

Schubert further notes that

> the most significant aspect of judicial review of presidential orders is its ineffectiveness. If the courts are the most important bulwark of freedom and liberty in the United States, then we have every right to view with alarm the future security of the republic.[138]

The Courts have been reluctant to challenge presidential power. In fact, they have often lent judicial support to presidential power grabs. As Clinton Rossiter states, "In the nature of things judicial and political, the Court can be expected to go on rationalizing most pretensions of most presidents. It is clearly one of the least reliable restraints on presidential activity. . . . For most practical purposes, the President may act as if the Supreme Court did not exist."[139] Clearly, the president understands this. Especially in the area of foreign policy, presidents do not fear the power of the courts as a check upon their power.[140]

The concurring opinion of Justice Robert H. Jackson in the case of *Youngstown Sheet and Tube Co. v. Sawyer* (1952) provides a classic description of presidential power from the Court's perspective. Jackson posits three levels of power. In the first level, the president acts in conjunction with the expressed or implied wishes of Congress. At this level, Jackson states, the president's "authority is at its maximum." Acting together, the president and Congress are granted "the widest latitude of judicial interpretation."

The second level is, to Jackson, a "zone of twilight." Here the president and Congress share power and authority, and "congressional inertia, indifference, or quiescence may sometimes, at least as a practical matter, enable, if not invite, measures of independent presidential responsibility." Here the legitimacy of a president's actions depends on "the imperatives of the events and contemporary imponderables."

In the third level, the president is on thin constitutional ice. Here, the president engages in actions "incompatible with the expressed or implied will of Congress." In such instances, according to Jackson, the president's power is "at its lowest ebb."

Presidents prefer the logic of *U.S. v. Curtiss-Wright Export Corp.* (1936) to that of *Youngstown*. In *Curtiss-Wright*, the Supreme Court came very close to recognizing presidential omnipotence in the area of foreign affairs. Essentially, the Court decided that the federal government's powers in foreign affairs are without constitutional limitation and, further, that the executive branch exercises the foreign affairs powers, positing—in Justice Sutherland's opinion—that the president is "the sole organ of the Federal Government in the field of international relations." Clearly the Framers had something else in mind.[141]

Thus the Court allows a wide scope for presidential power *unless* the president's actions run directly against the expressed will of the Congress (the Iran-Contra scandal, for example). This gives the president considerable room to maneuver. But presidents, unsatisfied with this restriction, *claim* very expansive powers under the Constitution. President George H. Bush went so far as to claim that he did not need a congressional declaration of support (i.e., of "war") prior to the Gulf War, but he did, in the end, seek and attain congressional approval.

Overall, the Court has not served as a consistent or effective check on presidential power. By accepting presidential claims of inherent and implied constitutional power, the Court has accepted a rather expansive view of presidential power. Thus, in decision making, presidents rarely fear the wrath of the Court.

Moving Beyond the Law

Given the numerous roadblocks and veto points that litter the president's path, it is not surprising that the more ambitious and goal-oriented presidents will get extremely frustrated as other actors block their way. An obstreperous Congress, demanding special interests, an uncooperative business community, an adversarial press, and others can at times seem to gang up on a president, preventing him from achieving his policy goals.

When faced with this myriad of opposing forces, most presidents feel caught between a rock and a hard place. Often their choice appears to be either to accept defeat or to take bold action (always, the president believes, in the national interest). To make the complex separation of powers work is difficult under the best of circumstances, and in normal times it may seem impossible to get the system moving. Thus, rather than accept defeat, some presidents are tempted to cut corners, go beyond the law, stretch the constitutional limits a bit.

When all else fails, as it often does, some presidents—knowing that their future political success, not to mention their historical reputation, is at stake—simply cannot resist going beyond the law. If the choice is gridlock or illegality, some presidents will choose the latter. After all, the president is absolutely convinced that what he wants is in the best interest of the nation, so why let a corrupt Congress, an uniformed public, or a hostile press stand in the way of progress (self-defined by the president)?

Presidents who are not well grounded in the virtues of the American system may see the system itself as the enemy and thus feel justified in going beyond the law. Richard Nixon with Watergate[142] and Ronald Reagan with the Iran-Contra scandal are but the two most pronounced examples.[143]

Sometimes a president gets away with it (e.g., Reagan); sometimes not (Nixon). But when the alternative is to stay within the law and fail (e.g. Ford, Carter), the temptation to go beyond the law—and maybe succeed and not get caught—is great, too great for some leaders to resist.

Of course, this is precisely what the Founders feared. The separation of powers and the checks and balances were set up so that ambition could counteract ambition and power could check power. The model of decision making was decidedly cooperative, not executive. But as the frustrations of high demands, high expectations, limited power, and falling approval eat away at presidents, they often cannot resist the temptation to go beyond the properly prescribed limits of the office.

Often, an attitude of arrogance overtakes the president and his top staff. "We know best" and "they are blocking progress" leads to the belief that the "slight" abuse of power is being done for the greater good. But such an attitude leads to the Imperial Presidency and its further abuses of power.[144]

The Reagan administration was absolutely convinced that communism was an evil that had to be fought at all costs, that the Marxist government in Nicaragua was a serious and direct threat to the United States, that the Congress was soft on communism, and that public opinion, which opposed U.S. intervention, was uninformed in spite of Herculean efforts by the administration. Therefore, Reagan was faced with the difficult choice either to accept the will of Congress, the voice of the people, and the law or to act on his own judgment of the national interest. Reagan acted.

Putting aside the question of whether Reagan was correct about the threat Nicaragua posed to the United States, one thing is absolutely clear: The Reagan administration decided that the law was wrong and that they would not be bound by it. This is the arrogance of power so feared by the Founders. This is a principal reason why the Founders insisted on checks and balances: to control executive tyranny and abuses of power.

The frustrations inherent in a president's inability to move the machinery of government may lead presidents to move beyond the law; they have also led scholars to articulate a more presidency-centered concept of government. In the frustrating years of Republican presidential "rule" in the 1980s, scholars on the political right—historically on the side of a more limited government and restrictions on executive power—relented to the temptation and began seeing the strong-presidency model as a tool for conservative ends. With conservatives in power but frustrated by the gridlock of the system, these scholars called for a strong president and weaker Congress.

Responding to the frustrations of Reagan's last seven years and of Bush's four years in office, writers on the political right produced calls for executive power such as Terry Eastland's *Energy in the Executive*, Corvitz and Rabkin's *The Fettered Presidency*, and Harvey C. Mansfield Jr.'s *Taming the Prince*.[145] Gridlock, like politics itself, makes strange intellectual bedfellows.

Is the president above the law? Of course not. Such a notion violates all precepts of the rule of law.[146] But are there certain prescribed circumstances that can justify a president's going beyond the law? Are there times when the president may exceed his constitutional powers?

The President's Emergency Power

When, if ever, is a president justified in stretching the Constitution? While the word *emergency* does not appear in the Constitution, there is some evidence to suggest that the Founders did envision the possibility of a president's exercising "supraconstitutional powers" in a time of national emergency.[147] The Constitution's silence, some suggest, leaves room for presidents to claim that certain constitutional provisions (e.g., Article 2, Section 1, the executive power clause, and the "faithfully execute" the law clause, along with Article 2, Section 2, the commander-in-chief clause) grant the president implied powers attendant to the performance of his job. Claims of such powers become especially pressing in times of crisis.

During a crisis, the president often assumes extraconstitutional powers.[148] The separate branches—which, under normal circumstances, are designed to check and balance the president—will usually defer to the president in times of national emergency. The president's institutional position offers him a vantage point from which he can more easily exert crisis leadership, and the Congress, Court, and public usually accept the president's judgments.

The notion of one set of legal and constitutional standards for normal conditions and another for emergency conditions raises some unsettling questions regarding democratic governments and constitutional systems.[149] Can democratic regimes function in any but prosperous, peaceful circumstances? Or must the United States constantly rely upon the strength of a despot or "constitutional dictatorship" to save it from disaster? Are constitutional governments incapable of meeting the demands of crisis? In short, can democracy work in the twenty-first century, or is it a relic of quieter times?

Democratic theory seems to be rather weak in addressing itself to the problem of crisis government and democratic objectives. In most instances, democratic political theorists have seen a need to revert to authoritarian leadership in times of crisis. Locke calls this executive "prerogative"; Rossiter refers to a "Constitutional Dictatorship"; and to Rousseau, it is an application of the "General Will." In cases of emergency, when extraordinary pressures are placed on democratic regimes, many theorists suggest that democratic systems—in order to save themselves from destruction—must defer to the ways of totalitarian regimes. In order to preserve democracy, one must, in other words, destroy democracy.

Laws decided upon by democratic means can be ignored and violated under this notion. To refer once again to Locke, in emergency situations the Crown retains the prerogative "power to act according to discretion for the public good, without the prescription of the law and sometimes even against it."[150] While this prerogative could properly be exercised only for the "public good," one cannot escape the conclusion that for democratic governments and democratic theory this is shaky ground on which to stand. And what if an executive acts wrongly? Here Locke is forced to abandon secular concerns and he writes that "the people have no other remedy in this, as in all other cases where they have no judge on earth, but to appeal to Heaven."[151]

Rousseau likewise recognized the need for a temporary suspension of democratic procedures in times of crisis. In the *Social Contract* he notes the following:

The inflexibility of the laws, which prevents them from adapting them-selves to circumstances, may, in certain cases, render them disastrous, and make them bring about a time of crisis, the ruin of the State.
... If ... the peril is of such a kind that the paraphernalia of the laws are an obstacle to their preservation, the method is to nominate a supreme ruler, who shall silence all the laws and suspend for a moment the sovereign authority. In such a case, there is no doubt about the gen-eral will, and it is clear that the people's first intention is that the State shall not perish.[152]

The major difference between Locke and Rousseau on this mat-ter rests in Rousseau's refusal to rely upon an "appeal to Heaven" in cases of possible abuse of the power of the "supreme magistracy." Rousseau emphasized that this power must have strictly enforced time limitations as a protection against a complete takeover of the system. But once extraordinary power is assumed by one individual ruler, who can be sure that such time limits can and will be adhered to?

John Stuart Mill, after defending representative government, makes this "uncharacteristic" comment: "I am far from condemning, in cases of extreme necessity, the assumption of absolute power in the form of a temporary dictatorship."[153]

Smith and Cotter sum up this problem in the writings of demo-cratic theorists when they note that

democratic political theorists tacitly admit the existence of a fatal defect in any system of constitutional democracy: Its processes are inadequate to confront and overcome emergency.[154]

And Niccolo Machiavelli, no great "democrat" himself, addresses this problem when he notes that

in a well-ordered republic it should never be necessary to resort to extra-constitutional measures; for although they may for the time be benefi-cial, yet the precedent is pernicious, for if the practice is once established of disregarding the laws for good objects, they will in a little while be disregarded under that pretext for evil purposes. Thus no republic will ever be perfect if she has not by law provided for everything, having a remedy for every emergency, and fixed rules for applying it.[155]

Clinton Rossiter's "Constitutional Dictatorship" is a modern ver-sion of the same problem that democratic theorists attempted (unsuccessfully, I suggest) to solve.[156] The "Constitutional Dictatorship" is an admission of the weakness of democratic theory, or of its failure to cover the full range of governing requirements. To save democracy, we escape from it. To protect democracy, we reject it. Democratic theory then, according to the democratic theorists, is incomplete; in cases of emergency, one is called upon to reject democracy for the more expedient ways of the dictator. In this manner, democratic theory opens the door to a strong, power-aggrandizing executive.

Nowhere in the Constitution is it specified that the president will have additional powers in times of crisis or emergency. But history has shown us that in times of national emergency, the powers of the president have greatly expanded, and while Abe Fortas writes that "Under the Constitution, the President has no implied powers which enable him to make or disregard laws,"[157] under the microscope of political reality we can see that this is precisely what American presidents have done.

The outcome of this view of an enlarged reservoir of presidential power in emergencies has been characterized by Edward S. Corwin as "constitutional relativity."[158] Corwin's view finds the Constitution broad and flexible enough to meet the needs of an emergency situation as defined and measured by its own provisions. By this approach, the Constitution can be adapted to meet the needs of the times. If the times call for quasi-dictatorial action by the executive, the Court could find this acceptable.

The problem of emergency situations in democratic systems is not easily answered. If the potential power of the state is used too little or too late, the democratic state faces the possibility of destruction. If used arbitrarily and capriciously, this power could lead the system to accept a form of permanent dictatorship. In a contemporary sense, the constant reliance on the executive to solve the many "emergencies" (self-defined by the executive) facing America could very well lead to the acceptance of the overly powerful executive and make the meaning of the term "emergency" shallow and susceptible to executive manipulation. With each new "emergency" in American history, the public and our political institutions seemed to become more accustomed to accepting a broader definition of presidential power to meet each new crisis.

The Court under Rossiter's constitutional dictatorship will generally recognize the need for the government to have inflated powers with which to deal with the impending crisis, and it will allow for a "flexible" interpretation of constitutional powers of the president, who is usually expected to deal with the emergency. Rossiter comes to this conclusion:

> In the last resort, it is always the executive branch in the government which possesses and wields the extraordinary powers of self-preservation of any democratic, constitutional state.[159]

The Court, under Rossiter's theory, recognizes the emergency and allows the president to assume additional powers. But the constitutional dictator must recognize the limits of his responsibilities. Franklin D. Roosevelt, in 1942, after claiming/requesting of Congress a grant of an unusually large amount of power, assured the legislature that "When the war is won, the powers under which I act automatically revert to the people—to whom they belong."[160] The executive, in short, will return the extraordinary powers he was granted during the crisis back to their rightful place. But serious questions remain as to (1) whether presidents have in fact returned this power, and (2) whether, even if the president desires to do so, a complete or even reasonable return to normality is possible after dictatorial or quasi-dictatorial power is placed in the hands of one man. In sum, can a democracy survive without a strong executive, and conversely, can a democracy exist with one?

Recognizing the need for expanded presidential power in order to meet the necessities of emergencies, political scientist Richard M. Pious attempts to distinguish between the legitimate and illegitimate use of emergency power by a president. Pious refers to seven "standards of behavior" that clarify this distinction:

1. The exercise of power should not involve personal or partisan advantage, nor should it interfere with the constitutional processes of election or succession to office.
2. The powers must be exercised in a national emergency, when the continued existence of the Union and the physical safety of the people is at stake, when delay might prove fatal, and when traditional constitutional procedures would involve such a delay.

3. The powers are exercised when no statute or precedent provides a visible alternative procedure, and nothing in the Constitution or laws of the land expressly prohibit the actions.
4. Use of prerogative powers should be preceded by the widest possible consultation within the government, including senior officials in the departments, and when possible, leaders of Congress. The president should try to create a consensus that emergency government must be instituted.
5. The president should make available to Congress and the judiciary a full record involving his actions as soon as practicable during or after the emergency. Courts should make the final determination if he claims executive privilege.
6. Once the emergency has passed Congress should legislate to routinize procedures, placing powers on a statutory basis, and should provide for legislative and judicial review if appropriate.
7. The checks and balances system must function throughout the emergency, permitting possible resolution of censure or an impeachment proceeding.[161]

Presidential Action in Times of Emergency

History has shown us that the President's emergency power has indeed been great in comparison to his powers under normal circumstances. When faced with a crisis situation, presidents have made exaggerated claims of power, acted upon these claims, and generally have gotten away with these excessive, and often extralegal, uses of power. History indeed provides us with clear examples of the enormous power of a president in an emergency situation.

The American political system has met crises with an expansion of presidential power. In emergency periods, the president may act with little regard for the wishes and dictates of the other branches. While the Constitution does not refer to any additional powers for the president during emergencies, the political reality has shown us that in times of crisis, the president becomes the prime mover of the

American system. The necessity for quick, decisive, often extracon-stitutional actions that the crisis may demand, places a heavy burden upon the president. Since he is the only leader able to move quickly, the burden of meeting the crisis "must" fall on his shoulders. According to Richard Longaker, "In times of crisis constitutional limitations bend to other needs."[162]

Lincoln during the Civil War and Franklin Roosevelt during the Depression serve as examples of presidents who, when faced with a crisis, acted boldly, assumed power, became constitutional dictators.[163] But what distinguishes the constitutional dictator from the Imperial President? What separates the actions of Lincoln and Roosevelt, generally considered to be appropriate, from those of Nixon and Reagan, generally considered inappropriate or imperial?

Essentially, several factors must occur for the crisis presidency to be valid: (1) the president must face a genuine and a widely recog-nized emergency; (2) the Congress and public must—more or less—accept that the president will exercise supra-constitutional powers; (3) the Congress *may*, if it chooses, override presidential acts; (4) the president's acts must be public so as to allow Congress and the pub-lic to judge them; (5) there must be no suspension of the next elec-tion; and (6) the president should consult with Congress where possible (see Pious's list in the previous section). We can see that Lincoln and Roosevelt met (more or less) all of these requirements; Nixon and Reagan, very few of them.

Even when the requirements are met, however, one should not be sanguine about presidential usurpations of power. As the Supreme Court reminded us in *Ex parte Milligan* (4 Wall. 2, 1866): "Wicked men, ambitious of power, with a hatred of liberty and contempt of law, may fill the place once occupied by Washington and Lincoln."

The events of September 11, 2001, brought the crisis presidency to a full fruition. Prior to that crisis, the Bush presidency was belea-guered and struggling. After 9/11, the Bush presidency resembled the Constitutional dictatorship Rossiter described. The president was granted wide latitude to act unilaterally not just to pursue and destroy terrorists abroad, but—absent a declaration of war—to dra-matically curtail constitutional due process rights at home. A crisis greatly expands a president's level of political opportunity and thus power.

Conclusion

Presidential leadership (true leadership as opposed to mere office holding) is a rare commodity. In those rare moments of leadership, presidents were able to animate citizens and mobilize government, develop a vision and establish an agenda, move the Congress and push the bureaucracy. Such presidents recast the arena of the politically possible. It hasn't happened often. The forces arrayed against a president usually have the upper hand. The power of lethargy is truly daunting.

The preconditions for effective presidential leadership are so rarely in syncopation: skill, the right timing, a consensus, a governing coalition, high popularity, vision, a clear mandate, and so forth. Presidents, to be effective leaders in a democratic system, must bring Hamiltonian energy, to a Madisonian system, for Jeffersonian ends. Lamentably, most presidents fail in this task.

For a leader to be effective, he needs the vision of John Kennedy, the political skills of Lyndon Johnson, the strategic insight of Richard Nixon, the genuineness of Gerald Ford, the character of Jimmy Carter, the charisma of Ronald Reagan, the experience of George H. Bush, and the interpersonal skills of Bill Clinton. It also helps, as Machiavelli reminds us, to have *fortuna* on our side.

This chapter has presented the building blocks of presidential leadership. Even so, how a president puts these blocks together—his strategic sense—tells only part of the story. For a president to succeed, he needs to have both a good strategic or power sense and also the benefit of circumstances or conditions (opportunities) that lend themselves to presidential leadership. The preconditions of power are of equal or greater than equal importance to skill in achieving success.

To succeed, presidents must be masters of the *light* (education, vision, mobilization) and the *heat* (power, bargaining). Given the incredible array of skills and circumstances necessary for presidents to succeed, it is no wonder that most of them either fail or at best give mediocre performances.

For Discussion

1. Can we really expect presidents to lead in domestic policy in normal (non-crisis) times? In normal times, does the president have sufficient resources to govern?
2. How can we (and should we) give the president more power in domestic affairs and less power in foreign affairs and war?
3. Do we overload the president? How can any president "do it all"?
4. Given that the presidency is an impossible job, what sorts of experiences or training best prepare someone for the office?
5. What limits can and should be placed on the "crisis or emergency presidency"?

Debate Questions

I. *Resolved:* That presidents have become slaves to public opinion polls and rarely exercise leadership.
II. *Resolved:* That the media, rather than serving as a check on the executive, are easily manipulated by presidents.

CHAPTER 4

Making the Presidency
Effective and Accountable

*Still the question recurs "can we do it better?" The dogmas of the
quiet past, are inadequate to the stormy present. The occasion is
piled high with difficulty, and we must rise with the occasion. As
our case is new, so* we must think anew, and act anew.

—ABRAHAM LINCOLN,
ANNUAL MESSAGE TO CONGRESS, DECEMBER 1, 1862

Two decades ago, Harold Barger began the concluding chapter
of his book *The Impossible Presidency* with the following:

Has the presidency become chronically unstable, or is it only suffering
from a temporary downturn not unlike earlier cycles in which Congress
dominated the Executive Branch? Is the decline of the office due to a
succession of less qualified chief executives, or has the presidency
become imperiled by a host of political and social problems at home and
abroad that defy solutions? Can any president serve out a full term and
still look forward to reelection, or is there no longer much hope that
there is "life after inauguration"?

Deep misgivings about the presidency have surfaced during the past
five administrations, paralleling a growing frustration and loss of confidence that have marked our nation at least since Vietnam and
Watergate. A yearning for strong national leadership has long since
extinguished fears about an imperial president. For Americans now
seem to be less concerned about presidential abuse of power than they
are by the inability of presidents to wield power at all.

Thoughtful observers of our politics grow uneasy over the chronic
inability of the United States to develop stable, coherent policies to deal
with domestic problems and global dangers. Chaotic swings in the

151

political fortunes of one president after another raise serious questions as to whether anyone can manage the U.S. store. An increasing number of political experts now wonder if the office can ever function with reasonable efficiency without major reforms in the selection process and in the constitutional powers of the presidency.[1]

It is amazing that two decades later those words sound as fresh as if they had been written this morning.

Having established in Chapter 1 that the presidents of the past thirty-five years have been inadequate to the task of governing; and having discussed in Chapter 2 the primary reasons why presidents usually have difficulty governing; and further, having discussed in Chapter 3 how presidents, under certain circumstances, can overcome the antileadership tendencies built into the American system, it is now time to turn our attention to a broader, perhaps more difficult question: What do we want of our presidents?

Is the current, inhibited state of presidential power/leadership acceptable, or do we want to trade in the eighteenth-century Constitution for a newer, more streamlined model, one perhaps better suited to the demands of the twenty-first century?

We have historically had a difficult time deciding what we want of our leaders: someone to pull us forward, or someone to follow our wishes; someone to act forcefully, or someone to execute the people's will. Likewise, we have historically had a difficult time reconciling leadership with our democratic aspirations. Having said this, it is equally (though no less problematically) true that "American political thought has not lacked admirers of leadership."[2]

Because of our ambivalence and confusion regarding the proper range and scope of powers to be invested in the presidency, we swing back and forth between the desire for heroic leaders to "save" us and the desire to contain, if not destroy, the leaders who disappoint us. The pendulum swings back and forth between eras when we invest too much hope in leaders and eras of disposable leaders and the dwarfing of the presidency. As Burns noted, "We search eagerly for leadership yet seek to cage and tame it."[3] But "power," if it be exercised wisely and in the interests of the people, cannot be so harnessed nor so liberated as to make it either ineffectual or dangerous.

Just what do we want of the presidency? Part of the difficulty inherent in such a question stems from a historical dilemma: The

Founders themselves were never quite clear as to what they wanted of the institution. Constitutionally, they left the presidency vague and unformed, hoping that the venerated George Washington would set appropriate precedents.[4] But how well do eighteenth-century precedents work in the twenty-first century? Perhaps it is time, in the spirit of Jefferson, who believed that no generation should be enslaved by the dogmas of the past, to ask anew: What do we want of the U.S. presidency? As Jefferson himself noted:

> Some men look at constitutions with sanctimonious reverence and deem them like the ark of the covenant, too sacred to be touched. They ascribe to the men of the preceding age a wisdom more than human, and suppose what they did to be beyond amendment. I knew that age well; I belonged to it, and labored with it. It deserved well of its country. It was very like the present, but without the experience of the present; and forty years of experience in government is worth a century of bookreading; and this they would say themselves, were they to rise from the dead. . . . Institutions must advance also, and keep pace with the times. We might as well require a man to wear still the coat which fitted him when a boy. . . .[5]

There is yet another compelling reason to reexamine the scope of presidential power: the end of the Cold War. In the Cold War era (1945–1989), it was widely believed that the United States, as the hegemonic power of the West, required strong presidential leadership (especially in foreign affairs).[6] But with the collapse of the Soviet empire, we are free from "some" of the burden of power imposed by the dangers of the Cold War. Freed of the weight of that burden we can ask: In the post–Cold War world, what power and limits do we wish to invest in the presidency in this new age of globalism?

Put another way, as we approach the new world before us, we must find out "how to empower the president without endangering the system."[7] While the president's formal powers are rather limited, his informal powers may help to overcome the limits of the office, but skill can go only so far. And, paradoxically, there are areas in which the president clearly has too little power (domestic and economic policy) and simultaneously areas where he has too much power (foreign policy and war).

Our confusion is complicated by the fact that leadership often seems at odds with democracy. We know leadership is important, but can we truly reconcile our need for leadership with our belief in democracy? Thomas E. Cronin believes we must:

> The challenge, for those who care about our nation and the dreams of constitutional democracy, is to seek ways to reconcile these concepts—leadership and democracy. Whether we like it or not, our democracy will stand or fall on the quality of leaders as well as on the quality of citizens we produce and nurture here.[8]

Cronin also attempts to provide guidance in how we can democratize leadership by calling for a rebirth of citizen politics:

> The challenge of reconciling leadership and democracy is part definition, part attitudinal, and part behavioral. We have too long held a view of leaders that is hierarchical, male, and upon which followers, like subjects or slaves, are dependent. That conception is antithetical to our democratic aspirations. The very word "followers" is a negative and demeaning word and ought, if possible, to be discarded or at least greatly modified. For a nation of subservient followers can never be a democratic one. A democratic nation requires educated, skeptical, caring, engaged, and contentious citizen-leaders—citizens who are willing to lead as well as follow, who are willing to point the way as often as they are persuaded in one way or another, and prize the spirit of liberty and free speech that animates our Bill of Rights.[9]

Only by creating a cadre of citizen-leaders can we hope to democratize (and thereby empower) leadership in the United States. But is this possible in the fractious, divisive, and petty politics of left versus right?

Presidents who lead in the democratic spirit create leaders, foster citizen responsibility, inspire and empower others to assume leadership responsibilities in their communities. Democratic leaders establish a moral vision; pursue egalitarian goals; question, challenge, engage, and educate citizens; offer hope. Emiliano Zapata said that "strong leaders make a weak people."[10] But strong *democratic leaders* help create *strong citizens*. Eugene Debs captured the dilemma when he said: "Too long have the workers of the world waited for some Moses to lead them out of bondage. He has not come; he will not come. I would not lead you out if I could; for if you would be led out, you could be led back again."[11]

Jefferson's Vision of Democratic Leadership[12]

Democratic theorists have long wrestled with a particularly vexing question: Is there such a thing as "Democratic Leadership" or are the two words mutually exclusive if not contradictory? Thomas E. Cronin has gone so far as to call them "warring concepts."[13] But can any system of government exist without leadership? For those who believe in the superiority of democracy over other forms of government, a way must be found to reconcile these two seemingly warring concepts into a sustainable whole.

The tension between the need for leadership and the demands of democracy was reinforced by James Bryce, who reminded us that "perhaps no form of government needs great leaders so much as democracy."[14] But what kind of leadership? The strong, forceful direction of a heroic leader, or the gentle guiding hand of a teacher?

Proponents of robust democracy realize, as Bruce Miroff has written, that

> leadership has rarely fit comfortably with democracy in America. The claim of leaders to political precedence violates the equality of democratic citizens. The most committed democrats have been suspicious of the very idea of leadership. When Thomas Paine railed against the "slavish custom of following leaders," he expressed a democrat's deepest anxiety.[15]

But such tensions have not prevented Americans from looking to strong leaders to guide the republic. Especially during a crisis, we turn to our leaders in hopes that strong heroic leadership can save the republic. Thus, while we are suspicious of strong leadership, we also admire it. As Arthur M. Schlesinger, Jr., has noted,

> The American democracy has readily resorted in practice to the very leadership it had disclaimed in theory. An adequate democratic theory must recognize that democracy is not self-executing: that leadership is not the enemy of self-government but the means of making it work; that followers have their own stern obligation, which is to keep leaders within rigorous constitutional bounds; and that Caesarism is more often produced by the failure of feeble governments than by the success of energetic ones.[16]

Dilemmas notwithstanding, is there a style of leadership compatible with political democracy? While a tension will always exist between leadership and democracy, there are ways to bring the two into a creative tension that both calls for a role for the leader and also promotes democratic participation and practice among the citizenry.

Just as Abraham Lincoln gave us a succinct, eloquent definition of democracy as *"government of the people, by the people, for the people,"*[17] so too did one of America's other Mt. Rushmore leaders give us an eloquent, even simple definition of democratic leadership. Thomas Jefferson believed that the primary duties of a leader in a democracy were *"to inform the minds of the people, and to follow their will"* (emphasis added).[18]

There are two key concepts contained in Jefferson's brief definition: (1) *inform minds* and (2) *follow their will*. Informing the minds of the people speaks to the role of leaders as educators. In a democracy, the leader has a responsibility to educate, enlighten, and inform the people. He or she must identify problems and mobilize the people to act. By informing or educating the citizenry, the leader also engages in a dialogue, the ultimate goal of which is to involve leader and citizen in the process of developing a vision, grounded in the values of the nation, which will animate future action.

The leader's task in a democracy is to look ahead, see problems, focus the public's attention on the work that must be done, provide alternative courses of action, chart a path for the future, and move the nation in support of his or her ideas. The leader must attempt to mobilize the public around a vision and secure a consensus on the proper way to proceed.

The second component of Jefferson's definition, to *"follow their will,"* suggests that after educating and involving the people, the leader must ultimately follow the will of the people. Several commentators have noted the distinction between the whim of the people (temporary and changing) and the will of the people (deeply held truths that speak to the nation's highest aspirations). The leader's job is to inform, educate, and persuade the public to embrace and work for a vision that taps into the deeper truths and higher purposes of the will of Americans. But whatever their judgment, the leader must serve the people and ultimately follow their direction.

In a democracy, following the will of the people is essential. Any leader who pursues policies contrary to the expressed wishes of the people can be accused of the democratic cardinal sin: defying the will of the people. Thus leadership requires, first, that a leader use all possible means to bring about informed judgments by the people. Then, the leader must *serve* the people. This form of democratic accountability calls for the leader to play an important role, but it ultimately relies upon the people to make final judgments.

The best democratic leadership, in Bruce Miroff's words, "not only serves people's interests but furthers their democratic dignity as well."[19] Thus, Thomas Jefferson's vision of democratic leadership that informs the public, then follows their will, elevates both leader and citizen. Such a form of leadership is difficult, time consuming, and fraught with pitfalls. But it is a style of leadership that builds strong citizens for a strong democracy.

A Powerful and Accountable President?

Can the presidency be made powerful *and* accountable? Can the president lead but not become an autocrat?

In some areas—foreign policy and war, for example—the president has perhaps too much power. In other areas, domestic and economic policy, the president seems too weak. The former means we often get heroic but undemocratic leadership; the latter means we often lead presidential lambs to political slaughter. Overall, the "system" of presidential leadership is dysfunctional. Presidents do not build coalitions, they do not generate consensus, and they sometimes act as independent policy entrepreneurs. This is not democratic leadership. It is not leadership.

In the beginning of this book, I offered a "theory" of presidential politics: *Presidents, facing a system of multiple veto points, seek to maximize power and influence.* How well, or poorly, does this theory explain presidential behavior? I fear that while it may capture the core of presidential behavior, there are still loose ends that remain unexplained. Presidential scholars have long bemoaned the absence of theory in the study of the presidency,[20] and this may be a function both of the complexity and the many-sideness of the institution. Can we find a single theory that truly explains presidential behavior, or must we move from president to president, trying to explain why *that one individual* succeeded or failed? I have argued that while individual presidents vary in skill, style, ideology, and other ways, they are also part of ongoing and recurrent patterns of behavior that shape the *presidency*. Thus, while any theory of presidential behavior will fall short of explaining every act by every individual president (which is not the job of a theory), a good theory captures the core, the essence of its subject. I hope that such a task was fulfilled by this theory of presidential behavior.

The United States needs a strong presidency and a democratically controlled presidency, a strong presidency and *strong citizenship*.[21] Benjamin R. Barber notes the difficulty inherent in such a hope:

> At the heart of democratic theory lies a profound dilemma that has afflicted democratic practice at least since the eighteenth century. Democracy requires both effective leadership and vigorous citizenship: yet the conditions and consequences of leadership often seem to undermine civic vigor. Although it cries for both, democracy must customarily make do either with strong leadership or with strong citizens. For the most part, depending on devices of representation in large-scale societies, democracy in the West has settled for strong leaders and correspondingly weak citizens.[22]

James Madison's caution in the *Federalist*, no. 51, speaks volumes in today's world:

> If men were angels, no government would be necessary. If angels were to govern man, neither external nor internal controls in government would be necessary. In framing a government which is to be administered by men over men the great difficulty lies in this, you must first enable the government to control the governed and in the next place oblige it to control itself. A dependence on the people is no doubt the primary control on the government. But experience has taught mankind the necessity for auxiliary precautions.

How can one give power but control it? Can the presidency be empowered but democratized?

Of course, our desire for strong presidential leadership seems contrary to the goal of holding presidents accountable. Leadership implies power; accountability implies limits. Paradoxes and contradictions aside, accountability is a fundamental piece of the democratic puzzle.[23] In essence it denotes that public officials are answerable for their actions. But to whom? Within what limits? Through what means?

There are three types of accountability: (1) *ultimate accountability* (which the United States has via the impeachment process); (2) *periodic accountability* (provided for by general elections); and (3) *daily accountability* (somewhat contained in the separation of powers).[24] James Madison believed that elections provided the "primary check on government" and that the separation of powers ("ambition will be made to counteract ambition") plus "auxiliary precautions" would take care of the rest.[25]

Of course, there *are* times when presidents abuse power or behave corruptly.[26] But even in the three most recent bouts with presidential abuses, Watergate, the Iran-Contra scandal, and the Clinton affair, the president was stopped by the countervailing forces of a free press, an independent Congress, an independent judiciary, and (belatedly) an aroused public.

Presidents can be held accountable, but can they be held responsible? That is, can they muster enough power to govern? One means to improve accountability and also empower leadership is to strengthen the party system in America. Our parties are—at least by European standards—weak, undisciplined, and nonideological. A stronger party system could organize and mobilize citizens and government, diminish the fragmentation of the separation of powers, and mitigate against the atomization of our citizenry. If the parties were more disciplined and programmatic, the government's ability to govern could be greatly enhanced.

A more responsible party system would also ground presidents in a more consensus-oriented style of leadership, and thereby diminish the independent, unconnected brand of leadership so often attempted by recent presidents. A stronger party system would be one way to help make the separation of powers work better. At present the institutional relation between the president and Congress is too often characterized as conflict if not combat. What is needed is cooperation. A more robust party system could help join the president and Congress together in a more cooperative relationship.[27]

The Ends and Means of Presidential Power

All presidents want to be successful, but what does it mean to be a success? High popularity? A good historical reputation? Achieving one's policy goals? A high congressional box score? Getting one's way?

If success is measured merely by getting one's way, then many bullies are successful. But success in leadership means more than getting what one wants. In determining success, we must always ask "power for what *ends?*" because power divorced from purpose is potentially dangerous and democratically undesirable.

In a democracy, people tend to get the government they deserve. If we look upon government as the enemy, and politics as a dirty word, our anger turns to apathy, allowing power (but not responsibility) to slip through our hands; we look at politics not as means to achieve public good, but as a necessary evil; we see elections as the choice between the lesser of two evils or the evil of the two lessers; we presume that our democratic responsibilities are satisfied merely by the act of voting every so often, or we drop out of politics. In short, if we abandon politics, power abandons us. So we return to a question asked earlier in this book: How do we bring Hamiltonian energy to the Madisonian system to achieve Jeffersonian ends?[28] If democracies have trouble finding and supporting leaders who seek to democratize power, they have an equally difficult time measuring success. While there is no easily computed presidential batting average to measure success, Emerson, answering the question "What is success?" came close:

> To laugh often and love much, to win the respect of intelligent persons and the affection of children; to appreciate beauty; to find the best in others; to give one's self; to leave the world a lot better whether by a healthy child, a garden patch, or a redeemed social condition; to have played and laughed with enthusiasm and sung with exaltation, to know even one life has breathed easier because you have lived—this is to have succeeded.[29]

In a *democracy*, a *successful leader* pursues and uses power, not for selfish ends, not to aggrandize his or her own status, but to achieve the goals of *empowerment*. Democratic leaders are *educators*, they are *visionaries.* they move the government in pursuit of the consensus generated from the values of the nation. They appeal to the best in citizens and attempt to lead the nation toward its better self.[30]

Franklin Roosevelt reminded us that the presidency "is preeminently a place of moral leadership."[31] Thus presidents may use their office as a "bully pulpit" to—when at their best—lead democratically. While the current cynicism and disdain about government sweeps the land—partly the result, I have argued, of the persistence of weak presidencies—let us not forget the great good to which government can and has been used. After all, it was through politics and government that the great social movements of the past century helped move us toward greater racial and gender equality, devised policies to expand education and opportunities to a wider segment of the population, attempted to protect and expand the rights of citizens. These battles are far from over. As a nation, we have a long way to go before we can truly grant the blessings of liberty and prosperity on all our fellow citizens, but it is through politics—and only through politics—that we can hope to achieve these noble goals. And if we want our politics (our government) to succeed, we must find ways for citizen power to guide, ennoble, and empower presidential leadership.

The ends that power serves are important, but in presidential terms, virtue is not enough. A successful president must have *character* and *competence.* Character without competence (resources, skill, power) gives us noble but ineffective leaders; competence without character may lead to government by demagogues.

Separation or Syncopation?

In theory, the separation of powers diminishes the chance of tyranny and increases the need for consensus and cooperation. In practice, there may very well be too much separation and too little power to act.[32]

In thinking about how to reform the presidency, the U.S. system of separating power is often compared with the British parliamentary model of the *fusion* of power. The British system brings the prime minister and Parliament together; it unifies power under a system of cabinet or prime ministerial rule in a strong-party model. The party in power selects the prime minister, who then has a considerable amount of power to achieve his or her policy goals.[33]

Most people (even most scholars) are comfortable with the idea of strong presidential leadership. On the left and right, the heroic-presidency model has begun to dominate the literature on presidential power. But what kind of strong presidency? One based on the Gaullist model? A presidency unhinged from the separation of powers?

As a gross overgeneralization, one could say that, historically, the political left has been more favorably disposed to the strong-presidency model, and the political right has been suspicious of a strong presidency. This reflected the old (outdated?) split between liberals and conservatives, with liberals inclined to use the power of the federal government to achieve liberal ends (the FDR model), and conservatives more inclined to rely on the "magic of the free market" to achieve social and economic goals.

But after years and years of failed or divided governments, a convergence has occurred. Today, all sides are drawn to the strong-presidency model. On the left, for example, former Carter administration official Lloyd Cutler calls for a parliamentary reform agenda, as do a number of academicians.[34]

What is surprising (and a historical anomaly) is that today, the political right embraces the strong-presidency model. Encouraged by the early days of Reagan's first term and seeing what George W. Bush could do after September 11, conservatives began to believe that the heroic presidency model could serve conservative ends. Conservative activists like Terry Eastland, academics like Jeremy Rabkin, and political philosophers like Harvey Mansfield, Jr.,[35] see the activist presidency as a conservative change agent worthy of support.

It seems that today the only place one can find defenses of the separation of powers, of the Framers' model, is in the academy. Scholars such as Tom Cronin, Robert Spitzer, and Harold Koh eloquently defend the legitimacy of the Founders' vision, arguing that our system is, after all, a tale of three branches, not one.[36] But they sometimes seem to be driving against traffic.

Reforming the Presidency

The American presidency, while the subject of much criticism and disappointment, has lasted for over two hundred years. The system created by Madison and the other Founders has lasted more or less intact for an amazingly long time by comparative standards. It is thus time to pay tribute to the Framers, but it is also time to honor their memory by reexamining the institution of the presidency and asking the right questions: Is this the best we can do? Is this eighteenth-century document adequate for governing in the twenty-first century?

The Framers would most certainly have been pleased to see how the system of checks and balances has thwarted executive tyranny. But they would perhaps have been less pleased with the excessive gridlock that so often characterizes relations between the president and Congress. The Founders wanted to limit presidential power, not spay and neuter the office.

"How," Bert Rockman asked in *The Leadership Question*, "can leadership be exerted yet restrained?"[37] It is a question that confounded the Founders and troubles us today.

Is the separation-of-powers model *the* problem? Does it create a magical gridlock machine? If one is the president, there must be times when it seems so. Woodrow Wilson—writing in 1884 *before* occupying the White House—saw the separation as creating a massive political escape clause for blame and responsibility:

> Power and strict accountability for its use are the essential constituents of good government. . . . It is, therefore, manifestly a radical defect in our federal system that it parcels out power and confuses responsibility as it does. The main purpose of the Convention of 1787 seems to have been to accomplish this grievous mistake. . . . Were it possible to call together again the members of that wonderful Convention. . . . they would be the first to admit that the only fruit of dividing power had been to make it irresponsible.[38]

But upon reflection we are reminded of the positive benefit of separating, sharing, and overlapping power. If one values deliberation, discussion, and debate; if we accept a model of democratic governing based on consensus and cooperation, then the reform agenda

will be short. But many see the separation as the likely suspect in the crime of gridlock.

Among reformers, there is a great deal of sympathy for the parliamentary alternative, but it must be admitted that with the American reverence for the Constitution, to make such a dramatic change is out of the question. Even if parliamentary reform were the panacea that some of its proponents suggest, there is simply no way to expect the American people to pursue such a radical restructuring of their system of government.

The choice, then, is not between radical restructuring *or* tinkering; not between dealing with root causes *or* symptoms; not between major surgery *or* an aspirin. The only choice we face, given the sacredness of the constitutional order, is to ask, which form of tinkering *might* make the system operate a bit better? Which Band-Aids might bring just a bit more fusion to a system so separated? While there is no surefire antidote to presidential failure, there *must* be a way to make the system operate better than its current performance levels.

Making the Presidency Work

To make the presidency work, to make it powerful but accountable, to help the presidency serve Jeffersonian ends, we must focus our attention widely on more than a single institution. The presidency does not exist in a vacuum, and presidential reforms, as important as they may be, cannot be instituted in isolation of the other important elements of the political system.

We must change the presidency, but *we* must change also. We must make the presidency work, but we must also reform Congress, change public expectations and demands, foster a rebirth of citizen interest and involvement, reform the party system, limit the pernicious impact of money on our political process, and more. Given the interconnectedness of the American system, not the reform of one branch but the reform of the American governmental system should be our goal. It is, after all, a tale of three branches, not one. And while ours is often a presidentially driven system (Congress leads only rarely[39]), it is also a system driven by cooperation and engagement between the separate institutions that share power.

First and foremost, we must accept the legitimacy of the separation of powers and the theory of government (consensus-building, cooperative) that rests behind it. Presidents and Congress must find reasons and ways to work together, lest they continue to face the deadlock and gridlock that has plagued recent years.[40] But can we make the separation of powers work better so that separation does not mean isolation? Can the president and Congress cooperate, or are they cursed to perpetually exhibit the most dysfunctional side of their separation?

The first precondition of making the separation of powers work better is the need to develop a *consensus*. This does not mean that all Americans must march in lockstep behind the will of the majority, but it does point to the need for Americans to feel like a nation once again: a people joined together in common pursuit of the common good—a nation, not merely an aggregation of individuals. The current division between Congress and the president reflects not merely the institutional battles between two branches of government but also the deeper conflicts and divisions that divide the nation and its people.

The only way to achieve a consensus is to begin a nationwide discussion, a dialogue of self-examination. We must ask: Who are we (as a people)? What do we want? Where do we wish to go? How can we get there?

If we are a people divided by race, class, religion, or ideology, we must find ways to move beyond the balkanization of cultures and develop a shared sense of national community. The end of the Cold War, rather than producing a sense of euphoria, has revealed a state of national confusion. Our national purpose, which seemed so clear in the Cold War era, is now characterized by self-doubt and drift. Even as we are united to fight a war against terrorism; the bonds holding us together seem quite fragile. Gone is the road map that guides us. In its place is the void. We have no useful interpretative framework to replace the Cold War consensus that so dominated the American psyche. We are left with a crisis of modernity in which the search for meaning has led to confusion. We can continue to drift aimlessly from one election to another, one party to another, one candidate to another, or we can engage in a dialogue focused on the search for the meaning of national community in a post–Cold War world.[41] The post 9/11 period, rather than generating a national discussion regarding our role in the world, has been a debateless series of presidential decisions with no public discussion. Most "leaders" fear the consequences of such a discussion. But the leader who can master this dilemma, the party that can mobilize the voters behind such a vision, will create the conditions for the next critical realignment of the American political system. Out of critical realignments comes the consensus that facilitates leadership.

We are a diverse nation, a complex nation, a multicultural nation, a heterogeneous nation. Can we truly get along? Can we become, once again, a nation? Can we pull together for the common good and the general welfare?

If we are to move ahead as a nation, we cannot rely simply on leaders taking us in new directions. Reform must percolate up as a result of national renewal and reinvention. Can we reinvent democracy and reinvent government for the public good?[42]

A rebirth of citizen democracy, to use Thomas Cronin's phrase, is needed if we are to recapture the lost essence of Jeffersonian democracy. Not the negative, hurtful activism that tears down the nation, but a hopeful, helpful, positive spirit of community and unity. For too long have we been at each other's throats; for too long have we been more inclined to tear down than to build up. Both the left and the right share in the blame for this "politics of contempt." In the late 1960s, many on the left misunderstood liberty to mean license, and freedom to mean free from responsibility. The right of today are currently engaged in their own version of "trash America." With their celebration of greed and the criticism of diversity, their attacks on anyone who questions President Bush's handling of the war on terrorism, they flock to the cynicism of a Rush Limbaugh and are made to feel temporarily better by mocking America. As the cynicism of the 1960s could not last, so too will the cynicism of the 1980s and 1990s wear thin after a time.

To replace the cynicism that has torn us apart, we need a sense of national identity that can bring us together. The needs of individualism (1980s–1990s) and the community (1960s) must be brought into balance. As citizens we must lower our political expectations and increase our political knowledge; we must embrace our diversity and build on our dreams. We must become a nation again.

A great deal needs to be done in Congress to reinvent the separation of powers in the twenty-first century. The system in which the Congress holds the president hostage or the system in which the president circumvents Congress must end. To make the separation of powers work better (as intended?), the Congress needs to (1) strengthen party leadership within Congress; (2) strengthen the parties (this wouldn't be a political science book without a call for stronger parties); (3) greatly diminish the importance of money in the congressional and political process; and (4) institute a form of the British model of "Question Time," in which the president appears before the Congress to answer questions.

What reforms might we implement so as to make the presidency work better? Of course, we want presidents with skill, judgment, experience, flexibility, intelligence, and vision. But even if we had an FDR, he would still face enormous roadblocks. How can we unclog the cholesterol-blocked arteries of the American system?

First, presidents must be *educators* and *visionaries*. Second, presidents must be *coalition builders*, opening lines of communication with Congress and developing bonds of mutual interest. Third, we should eliminate the twenty-second amendment's ban preventing presidents from seeking more than two terms. This might help repoliticize the president's second term and reinvigorate the political leverage of what have become "lame duck" presidents. And finally, we should synchronize the electoral terms of the presidents and Congress, with all (House, Senate, *and* president) serving four-year terms. This would give the president a greater opportunity to gain an electoral mandate and to govern with a stronger party.

These changes—reforms in the public, the Congress, *and* the presidency—should be seen not in isolation but in relation to one another. They are not a panacea, none exists; but they are designed to revive and reinvigorate the deadlocked separation of powers by fostering greater connection and cooperation. As Woodrow Wilson noted, "The rule of government action is necessary cooperation."[43]

The responsibility for reforming the presidency and the American political system generally falls upon the public, not upon our "leaders." Leaders rarely lead. They rarely can. Usually, leaders are mere officeholders who follow the public's mood or serve as caretakers. Unusual is the officeholder who truly tries to lead, to move the nation, to foment genuine (as opposed to cosmetic) change. We have no one to look to but ourselves. The American citizenry must re-create, empower, and reinvigorate American democracy: government of the people, by the people, and for the people.

But to do this, the American public must wake up and not passively accept the pretty word pictures painted by presidents who are better suited to filling the role of android game show host than to that of governing the nation. Perhaps the low point of the "citizen as ostrich" era came during the early 1980s, when we elected a president who promised the most absurdly far-fetched things, and we believed him! Ronald Reagan told us what we wanted to hear; he flattered us to death: huge tax cuts, huge defense increases, no pain, all gain. The president as Pied Piper played a magical tune and we followed, driving a beautiful new car (made in Japan or Germany), paid for on credit, all the way to the poorhouse. And did our support for a scandal-plagued Clinton reflect our being "bought off" by a strong economy?

How did this happen? James David Barber reminds us that we would rather live in Oz than in Kansas, but even so, where was our

Toto, the little dog who pulled back the Wizard's curtain to reveal that the Wizard was no wizard at all but a wrinkly old charlatan? Without a rebirth of citizen politics, new wizards can arise to mislead us. We must not let the pretty promises of photogenic people lead us to suspend our healthy skepticism so necessary in a robust and lively democracy.

If we are going to make the presidency and the American political system "work," we must decide what we want of government and of the presidency: an elective monarch? servant of the people? ruler of the people? a coequal branch of government? The presidency is confused because we are confused.

As Michael Lind reminds us, "Presidential democracy is not democracy."[44] But neither is deadlock or stagnation. As I get closer to AARP age, I more readily appreciate the Madisonian genius of the separation of powers. And while I look somewhat enviously at the ability of the prime ministers in parliamentary democracies to assert their will, I know that we will not and can not import parliamentary democracy onto our system. Thus let us embrace the separation of powers, make it work, and celebrate the stability and success of the Madisonian model.

The failure of leadership in the United States cannot be resolved overnight. The roots of the crisis run deep in our traditions, culture, and structure of government. Reforms such as those previously mentioned might help, but reforms can only do so much and go so far. If we as a people do not know in which direction we wish to go, no leader can do much to take command of the American system.

Conclusion

As should be clear, the presidency is a dynamic, not a static, institution. While there are standard role expectations and responsibilities faced by all occupants of the office, such uniformity must be seen as the other side of the coin of the rich variety each president brings to the office.

Each president brings a unique set of skills, experiences, goals, and styles to the presidency, but the office itself places certain demands on the president. It is this mix of the unique and the expected that makes the presidency such a fascinating institution. Since all presidents are expected to "lead," how individual differences (both inter- and intrapresidential) impact upon the institution often give us a clue of how well or poorly a president will perform. But being president is often like running in the sand; no matter how much energy you expend, you get nowhere slowly. Presidents rarely get to run on cinder tracks. In the United States, the president may be in office, but he is not necessarily in power.

The problems that plague the presidency (and the American political system) are not entirely new. Past presidents faced many of the antileadership obstacles that have confronted the recent occupants of the White House. Many of the problems inhibiting presidential leadership (e.g., intent of the Framers, structure of government) represent historical continuities, not radical departures from the past. *All* presidents have presided over a system that put leaders in chains. But there *are* some newer elements to add to the leadership aversion system that inhibits presidents (e.g., the decline of party support, weakness of congressional leadership, rise of globalism). The leadership aversion system is a constant reality; some of the components that make up its totality may change over time.

In order to attain progress and not merely change, we must know what to do (vision), how to go about doing it (skill), and hope that the system can be moved in that direction (resources and opportunity).

The United States is, for the most part, a *presidentially driven* system. Without presidential leadership, it is difficult for the government to sustain concerted action. While there are times and issues upon which the Congress takes the initiative and leads, this must be seen as the exception rather than the rule.[45]

While the "living" Constitution has evolved to Hamiltonian proportions, the written document still clings to a Madisonian architecture. To modern-day Hamiltonians, the Constitution is an empowering document; to Madisonians, it is a restricting document. In reality, it conforms to Corwin's dictum that it is an "invitation to struggle" for control of power. Since power floats in the American system, someone must grab and hold on to it. But power is slippery. The person best positioned to grab onto power (if only for a limited time) is the president. Thus presidential leadership is important, perhaps indispensable if the machinery of government is to move ahead.

While power is sometimes abused, often misused, and usually poorly used, we should not forget that the office and powers of the presidency are *potential* powers. And the power to do harm exists with the power to do good. If the presidency of the modern era has not been able to translate power potential into practical good, it must be remembered that it is not power itself that is good or ill, but the uses to which power is put. One could use government power to achieve good ends, but first, one must be able to use the power of government.

In this sense, the United States needs presidential power. The president must be a leader, but not just any kind of leader. Presidents must have the power to do good, but the system of checks and balances is important to put a halt to presidents whose actions may be suspect. Presidents need the power to achieve the ideals grounded in the Declaration of Independence and Bill of Rights, but the citizen needs the separation of powers to control abuse.

Perhaps that is why, as messy, confusing, frustrating, and aggravating as the separation of powers *can be*, it may still offer us the best available model for governing. If made to work properly—presidential leadership and persuasion moving the public around a vision that in turn leads to presidential influence in Congress—the separation of powers, and the theory of government that animates it, offers an opportunity for the government to be both powerful and democratically accountable.[46] In this way, respect for and reinvigoration of the separation of powers may offer presidents a way to overcome the failure so endemic in the American system.

Disappointment in the performance of presidents has become a reason (or excuse) for citizen cynicism and despair. The effect of failure and abuse of power on civic participation and participatory democracy has been devastating. Our citizens are democratic dropouts.

Thomas Cronin concluded his "Superman" article by noting that "we pay a price . . . for the way we have over-idealized the presidency." We also pay a price for overdenigrating the presidency. It becomes a self-fulfilling prophecy. We elect a president and almost immediately savage him.

In many ways, the presidency *is* a weak office. Designed with limits and checks, it takes a strong, forceful president in unusual times to overcome the limitations inherent in the office. To transcend weakness, presidents have pursued a combination of the following means: (1) the *formal* power to command; (2) the *informal* power to persuade and bargain; and (3) the *illegal* means of going beyond the law. As presidents get more and more frustrated by their inability to move the machinery of government with the first two methods, they are tempted to resort to the third. Can we have a presidency that is powerful, accountable, *and* constitutional?

The new textbook image of presidential weakness is a recognition of and response to thirty-five years of presidential inadequacy. Can the presidency be saved? In 1980, Thomas Cronin wrote that "the cult of the strong presidency is alive and well. . . . The American public . . . has not lost hope in the efficacy of strong purposive leadership."[47] The goal is to develop a responsive and responsible, powerful but accountable, constitutional and creative presidency. Waiting for Godot, or FDR, will not provide an answer.

The president is not Superman. In a democracy, all citizens are the Clark Kents, waiting to metamorphose into Super men and women. But, by the same token, the U.S. government is (almost always) a presidentially driven system. We need presidential leadership within democratic bounds. We need democratic leadership.

For Discussion

1. Write a new Constitution, one that fits the needs of the nation as it enters the twenty-first century.
2. In a post-hegemonic era, can we reduce the power of the president (and the role of the United States in the world) over foreign affairs?
3. Is strong presidential leadership compatible with political democracy? Does a strong presidency make for a weak people?
4. Should the president be a problem solver or an enabler/empowerer for the people?

Debate Questions

I. *Resolved:* That in the post–Cold War era, the president's power should be reduced in foreign affairs.

II. *Resolved:* That the United States should switch to a parliamentary form of government, similar to that of Britain.

Endnotes

Preface

1. I am indebted to James O'Toole for bringing the Ensor painting to my attention; see James O'Toole, *Leading Change* (San Francisco: Jossey–Bass, 1995), pp. 1–5.
2. David R. Mayhew, *Congress: The Electoral Connection* (New Haven, CT: Yale University Press, 1974).
3. The power-maximizing part of this theory is drawn from the pioneering work of Richard E. Neustadt, whose book *Presidential Power* (New York: Wiley, 1960) is still considered a classic work on presidential politics. The second part of the theory concerning the limits of power is drawn from Thomas E. Cronin's discussion of Neustadt's work that appears in *The State of the Presidency* (Boston: Little, Brown, 1980), pp. 121–136.
4. Michael A. Genovese, ed., *Women as National Leaders* (Newbury Park, CA.: Sage, 1993).

Chapter 1

1. Phil Williams, "The Limits of American Power: From Nixon to Reagan," *International Affairs* (Autumn 1987).
2. Thomas E. Cronin, *The State of the Presidency* (Boston: Little, Brown, 1980), p. vi.
3. Theodore J. Lowi and Benjamin Ginsberg, *Democrats Return to Power* (New York: Norton, 1994), p. 2.
4. Larry Berman, *Lyndon Johnson's War* (New York: Norton, 1991).

5. Michael A. Genovese, *The Nixon Presidency: Power and Politics in Turbulent Times*, (Westport, CT: Greenwood, 1990); Michael A. Genovese, *The Watergate Crisis* (Westport, CT: Greenwood, 1999).
6. Roger Porter, "Gerald Ford: A Healing Presidency," in Fred I. Greenstein, ed., *Leadership in the Modern Presidency* (Cambridge, MA: Harvard University Press, 1988), pp. 199–227.
7. Erwin C. Hargrove, *Jimmy Carter as President: A Study of Policy Leadership* (Baton Rouge: Louisiana State University Press, 1988).
8. Lou Cannon, *President Reagan: The Role of a Lifetime* (New York: Touchstone, 1991).
9. Colin Campbell and Bert A. Rockman, *The Bush Presidency: First Appraisals.* (Chatham, NJ: Chatham House, 1991).
10. Susan Schmidt and Michael Weisskopf, *The Truth at Any Cost: Ken Starr and the Unmasking of Bill Clinton* (New York: Perennial, 2000); Jeffrey Toobin, *A Vast Conspiracy: The Real Story of the Sex Scandal That Nearly Brought Down a President* (New York: Touchstone, 1999).
11. William E. Leuchtenburg, *In the Shadow of FDR: From Harry Truman to Ronald Reagan* (Ithaca, NY: Cornell University Press, 1983). See also Philip Abbott, *The Exemplary Presidency* (Amherst: University of Massachusetts Press, 1990).
12. Terry M. Moe, "Presidential Style and Presidential Theory" (paper presented at the Presidency Research Conference, Pittsburgh, 1990), p. 8.
13. Thomas E. Cronin, "Superman, Our Textbook President," *Washington Monthly*, October 1970, pp. 7–18.
14. Robert J. Spitzer, *President and Congress* (New York: McGraw-Hill, 1992), pp. 36–37.
15. Fred J. Greenstein, *The Hidden-Hand Presidency: Eisenhower as Leader* (New York: Basic Books, 1982).
16. Adapted from William G. Andrews, "The Presidency, Congress, and Constitutional Theory," in Norman C. Thomas, ed., *The Presidency in Contemporary Context* (New York: Dodd, Mead, 1973). Andrew refers only to two categories of evaluation, "Hallowed Be the President" and "Deliver Us from Presidents." I have added all others.
17. Alfred DeGrazia, *Congress and the Presidency* (Washington, DC: American Enterprise Institute, 1967) and *Republic in Crisis: Congress Against the Executive Force* (New York: Federal Legal Publications, 1965).
18. Richard E. Neustadt, *Presidential Power: The Politics of Leadership* (New York: Free Press, 1990).
19. Clinton Rossiter, *The American Presidency* (New York: Harcourt, Brace and World, 1956), p. 250.

20. Ibid., p. 251.
21. Neustadt, *Presidential Power*, p. 195.
22. Thomas E. Cronin, *The State of the Presidency*, 2nd ed. (Boston: Little, Brown, 1980), pp. 75–116. See also William W. Lammers, *Presidential Politics* (New York: HarperCollins, 1976); Richard M. Pious, *The American Presidency* (New York: Basic Books, 1979).
23. Herman Finer, *The Presidency* (Chicago: University of Chicago Press, 1960), pp. 111, 119.
24. James MacGregor Burns, *Presidential Government: The Crucible of Leadership* (Boston: Houghton Mifflin, 1965), p. 330.
25. Grant McConnell, *The Modern Presidency* (New York: St. Martin's Press, 1967), p. 87.
26. Albert Cantrill, *The American People, Vietnam, and the Presidency* (Princeton, NJ: Princeton University Press, 1976); David Halberstam, *The Best and the Brightest* (New York: Random House, 1972); Stanley Karnow, *Vietnam: A History* (New York: Viking, 1983).
27. Berman, *Lyndon Johnson's War*.
28. Genovese, *The Nixon Presidency*.
29. Michael A. Genovese, "Presidential Corruption: A Framework" (paper presented at annual meeting of the American Political Science Association, New York, September 1–5, 1994); Michael A. Genovese, *The Watergate Crisis* (Westport, CT, 1999).
30. Arthur M. Schlesinger, Jr., *The Imperial Presidency* (Boston: Houghton Mifflin, 1973).
31. Marcus Cunliffe, "A Defective Institution?" *Commentary*, February 1968, p. 28.
32. Schlesinger, *The Imperial Presidency*.
33. Quoted in Joseph Kraft, "The Post Imperial Presidency," *New York Times*, November 2, 1980, p. 31.
34. Michael A. Genovese, *The Presidency in an Age of Limits* (Westport, CT: Greenwood Press, 1993), ch. 3.
35. For a more extensive analysis of the modern presidents, see Genovese, *The Presidency in an Age of Limits*.
36. Genovese, "Presidential Corruption."
37. See Terrel H. Bell, *The Thirteenth Man: A Reagan Cabinet Memoir* (New York: Free Press, 1987); Alexander M. Haig, Jr., *Caveat: Realism, Reagan and Foreign Policy* (New York: Macmillan, 1984); David A. Stockman, *The Triumph of Politics: The Inside Story of the Reagan Revolution* (New York: Avon, 1987); Michael K. Deaver, *Behind the Scenes* (New York: William Morrow, 1988); Larry Speakes,

Speaking Out (New York: Scribners, 1988); Donald T. Regan, *For the Record: From Wall Street to Washington* (New York: Harcourt Brace Jovanovich, 1988).

38. Michael A. Genovese, "The Return of the Imperial Presidency," *Presidency Research* (Fall 1986): 7–9.

39. For a full account of how the modern presidents understood and attempted to deal with the decline of U.S. power, see Genovese, *The Presidency in an Age of Limits.*

40. Michael Nelson, "Evaluating the Presidency," in Nelson, *The Presidency and the Political System* (Washington, DC: CQ Press, 1984), p. 10.

41. Cronin, "Superman: Our Textbook President."

42. Michael A. Genovese, "Wimpyman, Our Textbook President," *Presidency Research* (Winter 1988–89): 3–5.

43. George Will, "The Veep and the Blatherskite," *Newsweek*, June 29, 1992, p. 72.

44. Lowi and Ginsberg, *Democrats Return to Power*, p. 18.

45. Haynes Johnson, *The Best Times: America in the Clinton Years* (New York: Harcourt, 2001); see also William C. Berman, *From the Center to the Edge: The Politics and Policies of the Clinton Presidency* (Lanham, MD: Rowman and Littlefield, 2001).

46. With apologies to Guatemala, this title is attributed to Ron Klair, Gore Florida campaign advisor. See Editorial Staff, *The Washington Post, Deadlock* (New York: Public Affairs, 2001), p. 71.

47. Quoted in David Remnick, "The Talk of the Town" *New Yorker*, December 4, 2000, p. 35.

48. Louis Menand, "The Talk of the Town," *New Yorker*, November 27, 2000, p. 67.

49. James W. Ceasar and Andrew Busch, *The Perfect Tie: The Story of the 2000 Presidential Election* (Lanham, MD: Rowman and Littlefield, 2001.), p. 171.

50. See Vincent Bugliosi, *The Betrayal of America* (New York: Thunder's Month Press, 2001); E. J. Dionne and William Kristol, *Bush vs. Gore: The Court Cases and Commentary* (Washington, DC: Brookings, 2001); Samuel Issacharoff, Pamela Karlan, and Richard Pildes, *When Elections Go Bad* (New York: Foundation Press, 2001); Howard Gillman, *The Votes That Counted* (Chicago: University of Chicago Press, 2002); Alan M. Dershowitz, *Supreme Injustice* (New York: Oxford University Press, 2001); and Richard A. Posner, *Breaking the Deadlock* (Princeton, NJ: Princeton University Press, 2001).

51. Harold M. Barger, *The Impossible Presidency: Illusions and Realities of Executive Power* (Glenview, IL: Scott, Foresman, 1984), p. 2.

52. Ibid., p. 12.
53. Godfrey Hodgson, *All Things to All Men* (New York: Touchstone, 1980), p. 13.
54. Robert K. Murray and T. H. Blessing, "The Presidential Performance Study: A Progress Report," *Journal of American History* 170 (1983). Reagan is included in a 1991 update of the survey.
55. Stephen Skowronek, "Presidential Leadership in Political Time," in Michael Nelson, ed., *The Presidency and the Political System*, 4th ed. (Washington, DC: CQ Press, 1994).
56. Jimmy Breslin, *How the Good Guys Finally Won* (New York: Ballantine, 1975), p. 29
57. Schlesinger, *The Imperial Presidency*, p. 431. See also Robert E. DiClerico, *The American President* (Englewood Cliffs, NJ: Prentice-Hall, 1979).
58. James David Barber, "The Nixon Brush with Tyranny," *Political Science Quarterly* (Winter 1977–1978): 581.
59. Peter Drucker, *The Effective Executive* (New York: HarperCollins, 1966), p. 79.

Chapter 2

1. Hugh Heclo and Lester Salamon, *The Illusion of Presidential Government* (Boulder, Co.: Westview Press, 1981), p. 1.
2. Quoted in Thomas E. Cronin, "Presidential Power Revised and Reappraised," *Western Political Quarterly* 32, no.4 (December 1979), p. 381.
3. Alexander Hamilton, James Madison, and John Jay, *The Federalist Papers*, no. 51 (New York: New American Library, 1961), p. 322.
4. Madison, *Federalist*, no. 45; Hamilton, *Federalist*, no. 70, respectively.
5. Edward S. Corwin, *The President: Office and Powers, 1978–1984*, 5th ed. (New York: New York University Press, 1984), originally published in 1940. See also Joseph M. Bessette and Jeffrey Tulis, *The Presidency in the Constitutional Order* (Baton Rouge: Louisiana State University Press, 1981); Louis Fisher, *The Constitution Between Friends* (New York: St. Martin's Press, 1978).
6. Thomas E. Cronin, ed., *Inventing the American Presidency* (Lawrence: University Press of Kansas, 1989).
7. Lyn Ragsdale, *Presidential Politics* (Boston: Houghton Mifflin, 1993), p.30.
8. Bert A. Rockman, *The Leadership Question: The Presidency and the American System* (New York: Praeger, 1984), p. 42.

9. James Pfiffner, *The Modern Presidency* (New York: St. Martin's Press, 1993), p. 13.

10. Rockman, *The Leadership Question*, pp. 39, 40, 41.

11. David Mayhew argues in *Divided We Govern* (New Haven, CT: Yale University Press, 1991) that divided government has not had a significant impact upon deadlock/gridlock. For works that see divided government as a problem, see Lance T. LeLoup and Steven A. Shull, *Congress and the President: The Policy Connection* (Belmont, CA: Wadsworth, 1993); James A. Thurber, *Divided Democracy* (Washington, DC: CQ Press, 1991); and Cary W. Cox and Samuel Kernell, *The Politics of Divided Government* (Boulder, CO: Westview Press, 1991). For an excellent overview, see Charles O. Jones, *The Presidency in a Separated System* (Washington, DC: Brookings, 1994); and Donald L. Robinson, *"To the Best of My Ability": The Presidency and the Constitution* (New York: Norton, 1987).

12. Rockman, *The Leadership Question*, p. 43.

13. Arthur M. Schlesinger, Jr., "Leave the Constitution Alone," in Donald Robinson, ed., *Reforming American Government: The Bicentennial Papers of the Committee on the Constitutional System* (Boulder, CO: Westview Press, 1985), p. 53.

14. Neustadt, *Presidential Power: The Politics of Leadership* (New York: Free Press, 1990).

15. James MacGregor Burns, "More Than Merely Power: II," *New York Times*, November 17, 1978, p. A29.

16. For an excellent overview of Gardner's view on leadership, see John Gardner, *On Leadership* (New York: Free Press, 1990).

17. Clinton Rossiter, *Conservatism in America* (New York: Vintage, 1962), p. 72.

18. Cronin, *The State of the Presidency*, p. 24.

19. Max Lerner, *America as a Civilization* (New York: Knopf, 1957), p. 718.

20. Alexis de Tocqueville, *Democracy in America* (New York: Knopf, 1969), p. 430.

21. Michel Crozier, *The Trouble with America* (Berkeley: University of California Press, 1984), p. 71.

22. See Robert Bellah, Richard Masden, William Sullivan, Ann Swidel, and Steven Tipton, *Habits of the Heart* (New York: HarperCollins, 1985).

23. Warren Bennis, *Why Leaders Can't Lead: The Unconscious Conspiracy Continues* (San Francisco: Jossey-Bass, 1989), p. 46.

24. David F. Schuman, *A Preface of Politics* (Itasca, IL: F. E. Peacock, 1991), p. 6.

25. Samuel P. Huntington, *American Politics: The Promise of Disharmony* (Cambridge, MA: Harvard University Press, 1981), pp. 4, 33.
26. Madison, *Federalist*, no. 10.
27. See Stephen Skowronek, *The Politics Presidents Make* (Cambridge, MA: Belknap Press, 1993).
28. Rockman, *The Leadership Question*, p. 84.
29. Stephen Skowronek, "Presidential Leadership in Political Time," in Michael J. Nelson, ed., *The President and the Political System*, 3rd ed. (Washington, DC: CQ Press, 1990), pp. 117–162.
30. See Michael A. Genovese, "Presidential Leadership and Crisis Management," *Presidential Studies Quarterly* (Spring 1986), pp. 300–309.
31. Valerie Bunce, *Do New Leaders Make a Difference? Executive Succession and Public Policy Capitalism and Socialism* (Princeton, NJ: Princeton University Press, 1981).
32. Paul C. Light, *The President's Agenda* (Baltimore: Johns Hopkins University Press, 1982).
33. Arthur M. Schlesinger, Jr., *The Cycles of American History* (Boston: Houghton Mifflin, 1986), pp. 22–27.
34. Ibid. p. 34.
35. Erwin C. Hargrove, *The Power of the Modern Presidency* (New York: Knopf, 1974), p 186.
36. Ibid.
37. Thomas E. Cronin, "If Bush Is to Be the 'Education President' Much Work Must Be Done at the Grassroots," *Chronicle of Higher Education* 35 (February 1, 1989): B-2.
38. Ibid., p. 2.
39. James MacGregor Burns, *Leadership* (New York: HarperCollins, 1978).
40. James W. Davis, *The President as Party Leader* (New York: Praeger, 1992). See also Sidney M. Milkis, *The President and the Parties* (New York: Oxford University Press, 1993).
41. James MacGregor Burns, *The Power to Lead: The Crisis of the American Presidency* (New York: Simon and Schuster, 1984), p. 214.
42. Quoted in Richard Hofstadter, *The Idea of a Party System* (Oxford, England: Oxford University Press, 1969), p. 123.
43. George C. Edwards, *At the Margins: Presidential Leadership in Congress* (New Haven, CT: Yale University Press, 1989).
44. Samuel M. Kernell, *Going Public: New Strategies of Presidential Leadership* (Washington DC: CQ Press, 1989).

45. Milkis, *The President and the Parties*, p. 10; Craig A. Rimmerman, *Presidency by Plebiscite* (Boulder, CO: Westview Press, 1993).

46. Lester G. Seligman and Cary R. Covington, *The Coalition Presidency* (Chicago: Dorsey Press, 1989).

47. Burns, *The Power to Lead*, p. 43.

48. See Richard A. Watson, *The Presidential Contest* (New York: Wiley, 1984); Stephen J. Wayne, *The Road to the White House* (New York: St. Martin's Press, 1988); Nelson W. Polsby and Aaron Wildavsky, *Presidential Elections* (New York: Free Press, 1991); Herbert B. Asher, *Presidential Elections and American Politics* (Homewood, IL: Dorsey Press, 1984); James W. Ceaser, *Presidential Selection* (Princeton, NJ: Princeton University Press, 1979).

49. James A. Barnes, "Ready or Not," *National Journal*, September 4, 1993, pp. 2136–141.

50. Hubert Humphrey, quoted in the *New York Times*, October 13, 1974, p. E18. Quoted in Herbert B. Asher, *Presidential Elections and American Politics* (Homewood, IL: Dorsey Press, 1984), p. 186. See also Anthony Corrado, *Creative Campaigning* (Boulder, CO: Westview Press, 1992); John H. Kessel, *Presidential Campaign Politics* (Chicago: Dorsey Press, 1988); Joseph A. Pika, Zelna Mosley, and Richard A. Watson, *The Presidential Contest* (Washington, DC: CQ Press, 1992).

51. Charles E. Lindblom, "The Market as Prison," *Journal of Politics* 44 (1982): 324–336.

52. Ibid., p. 325.

53. Ibid., p. 325.

54. Ibid., pp. 328–329.

55. James O'Connor, *The Fiscal Crisis of the State* (New York: St. Martin's Press, 1973); Alan Wolfe, *The Limits of Legitimacy* (New York: Free Press, 1977).

56. Edward S. Greenberg, *The American Political System* (Boston: Little, Brown, 1986), p. 344. See also William F. Grover, *The President as Prisoner* (New York: SUNY Press, 1989).

57. See Ray C. Fair, "The Effect of Economic Events on Votes for President," *Review of Economics and Statistics* 60 (1978): 159–173; David G. Golden and James M. Poterba, "The Price of Popularity: The Political Business Cycle Reexamined," *American Journal of Political Science* 24 (1980): 696–714; Sam Kernell, "Explaining Presidential Popularity," *American Political Science Review* 72 (1978): 506–533.

58. See Frank E. Meyers, "Social Classes and Political Change in Western Industrial Systems," *Comparative Politics* 2 (1970): 389–412.
59. Quoted in Arthur M. Schlesinger, Jr., *A Thousand Days: John F. Kennedy in the White House* (Boston: Houghton Mifflin, 1965), p. 641.
60. Quoted in Ronald F. King, "The Politics of Regressive Taxation Changes" (paper presented at the annual meeting of the Midwest Political Science Association, Chicago, 1977), p. 12.
61. Thomas E. Cronin, "Presidential Power Revised and Reappraised," *Western Political Quarterly* 32 (1979): 389.
62. Bruce Mirott, *Pragmatic Illusions* (New York: David McKay, 1976), p. 273.
63. Ibid., p. 274.
64. Ibid., p. 276.
65. Jeff Fauz, "Whose Rules for Globalization?" *The American Prospect*, June 5, 2000.; Wayne Ellwood, *The No-Nonsense Guide to Globalization* (London: Verso, 2001). Anthony Giddens, *Runaway World: How Globalization Is Reshaping Our Lives* (New York: Routledge, 2002).

Chapter 3

1. Hedrick Smith, *The Power Game: How Washington Works* (New York: Ballantine, 1988).
2. William W. Lammers, and Michael A. Genovese, *The Presidency and Domestic Policy: Comparing Leadership Styles, FDR to Clinton* (Washington, DC: CQ Press, 2000).
3. Michael A. Genovese and Seth Thompson, "Women as Chief Executives: Does Gender Matter?" in Michael A. Genovese, ed., *Women as National Leaders*, (Newbury Park, CA: Sage, 1993), pp. 1–2.
4. Cronin, *The State of the Presidency*, p. 145.
5. Robert Shogan, *The Riddle of Power* (New York: Dutton, 1991), p.5.
6. Michael A. Genovese, *The Power of the American Presidency* (New York: Oxford University Press, 2001).
7. Robert A. Dahl, *Pluralist Democracy in the United States* (New York: Rand McNally, 1967), p. 90.
8. James P. Pfiffner, *The Strategic Presidency: Hitting the Ground Running* (Chicago: Dorsey Press, 1988).

9. James MacGregor Burns, *Roosevelt: The Lion and the Fox* (San Diego, CA: Harvest/HBI, 1984), p. 197.
10. Edward S. Cronin, *The President: Office and Powers* (New York: New York University Press, 1957).
11. Neustadt, *Presidential Power.*
12. Burns, *Leadership,* p. 18.
13. John F. Kennedy, Foreword to Theodore C. Sorenson, *Decision-Making in the White House* (New York: Columbia University Press, 1963), p. xi.
14. Burns, *Leadership,* part 3.
15. Donald T. Phillips, *Lincoln on Leadership* (New York: Warner, 1992), p. 137.
16. Burt Nanus, *Visionary Leadership* (San Francisco, CA: Jossey-Bass, 1992), p. 3.
17. Ibid., p. 4.
18. Sheldon Wolin, *Politics and Vision* (Boston: Little, Brown, 1960), p. 436.
19. Warren Bennis and Burt Nanus, *Leaders: Strategies for Taking Charge* (New York: HarperCollins, 1985), pp. 39, 42.
20. Lester Salamon, *The Illusion of Presidential Government* (Boulder, CO: Westview Press, 1981), p. 292.
21. Lance Blakesley, *The President as a Strategically Versatile Leader* (Chicago: Nelson-Hall, 1995).
22. Quoted in Sidney Blumenthal, "The Education of a President," *New Yorker,* January 24, 1994, p. 33.
23. Fred I. Greenstein and Nelson Polsby, eds., *The Handbook of Political Theory: Micro-Political Theory* (Reading, MA.: Addison-Wesley, 1975), pp. 19–21.
24. Erwin C. Hargrove, "Presidential Personality and Leadership Style," in George C. Edwards III, John H. Kessel, and Bert A. Rockman, eds., *Researching the Presidency: Vital Questions, New Approaches* (Pittsburgh: University of Pittsburgh Press, 1993), p. 70.
25. Ibid., p. 82
26. Ibid., p. 69.
27. For a view that suggests we should spend less time studying skill and more on institutional pressures, see Terry M. Moe, "Presidents, Institutions, and Theory," in Edwards, Kessel, and Rockman, op. cit., pp. 337–385. For an attempt to understand the role of skill in domestic policy achievement, see Lammers and Genovese, *The Presidency and Domestic Policy.*

28. Robert K. Murray and Tim H. Blessing, *Greatness in the White House: Rating the Presidents, Washington Through Carter* (University Park: Pennsylvania State University Press, 1988).
29. Burns, *Roosevelt: The Lion and the Fox*, p. 264.
30. See James David Barber's often criticized but influential work, *The Presidential Character: Predicting Performance in the White House* (Englewood Cliffs, NJ: Prentice Hall, 1992).
31. James P. Pfiffner, ed., *The Managerial Presidency* (Pacific Grove, CA.: Brooks/Cole, 1991).
32. Pfiffner, *The Strategic Presidency*.
33. For an excellent review of how the press treated President Clinton in the early stages of his administration, see the three-part series by David Shaw, *Los Angeles Times*, September 15–17, 1993
34. Pfiffner, *The Strategic Presidency*, p. 4.
35. Quoted in Hedrick Smith, *The Power Game*, p. 331.
36. Light, *The President's Agenda*, pp. 41–45.
37. Alexander Haig, *Caveat: Realism, Reagan, and Foreign Policy* (New York: Macmillan, 1984).
38. James P. Pfiffner, "The Carter-Reagan Transition: Hitting the Ground Running," *Presidential Studies Quarterly*, (Fall 1983): 522–544.
39. Bunce, *Do New Leaders Make a Difference?*
40. Light, *The President's Agenda*, p. 36.
41. Quoted in Light, *The President's Agenda*, p. 36.
42. See Hedrick Smith, *The Power Game*, pp. 340–342.
43. Cronin, *The State of the Presidency*, p. 168.
44. Benjamin Ginsberg and Martin Shefter, *Politics by Other Means* (New York: Basic Books, 1990), pp. 164–165.
45. James MacGregor Burns, quoted in Hedrick Smith, *The Power Game*, p. 679.
46. Hedrick Smith, *The Power Game*, p. 680.
47. Ibid.
48. James A. Davis and David L. Nixon, "The President's Party," *Presidential Studies Quarterly* 24:2 (Spring 1994): 363–365.
49. Paul Brace and Barbara Hinckley, *Follow the Leader: Opinion Polls and the Modern Presidents* (New York: Basic Books, 1992).
50. Richard E. Neustadt, *Presidential Power and the Modern Presidents* (New York: Free Press, 1990).
51. George C. Edwards, *Presidential Influence in Congress* (San Francisco, CA: Freeman, 1980), pp. 86–100.

52. Neustadt, *Presidential Power*, p. 76.

53. Quoted in George C. Edwards III and Stephen J. Wayne, *Presidential Leadership: Politics and Policy Making* (New York: St. Martin's Press, 1990) p. 90.

54. Edwards and Wayne, op. cit., p. 90.

55. Quoted in Edwards and Wayne, op. cit., p. 91.

56. Jody Powell, quoted in Michael Baruch Grossman and Martha Joynt Kumar, "Carter, Reagan, and the Media: Have the Rules Changed on the Poles of the Spectrum of Success?" (paper presented at the annual meeting of the American Political Science Association, New York, September 3–6, 1981), p. 18.

57. Fred Greenstein, "What the President Means to Americans," in James David Barber, ed., *Choosing the President* (New York: American Assembly, 1974), pp. 130–131.

58. Theodore J. Lowi, *The Personal President: Power Invested Promise Unfulfilled* (Ithaca, NY: Cornell University, 1985).

59. Brace and Hinckley, *Follow the Leader*, p. 1.

60. Jeffrey K. Tulis, *The Rhetorical Presidency* (Princeton, NJ: Princeton University Press, 1987), ch. 2.

61. Pfiffner, *The Modern Presidency*, ch. 2.

62. Mary E. Stuckey, *The President as Interpreter-in-Chief* (Chatham, NJ: Chatham House, 1991).

63. Bruce Miroff, *Icons of Democracy* (New York: Basic Books, 1993), p. 2.

64. Thomas E. Cronin, "Leadership and Democracy," *Liberal Education* 73:2 (March/April 1987): 35–38; Benjamin R. Barber, "Neither Leaders nor Followers: Citizenship Under Strong Democracy," in Michael R. Beschloss and Thomas E. Cronin, *Essays in Honor of James MacGregor Burns* (Englewood Cliffs, NJ: Prentice-Hall, 1989), pp. 117–132.

65. Genovese, *The Presidency in an Age of Limits*.

66. Harvey G. Zeidenstein, "Presidents' Popularity and Their Wins and Losses on Major Issues: Does One Have a Greater Influence over the Other?" *Presidential Studies Quarterly* (Spring 1985): 287–300.

67. Richard A. Brody, *Assessing the President: The Media, Elite Opinion, and Public Support* (Stanford, CA: Stanford University Press, 1991).

68. Ibid.

69. Summaries of the literature on the impact of the economy can be found in Samuel Kernell, *Going Public* (Washington, D.C.: CQ, 1986), ch. 7; George C. Edwards III, *The Public Presidency* (New York: St. Martin's Press, 1983), ch. 6.

70. Robert H. Ferrel, ed., *Off the Record: The Private Papers of Harry S Truman* (New York: HarperCollins, 1980), p. 310.
71. Brace and Hinckley, *Follow the Leader*, p. 45.
72. Roderick Hart, *The Sound of Leadership* (Chicago: University of Chicago Press, 1987).
73. Edwards and Wayne, *Presidential Leadership*, p. 131.
74. Barger, *The Impossible Presidency*, p. 357.
75. John Orman, "Covering the American Presidency: Balanced Reporting in the Presidential Press," *Presidential Studies Quarterly* 14 (1984): 381–382.
76. Norman Ornstein and Michael Robinson, "The Case of Our Disappearing Congress," *TV Guide*, January 11, 1986, pp. 4–10.
77. Hedrick Smith, *The Power Game*, p. 10.
78. Cronin, *The State of the Presidency*, pp. 140–151.
79. Deaver, *Behind the Scenes*, p. 73.
80. John Maltese, *Spin Control: The White House Office of Communications and the Management of Presidential News* (Chapel Hill: University of North Carolina Press, 1992).
81. Hedrick Smith, *The Power Game*, p. 10.
82. Samuel Kernell, *Going Public: New Strategies of Presidential Leadership* (Washington, DC: CQ, 1986).
83. Jeffrey K. Tulis, *The Rhetorical Presidency* (Princeton, NJ: Princeton University Press, 1987), p. 95.
84. James W. Davis, *The American Presidency: A New Perspective* (New York: HarperCollins, 1987), p. 121.
85. Genovese, *The Nixon Presidency*, ch. 2.
86. Quoted in Michael J. Robinson and Margaret A. Sheehan, *Over the Wire and on TV* (New York: Russell Sage Foundation, 1983), p. 103.
87. Mark Hertsgaard, *On Bended Knee: The Press and the Reagan Presidency* (New York: Schocken Books, 1989).
88. See David Shaw, *Los Angeles Times*, September 15, 16, and 17, 1993, for an examination of the media's treatment of the Clinton presidency.
89. Larry Sabato, *Feeding Frenzy* (New York: Free Press, 1991).
90. James S. Young, *The Washington Community, 1800–1828* (New York: Columbia University Press, 1966), pp. 75–76.
91. Emmet John Hughes, *The Living Presidency* (New York: Coward, MacCann and Geoghegan, 1973), p. 208.
92. Robert J. Spitzer, *The Presidential Veto: Touchstone of the American Presidency* (Albany: State University of New York Press, 1988).

93. Arthur M. Schlesinger, Jr., and Alfred de Grazia, *Congress and the Presidency: Their Role in Modern Times* (Washington, DC: American Enterprise Institute, 1967), pp. 4–5.

94. Robert J. Spitzer, *President and Congress: Executive Hegemony at the Crossroads of American Government* (New York: McGraw-Hill, 1993), p. xx.

95. Lance T. LeLoup and Steven A. Shull, *Congress and the President: The Policy Connection* (Belmont, CA: Wadsworth, 1993).

96. Rossiter, *The American Presidency*, p. 26.

97. Roger H. Davidson, "The Presidency and Congress," in Michael Nelson, ed., *The Presidency and the Political System* (Washington, DC, CQ, 1984), pp. 363–391.

98. George C. Edwards III, *At the Margins: Presidential Leadership in Congress* (New Haven, CT: Yale University Press, 1989).

99. *Youngstown Sheet and Tube Co. v. Sawyer*, 343 US 579,635 (1952).

100. Edwards, *At the Margins*; Jon R. Bond and Richard Fleisher, *The President in the Legislative Arena* (Chicago: University of Chicago Press, 1990).

101. Brace and Hinckley, *Follow the Leader*; see also Douglas Rivers and Nancy Rose, "Passing the President's Program: Public Opinion and Presidential Influence in Congress," *American Journal of Political Science* 29 (May 1985): 183–196; and Richard Brody, *Assessing the President: The Media, Elite Opinion, and Public Support* (Stanford, CA: Stanford University Press, 1991), p. 21.

102. Brody, *Assessing the President*, p. 22.

103. Bond and Fleisher, *The President in the Legislative Arena*, p. 218; Edwards, *At the Margins*; Aage R. Clausen, *How Congressmen Decide: A Policy Focus* (New York: St. Martin's Press, 1973).

104. Terry Sullivan, "Headcounts, Expectations, and Presidential Coalitions in Congress," *American Journal of Political Science* 32:3 (August 1988): 567–589.

105. Edwards, *At the Margins*, p. 216.

106. Quoted in Barger, *The Impossible Presidency*, p. 127.

107. Rowland Evans and Robert Novak, *Lyndon B. Johnson: The Exercise of Power* (New York: New American Library, 1966), p. 104.

108. Quoted in George C. Edwards III, "Legislative Leadership," in Leonard W. Levy and Louis Fisher, eds., *Encyclopedia of the American Presidency*, vol. 3, (New York: Simon and Schuster, 1993), p. 950.

109. Douglas Jehl, "Clinton Assails G.O.P Delays in Bitter Tones," *New York Times*, July 27, 1993, p. A1.

110. See Paul Richter and Karen Tamulty, "Clinton's Use of the Soft Sell Worries Allies," *Los Angeles Times*, July 31, 1993, p.1.; R. W. Apple, Jr., "An Excess of the Pulpit and Not Enough Bully," *New York Times*, August 5, 1993, p. A12.

111. James Gerstenzang and Paul Richter, "Clinton Lobbying Wins More Votes for NAFTA Pact," *Los Angeles Times*, November 17, 1993, p. A1.

112. Karen Tamulty, "Clinton Piles Up Record Legislative Wins," *Los Angeles Times*, November 13, 1993, p. A23.

113. Bruce Buchanan, *The Presidential Experience: What the Office Does to the Man* (Englewood Cliffs, NJ: Prentice Hall, 1978).

114. For excellent works on the managerial aspects of the presidency, see Pfiffner, *The Managerial Presidency*; Peri E. Arnold, *Making the Managerial Presidency* (Princeton, NJ: Princeton University Press, 1986); Colin Campbell, *Managing the Presidency: Carter, Reagan, and the Search for Executive Harmony* (Pittsburgh: University of Pittsburgh Press, 1986); Stephen Hess, *Organizing the Presidency* (Washington, DC: Brookings, 1976); Hugh Heclo, *A Government of Strangers: Executive Politics in Washington* (Brookings, 1977); Samuel Kernell and Samuel Popkin, eds., *Chief of Staff* (Berkeley: University of California Press, 1986); and John P. Burke, *The Institutional Presidency* (Baltimore: Johns Hopkins University Press, 1992).

115. Colin Campbell, "Political Executives and Their Officials," in Ada W. Finifter, ed., *Political Science: The State of the Discipline, II* (Washington, DC: American Political Science Association, 1993).

116. Bennis and Nanus, *Leaders: The Strategies for Taking Charge*, p. 21.

117. Warren Bennis, *On Becoming a Leader* (Reading, MA: Addison-Wesley, 1989), p. 45.

118. James P. Pfiffner, "The President's Chief of Staff: Lessons Learned," Working Paper 92:19, October 1992, Institute of Public Policy, George Mason University.

119. Richard T. Johnson, *Managing the White House* (New York: HarperCollins, 1974).

120. Charles E. Walcott and Kara M. Holt, *Governing the White House* (Lawrence: University Press of Kansas, 1995); Richard W. Waterman, *Presidential Influence and the Administrative State*, (Knoxville: University of Tennessee Press, 1989).

121. Robert F. Durant and Adam L. Warber, "Networking in the Shadow of Hierarchy: Public Policy, the Administrative Presidency, and the Neoadministrative State," *Presidential Studies Quarterly* 31, no. 2 (June 2001): 221–222.

122. Richard Nathan, *The Administrative Presidency* (New York: Wiley, 1983); Robert F. Durant, *The Administrative Presidency Revisited* (New York: State University of New York Press, 1992); Peri E. Arnold, *Making the Managerial Presidency* (Lawrence: University Press of Kansas, 1998).
123. See *Jenkins v. Collard*, 145 U.S. 557, 560–561 (1891).
124. Phillip J. Cooper, *By Order of the President* (Laurence: University of Kansas, 2002); Kenneth R. Mayer, *With the Stroke of a Pen: Executive Orders and Presidential Power* (Princeton, NJ: Princeton University Press, 2001).
125. Dick Morris, *The New Prince* (Los Angeles: Renaissance Books, 1999), p. 89.
126. Richard Nathan, *The Administrative Presidency* (New York: Wiley, 1983).
127. Terry Moe, "The Politicized Presidency," in John E. Chubb and Paul E. Peterson, eds., *The New Direction in American Politics* (Washinton, DC: Brookings, 1985).
128. Aaron Wildavsky, "The Two Presidencies," in *Trans-Action*, December 1966, p. 7. See also Barbara Kellerman and Ryan J. Barilleaux, *The President as World Leader* (New York: St. Martin's Press, 1991); and Cecil V. Crabb and Kevin V. Mulcahy, *American National Security* (Pacific Grove, CA: Brooks/Cole, 1991).
129. Lance T. LeLoup and Steven A. Shull, "Congress Versus the Executive: The 'Two Presidencies' Reconsidered," *Social Science Quarterly* 59 (March 1979): 704–719; Lee Sigelman, "A Reassessment of the 'Two Presidencies' Thesis," *Journal of Politics* 41 (November 1979): 1195–205; exchange between Shull/LeLoup and Sigelman in *Journal of Politics* 43 (May 1981); Jeffrey E. Cohen, "A Historical Reassessment of Wildavsky's 'Two Presidencies' Thesis," *Social Science Quarterly* 63 (September 1982): 549–555. See also Steven A. Shull, ed., *The Two Presidencies: A Quarter Century Assessment* (Chicago, IL: Nelson-Hall, 1991).
130. Duane M. Oldfield and Aaron Wildavsky, "Reconsidering the Two Presidencies," *Society* (July/August 1989): 55.
131. James M. Lindsay and Wayne P. Steger, "The 'Two Presidencies' in Future Research: Moving Beyond Roll-Call Analysis," *Congress and the Presidency* 20:2 (Autumn 1993): pp. 103–117.
132. Bond and Gleisher, *The President in the Legislative Arena*, p. 171.
133. Genovese, "Presidential Leadership and Crisis Management."
134. Marcia Lynn Whicker, Jamer P. Pfiffner, and Raymond A. Moore, eds., *The Presidency and the Persian Gulf War* (Westport, CT: Praeger, 1993).

135. R. W. Apple, Jr., "Reagan Curse on Clinton," *New York Times*, August 1, 1993, p. A1; Sidney Blumenthal, "The Sorcerer's Apprentices," *New Yorker*, July 9, 1993, p. 29.

136. Michael A. Genovese, "The Supreme Court as a Check on Presidential Power," *Presidential Studies Quarterly* winter-spring 1976; and Michael A. Genovese, *The Supreme Court, the Constitution, and Presidential Power* (Lanham, Md.: University Press of America, 1980).

137. Glendon Schubert, *The Presidency in the Courts* (Minneapolis: University of Minnesota Press, 1957), p. 4.

138. Ibid., p. 3.

139. Rossiter, *The American Presidency*, pp. 45 and 42.

140. Koh, *The National Secureity Constitution*; Thomas M. Franck, *Political Questions/Judicial Answers* (Princeton, NJ: Princeton Univerity Press, 1992); and Henry J. Abraham, *Justices and Presidents* (New York: Oxford University Press, 1985).

141. David Gray Adler, "The Court and the Ghost of Curtiss-Wright" (paper presented at the annual meeting of the American Political Science Association, Washington, DC, September 1989).

142. Genovese, *The Nixon Presidency*; Stanley K. Kutler, *The Wars of Watergate* (New York: Knopf, 1990).

143. Theodore Draper, *A Very Thin Line: The Iran-Contra Affairs* (New York: Touchstone, 1991); Jane Mayer and Doyle McManus, *Landslide: The Unmaking of the President, 1984–1988* (Boston: Houghton Mifflin, 1988).

144. Nancy V. Baker, *Conflicting Loyalties: Law and Politics in the Attorney General's Office, 1789–1990* (Lawrence: University Press of Kansas, 1992); Katy J. Harriger, *Independent Justice: The Federal Special Prosecutor in American Politics* (Lawrence: University Press of Kansas, 1992); Rebecca Mae Salokar, *The Solicitor General: The Politics of Law* (Philadelphia: Temple University Press, 1992).

145. Terry Eastland, *Energy in the Executive: The Case for the Strong Presidency* (New York: Free Press, 1992); L. Gordon Corvitz and Jeremy A. Rabkin, eds., *The Fettered Presidency: Legal Constraints on the Executive Branch* (Washington, DC: American Enterprise Institute, 1989); Harvey C. Mansfield, Jr., *Taming the Prince: The Ambivalence of Modern Executive Power* (New York: Free Press, 1989).

146. Koh, *The National Security Constitution*.

147. Daniel P. Franklin, *Extraordinary Measures: The Exercise of Prerogative Powers in the United States* (Pittsburgh: University of Pittsburgh Press, 1991).

148. Genovese, "Presidential Leadership and Crisis Management"; Genovese, "Presidents and Crisis: Developing a Crisis Management System in the Executive Branch," *International Journal on World Peace* (Spring 1987): pp. 108–117.
149. Michael A. Genovese, "Democratic Theory and the Emergency Powers of the President," *Presidential Studies Quarterly* (Summer 1979): pp. 283–289.
150. John Locke, *Treatise on Civil Government and a Letter Concerning Toleration* (New York: Appleton-Century-Crofts, 1937), ch. 14, p. 109.
151. Ibid., p. 113.
152. Jean-Jacques Rousseau, *The Social Contract and Discourses* (New York: Dutton, 1950), book 4, ch. 6, p. 123.
153. John Stuart Mill, *Considerations on Representative Government* (New York: Liberal Arts Press, 1958), p. 274.
154. J. Malcolm Smith and Cornelius P. Cotter, *Powers of the President During Crises* (Washington, DC: Public Affairs Press, 1960), p. 7.
155. Niccolo Machiavelli, *The Prince and the Discourses* (New York: Modern Library, 1950), book 1, ch. 34, p. 203.
156. Clinton Rossiter, *Constitutional Dictatorship: Crisis Government in the Modern Democracy* (Princeton, NJ: Princeton University Press, 1948).
157. Abe Fortas, "The Constitution and the Presidency," *Washington Law Review 49* (August 1974): 100.
158. Edward S. Corwin, *Total War and the Constitution* (Westminster, MD.: Knopf, 1947), p. 80.
159. Rossiter, *Constitutional Dictatorship*, p. 12.
160. "President Speaks," *New York Times*, September 8, 1942, p. 1 (text of speech on pg. 17).
161. Richard M. Pious, *The American Presidency* (New York: Basic Books, 1979), p. 84.
162. Richard Longaker, Introduction to Rossiter, *The Supreme Court and the Commander in Chief*, expanded ed. (Ithaca, NY: Cornell University Press, 1976), p. xii.
163. Genovese, *The Supreme Court, the Constitution, and Presidential Power*, ch. 3.

Chapter 4

1. Harold Barger, *The Impossible Presidency: Illusions and Realities of Executive Power* (Glenview, IL: Scott, Foresman, 1984), pp. 396–397.
2. Bruce Miroff, *Icons of Democracy* (New York: Basic Books, 1993), p. 1.

3. James MacGregor Burns, *Leadership* (New York: HarperCollins, 1978), p. 9.
4. Glen A. Phelps, *George Washington and American Constitutionalism* (Lawrence: University Press of Kansas, 1993).
5. Quoted in Larry Berman, *The New American Presidency* (Boston: Little, Brown, 1987), p. 339.
6. Michael A. Genovese, *The Presidency in an Age of Limits* (Westport, CT: Greenwood Press, 1993).
7. Norman C. Thomas, Joseph A. Pika, and Richard A. Watson, *The Politics of the Presidency* (Washington, DC: CQ Press, 1993), p. 434.
8. Thomas E. Cronin, "Leadership and Democracy," *Liberal Education* 73, no. 2 (March/April 1987): p 36.
9. Ibid., pp. 36–37.
10. Quoted in Benjamin R. Barber, "Neither Leaders nor Followers," in *Essays in Honor of James MacGregor Burns*, edited by Thomas E. Cronin and Micheal R. Beschloss (Englewood Cliffs, NJ: Prentice-Hall, 1989), op. cit., p. 117.
11. Quoted in Mark E. Kann, "Challenging Lockean Liberalism in America: The Case of Debs and Hillquit," *Political Theory*, no. 8 (May 1980): 214.
12. Adapted from Michael A. Genovese, "Thomas Jefferson and the Vision of Democratic Leadership," *Journal of Leadership Studies* (June 1994): pp. 101–109.
13. Cronin, "Leadership and Democracy," p. 36.
14. James Bryce, *The American Commonwealth* (New York: MacMillan, 1888), vol. 2, p. 460.
15. Miroff, *Icons of Democracy*, p. 1.
16. Arthur M. Schlesinger, Jr., *The Cycles of American History* (Boston: Houghton Mifflin, 1986), p. 430.
17. Abraham Lincoln, *The Gettysburg Address*. See Mario Cuomo and Harold Holzer, eds., *Lincoln on Democracy* (New York: HarperCollins, 1990).
18. Willard Sterne Randall, *Thomas Jefferson: A Life* (New York: Henry Holt, 1993). See also Merrill D. Peterson, ed., *The Portable Thomas Jefferson* (New York: Viking, 1975).
19. Miroff, *Icons of Democracy*, p. 354.
20. George C. Edwards, John H. Kessel, and Bert A. Rockman, *Researching the Presidency* (Pittsburgh, PA: University of Pittsburgh Press, 1993).
21. Benjamin R. Barber, *Strong Democracy: Participatory Politics for a New Age* (Berkeley: University of California Press, 1984).

22. Benjamin R. Barber, "Neither Leads nor Follows," in *Essays in Honor of James MacGregor Burns,* edited by Thomas E. Cronin and Michael R. Beschloss (Englewood Cliffs, NJ: Prentice-Hall, 1989). p. 117.

23. Thomas E. Cronin and Michael A. Genovese, *The Paradoxes of the American Presidency* (New York: Oxford University Press, 1998).

24. Theodore C. Sorensen, *Watchmen in the Night* (Cambridge, MA: MIT Press, 1975).

25. James Madison, *The Federalist Papers,* no. 51.

26. Michael A. Genovese, "Presidential Corruption." Paper presented at annual meeting of the America Political Science Association, New York, September 1994.

27. Sidney M. Milkis, *The President and the Parties* (New York: Oxford University Press, 1993).

28. I first heard Thomas Cronin use this phrase: He believes its genesis might be traced to James M. Burns.

29. Quoted in Thomas E. Cronin, "Thinking and Learning About Leadership," *Presidential Studies Quarterly* (Winter 1984): 31.

30. Miroff, *Icons of Democracy,* ch. 1.

31. James MacGregor Burns, *Roosevelt: The Lion and the Fox* (San Diego, CA: Harvest/HBJ, 1984), p. 151.

32. James L. Sundquist, *Constitutional Reform and Effective Government* (Washington, DC: Brookings, 1986); James MacGregor Burns, *The Power to Lead: The Crisis of the American Presidency* (New York: Simon and Schuster, 1984); Donald L. Robinson *To the Best of My Ability The Presidency and the Constitution* (New York: Norton, 1987).

33. For an examination of how Margaret Thatcher used the power of her office to achieve policy and political goals, see Michael A. Genovese, "Margaret Thatcher and the Politics of Conviction Leadership," in Michael A. Genovese, ed., *Women as National Leaders* (Newbury Park, CA: Sage, 1993). pp. 177–210.

34. Lloyd Cutler, "Party Government Under the Constitution," in Donald L. Robinson, ed., *Reforming American Government: The Bicentennial Papers of the Committee on the Constitutional System* (Boulder, CO: Westview Press, 1985); and Sundquist, *Constitutional Reform and Effective Government.*

35. See Terry Eastland, *Energy in the Executive: The Case for the Strong Presidency* (New York: Free Press, 1992); L. Gordon Corvitz and Jeremy A. Rabkin, *The Fettered Presidency: Legal Constraints on the Executive Branch* (Washington, DC: American Enterprise Institute, 1989); and Harvey C. Mansfield, Jr., *Taming the Prince: The Ambivalance of Modern Executive Power* (New York: Free Press, 1989).

36. See Thomas E. Cronin, *The State of the Presidency*, 2nd ed. (Boston, MA: Little, Brown, 1980). Harold Kongju Koh, *The National Security Constitution* (New Haven, CT: Yale University Press, 1990). and Robert J. Spitzer, *President and Congress* (New York: McGraw-Hill, 1993).

37. Bert Rockman, *The Leadership Question* (New York: Praeger, 1984). p. 221.

38. Quoted in Larry Berman, *The New American Presidency* (Boston: Little, Brown, 1987), p. 344.

39. See Lance T. LeLoup and Steven A. Shull, *Congress and the President* (Belmont, CA: Wadsworth, 1993).

40. See: Spitzer, *President and Congress*, and Koh, *The National Security Constitution*.

41. Robert Jay Lifton, *The Protean Self: Resilience in an Age of Fragmentation* (New York: Basic Books, 1993).

42. David Osborne and Ted Gaehler, *Reinventing Government* (New York: Plume, 1992).

43. Woodrow Wilson, *The State* (Boston: D.C. Heath, 1903), p. 639.

44. Michael Lind, "The Out-of-Control Presidency," *New Republic*, August 14, 1995, p. 21.

45. LeLoup and Shull, *Congress and the President*.

46. Spitzer, *President and Congress*.

47. Cronin, *The State of the Presidency*.

Internet Links

Presidency

www.whitehouse.gov
www.theamericanpresidency.net
www.americanpresident.org/presidentialresources.htm
www.ipl.org/ref/POTUS
http://fedbbs.access.gpo.gov
http://www.whitehouse.gov,WH/html/briefroom.html
http://www.infoctr.edu/fwl/

Congress

www.senate.gov
www.house.gov
http://web.loc gov/global/executive/fed.html
www.govspot.com/must/congress.htm
www.congressweb.com
http://thomas.loc.gov
www.access.gpo.gov/congress/index.html
http://cq.com
www.hillnews.com
http://lcweb.loc.gov/global/legislative/abtcong.html
http://voxpop.org/classic/index.morph
http://www.loc.gov

Courts

www.supremecourts.gov

http://supct.law.cornell.edu/supct

http://usgovinfo.about.com/library weekly/aa081400a.htm?once=true&

http://jurist.law.pitt.edu/supremecourt.htm

www.lawguru.com/ilawlib/index.html

http://www.law.ou.edu/hist

www.law.cornell.edu

http://caselaw.findlaw.com/scripts/getcase.pl?court=us$navby=year$year=
recent

National Opinion

Gallup opinion polls:	roperweb.ropercenter.uconn.edu
ABC News/*Washington Post:*	roperweb.ropercenter.uconn.edu
CBS News/*New York Times:*	roperweb.ropercenter.uconn.edu
NBC News/*Wall Street Journal:*	roperweb.ropercenter.uconn.edu

---

Note: www.whitehouse.gov, www.senate.gov., www.house.gov, www
.supremecourt.gov are the main sites. From there you will find links to more
spccific areas.

Bibliography

Abbot, Philip. *The Exemplary Presidency*. Amherst: University of Massachusetts Press, 1990.

Abraham, Henry J. *Justices and Presidents*. New York: Oxford University Press, 1985.

Adler, David G. "The Court and the Ghost of Curtiss-Wright." Paper presented at the annual meeting of the American Political Science Association. Washington, DC, September 1989.

Adler, David Gray, and Larry N. George, eds. *The Constitution and the Conduct of Foreign Policy*. Lawrence: University Press of Kansas, 1996.

Andrews, William G. "The Presidency, Congress and Constitutional Theory." In *The Presidency in Contemporary Context*, edited by Norman C. Thomas. New York: Dodd, Mead, 1973.

Apple, R.W., Jr. "An Excess of the Pulpit, and Not Enough Bully." *New York Times*, August 5, 1993.

Arnold, Peri E. *Making the Managerial Presidency*. Princeton, NJ: Princeton University Press, 1986.

Asher, Herbert. *Presidential Elections and American Politics*. Homewood, IL: Dorsey Press, 1984.

Baker, Nancy V. *Conflicting Loyalties: Law and Politics in the Attorney General's Office, 1789–1990*. Lawrence: University Press of Kansas, 1992.

Barber, Benjamin R. "Neither Leaders nor Followers: Citizenship Under Strong Democracy." In *Essays in Honor of James MacGregor Burns*, edited by Thomas E. Cronin and Michael R. Beschloss. Englewood Cliffs, NJ: Prentice-Hall, 1989.

———. *Strong Democracy: Participatory Politics for a New Age*. Berkeley: University of California Press, 1984.

199

Barber, James David. *Choosing the President*. New York: American Assembly, 1974.

———. "The Nixon Brush with Tyranny," *Political Science Quarterly* 92, no. 4 (Winter 1977–1978): pp. 581–605.

———. *The Presidential Character: Predicting Performances in the White House*. Englewood Cliffs, NJ: Prentice-Hall, 1992.

Barger, Harold. *The Impossible Presidency: Illusions and Realities of Executive Power*. Glenview, IL: Scott, Foresman, 1984.

Barilleaux, Ryan J., and Barbara Kellerman. *The President as World Leader*. New York: St. Martin's Press, 1991.

Barnes, James A. "Ready or Not." *National Journal*, September 4, 1993, pp. 2136–2141.

Bell, Terrel. *The Thirteenth Man: A Reagan Cabinet Memoir*. New York: Free Press, 1987.

Bellah, Robert N., William Sullivan, Ann Swidel, and Steven Tipton. *Habits of the Heart*. New York: HarperCollins, 1985.

Bennis, Warren. *On Becoming a Leader*. Readng, MA: Addison-Wesley, 1989.

———. *Why Leaders Can't Lead: The Unconscious Conspiracy Continues*. San Francisco: Jossey-Bass, 1989.

Bennis, Warren, and Burt Nanus. *Leaders: Strategies for Taking Charge*. New York: Harper-Collins, 1985.

Berman, Larry. *Lyndon Johnson's War*. New York: Norton, 1991.

———. *The New American Presidency*. Boston: Little, Brown, 1987.

Beschloss, Michael R., and Thomas E. Cronin. *Essays in Honor of James MacGregor Burns*. Englewood Cliffs, NJ: Prentice-Hall, 1989.

Bessette, Joseph M., and Jeffrey Tulis. *The Presidency in the Constitutional Order*. Baton Rouge: Louisiana State University Press, 1984.

Blakesley, Lance. *The President as a Strategically Versatile Leader*. Chicago: Nelson-Hall, 1995.

Blessing, Tim H., and Robert K. Murray. *Greatness in the White House: Rating the Presidents, Washington Through Carter*. University Park: Pennsylvania State University Press, 1988.

———. "The Presidential Performance Study: A Progress Report." *Journal of American History* 170 (1983): pp. 535–555.

Blumenthal, Sidney. "The Education of a President." *New Yorker*, January 24, 1994, pp 31–43.

Bond, Jon, and Richard Fleisher. *The President in the Legislative Arena.* Chicago: University of Chicago Press, 1990.

Brace, Paul, and Barbara Hinckley. *Follow the Leader: Opinion Polls and the Modern Presidents.* New York: Basic Books, 1992.

Breslin, Jimmy. *How the Good Guys Finally Won.* New York: Ballantine Books, 1975.

Brody, Richard A. *Assessing the President: The Media, Elite Opinion, and Public Support.* Stanford, CA: Stanford University Press, 1991.

Bryce, James. *The American Commonwealth.* New York: MacMillan, 1888.

Buchanan, Bruce. *The Presidential Experience: What the Office Does to the Man.* Englewood Cliffs, NJ: Prentice-Hall, 1978.

Bunce, Valerie. *Do New Leaders Make a Difference?: Executive Successions and Public Policy Capitalism and Socialism.* Princeton, NJ: Princeton University Press, 1981.

Burke, John P. *The Institutional Presidency.* Baltimore: Johns Hopkins University Press, 1992.

Burns, James MacGregor. *Leadership.* New York: HarperCollins, 1978.

———. "More Than Merely Power: II." *New York Times,* November 17, 1978, Section A, p. 29.

———. *The Power to Lead: The Crisis of the American Presidency.* New York: Simon and Schuster, 1984.

———. *Presidential Government: The Crucible of Leadership.* Boston: Houghton Mifflin, 1965.

———. *Roosevelt: The Lion and the Fox.* San Diego: Harvest/HBJ, 1984.

Campbell, Colin. *Managing the Presidency: Carter and Reagan, and the Search for Executive Harmony.* Pittsburgh: University of Pittsburgh Press, 1986.

———. "Political Executives and their Officials," *Political Science: The State of the Discipline, II.* Washington, DC: American Political Science Association, 1993.

Campbell, Colin, and Bert Rockman. *The Bush Presidency: First Appraisals.* Chatham, NJ: Chatham House, 1991.

Cannon, Lou. *President Reagan: The Role of a Lifetime.* New York: Touchstone, 1991.

Cantrill, Albert. *The American People, Vietnam and the Presidency.* Princeton, NJ: Princeton University Press, 1976.

Ceaser, James W. *Presidential Selection*. Princeton, NJ: Princeton University Press, 1979.

Ceaser, James W., and Andrew Busch. *The Perfect Tie: The True Story of the 2000 President Election*. Lanham, MD: Rowman & Littlefield, 2001.

Chubb, John E., and Paul E. Peterson. *Can the Government Govern?* Washington, DC: Brookings, 1989.

———. *The New Direction in American Politics*. Washington, DC: Brookings, 1985.

Clausen, Aage R. *How Congressmen Decide: A Policy Focus*. New York: St. Martin's Press, 1973.

Cohen, Jeffrey E. "A Historical Reassessment of Wildavsky's 'Two Presidencies' Thesis," *Social Science Quarterly* 63 (September 1982): pp 549–555.

Corrado, Anthony. *Creative Campaigning*. Boulder, CO: Westview, 1992.

Corvitz, L. Gordon, and Jeremy A. Rabkin. *The Tethered Presidency*. Washington, DC: American Enterprise Institute, 1989.

Corwin, Edward S. *The President: Office and Powers, 1978–1984*, 5th ed. New York: New York University Press, 1984.

———. *Total War and the Constitution*. Westminster, MD.: Knopf, 1947.

Cotter, Cornelius P. and J. Malcolm Smith. *Powers of the President During Crises*. Washington, DC: Public Affairs Press, 1960.

Covington, Cary R., and Lester G. Seligman. *The Coalition Presidency*. Chicago: Dorsey Press, 1989.

Cox, Gary W., and Samuel Kernell. *The Politics of Divided Government*. Boulder, CO: Westview Press, 1991.

Crabb, Cecil V., and Kevin V. Mulcahy. *American National Security*. Pacific Grove, CA: Brooks/Cole, 1991.

Cronin, Thomas E. "If Bush Is to Be the 'Education President' Much Work Must Be Done at the Grassroots." *Chronicle of Higher Education* 35 (February 1, 1989): pp. B1–B2.

———. *Inventing the American Presidency*. Lawrence: University Press of Kansas, 1989.

———. "Leadership and Democracy," *Liberal Education* 73, no. 2 (March/April 1987).

———. "Presidential Power Revised and Reappraised," *Western Political Quarterly*, December 1979.

———. *The State of the Presidency*, 2nd ed. Boston: Little, Brown, 1980.

———. "Superman, Our Textbook President," *Washington Monthly*, October 1970.

———. "Thinking and Learning About Leadership," *Presidential Studies Quarterly* (Winter 1984): pp. 22–34.

Cronin, Thomas E., and Michael R. Beschloss. *Essays in Honor of James MacGregor Burns*. Englewood Cliffs, N.J.: Prentice-Hall, 1989.

Crozier, Michael. *The Trouble with America*. Berkeley: University of California Press, 1984.

Cunliffe, Marcus. "A Defective Institution?" *Commentary*, February 1968, pp. 71–80.

Cutler, Lloyd. "Party Government Under the Constitution." In Donald Robinson, ed., *Reforming American Government: The Bicentennial Papers of the Committee on the Constitutional System*. Boulder, CO: Westview Press, 1985.

Dahl, Robert A. *Pluralist Democracy in the United States*. New York: Rand McNally, 1967.

Davidson, Roger H. "The Presidency and Congress." In *The Presidency and the Political System*. Washington, DC: Congressional Quarterly Press, 1984.

Davis, James A., and David I. Nixon. "The President's Party." *Presidential Studies Quarterly* 24, no.2 (Spring 1994): pp. 363–373.

Davis, James W. *The American Presidency: A New Perspective*. New York: HarperCollins, 1987.

———. *The President as Party Leader*. New York: Praeger, 1992.

Deaver, Michael K. *Behind the Scenes*. New York: William Morrow, 1988.

DeGrazia, Alfred. *Congress and the Presidency*. Washington, DC: American Enterprise Institute, 1967.

———. *Republic in Crisis: Congress Against the Executive Force*. New York: Federal Legal Publications, 1965.

DiClerico, Robert E. *The American President*. Englewood Cliffs, NJ: Prentice-Hall, 1979.

Draper, Theodore. *A Very Thin Line: The Iran-Contra Affairs*. New York: Touchstone Books, 1991.

Drew, Elizabeth. *On the Edge: The Clinton Presidency*. New York: Simon and Schuster, 1994.

Drucker, Peter. *The Effective Executive*. New York: HarperCollins, 1966.

Eastland, Terry. *Energy in the Executive*. New York: Free Press, 1992.

Edwards, George C. *At the Margins: Presidential Leadership in Congress.* New Haven, CT: Yale University Press, 1989.

———. *The Public Presidency.* New York: St. Martin's Press, 1983.

Edwards, George C., John H. Kessel, and Bert A. Rockman. *Researching the Presidency: Vital Questions, New Approaches.* Pittsburgh: University of Pittsburgh Press, 1993.

Edwards, George C., and Stephen Wayne. *Presidential Leadership: Politics and Policy Making.* New York: St. Martin's Press, 1990.

Evans, Rowland, and Robert Novak. *Lyndon B. Johnson: The Exercise of Power.* New York: New American Library, 1966.

Fair, Ray C. "The Effect of Economic Events on Votes for President." *Review of Economics and Statistics* 60 (1978): pp. 159–173.

Ferrel, Robert H., ed. *Off the Record: The Private Papers of Harry S Truman.* New York: HarperCollins, 1980.

Finer, Herman. *The Presidency.* Chicago: University of Chicago Press, 1960.

Finifter, Ada W. *Political Science: The State of the Discipline, III.* Washington, DC: American Political Science Association, 1993.

Fishel, Jeff. *Presidents and Promises.* Washington, DC: CQ Press, 1985.

Fisher, Louis. *The Constitution Between Friends.* New York: St. Martin's Press, 1978.

Fleisher, Richard, and Jon Bond. *The President in the Legislative Arena.* Chicago: University of Chicago Press, 1990.

Fortas, Abe. "The Constitution and the Presidency." *Washington Law Review* 49 (August 1974): pp. 233–244.

Franck, Thomas M. *Political Questions/Judicial Answers.* Princeton, NJ: Princeton University Press, 1992.

Franklin, Daniel P. *Extraordinary Measures.* Pittsburgh: University of Pittsburgh Press, 1991.

Gaebler, Ted, and David Osbourne. *Reinventing Government.* New York: Plume, 1992.

Gardner, John. *On Leadership.* New York: Free Press, 1990.

Genovese, Michael A. "Democratic Theory and the Emergency Powers of the President." *Presidential Studies Quarterly* (Summer 1979): pp. 283–289.

———. *The Nixon Presidency: Power and Politics in Turbulent Times.* Westport, CT: Greenwood Press, 1990.

————. *The Presidency in an Age of Limits*. Westport, CT: Greenwood Press, 1993.

————. "Presidents and Crisis: Developing a Crisis Management System in the Executive Branch." *International Journal on World Peace* (Spring 1987): pp. 301–311.

————. "Presidential Leadership and Crisis Management." *Presidential Studies Quarterly* (Spring 1986): pp. 300–309.

————. "The Return of the Imperial Presidency." *Presidency Research* (Fall 1986): pp. 11–13.

————. *The Supreme Court, the Constitution, and the Presidential Power.* Lanham, MD: University Press of America, 1980.

————. "The Supreme Court, as a Check on Presidential Power." *Presidential Studies Quarterly* (Winter/Spring 1976): pp. 40–44.

————. "Wimpyman, Our Textbook President." *Presidency Research* (Winter 1988–1989): pp. 21–23.

Genovese, Michael A., and Seth Thompson. "Women as Chief Executives: Does Gender Matter?" In *Women as National Leaders*, edited by Michael A. Genovese. Newbury Park, CA: Sage, 1993.

Gerstenzang, James, and Paul Richter. "Clinton Lobbying Wins More Votes for NAFTA Pact." *Los Angeles Times*, November 17, 1993, p. A1.

Ginsberg, Benjamin, and Martin Shefter. *Politics by Other Means*. New York: Basic Books, 1990.

Ginsberg, Benjamin, and Theodore J. Lowi. *Democrats Return to Power.* New York: Norton, 1994.

Golden, David G., and James M. Poterba. "The Price of Popularity: The Political Business Cycle Reexamined." *American Journal of Political Science* 24 (1980): pp. 696–715.

Greenberg, Edward. *The American Political System*. Boston: Little Brown, 1986.

Greene, John Robert. *The Presidency of Gerald R. Ford*. Lawrence: University Press of Kansas, 1995.

Greenstein, Fred. "What the President Means to Americans." In *Choosing The President*, edited by James D. Barber. New York: American Assembly, 1974.

————. *The Hidden-Hand Presidency: Eisenhower as Leader.* New York: Basic Books, 1982.

Greenstein, Fred I., and Nelson Polsby. *The Handbook of Politcal Theory: Micro-Political Theory*. Reading, MA: Addison-Wesley, 1975.

Grossman, Michael Bruch, and Martha Joynt Kumar. "Carter, Reagan and the Media: Have the Rules Changed or the Poles of the Spectrum of Success?" Paper presented at the annual meeting of the American Political Science Association, New York, September 1981.

Grover, William F. *The President as Prisoner*. New York: State University of New York Press, 1989.

Haig, Alexander M. *Caveat: Realism, Reagan and Foreign Policy*. New York: Macmillan, 1984.

Halberstam, David. *The Best and the Brightest*. New York: Random House, 1972.

Hamilton, Alexander, James Madison, and John Jay. *Federalist Papers*. New York: New American Library, 1961.

Han, Lori Cox. *Governing From Center Stage: White House Communication Strategies During the Television Age of Politics*. Cresskill, NJ: Hampton Press, 2001.

Hargrove, Erwin C. *Jimmy Carter as President: A Study of Policy Leadership*. Baton Rouge: Louisiana State University Press, 1988.

———. *The Power of the Modern Presidency*. New York: Knopf, 1974.

———. "Presidential Personality and Leadership Style." In *Researching the Presidency: Vital Questions, New Approaches*. Pittsburgh: University of Pittsburgh Press, 1993.

———. *The President as Leader: Appealing to the Better Angels of Our Nature*. Lawrence: University Press of Kansas, 1998.

Harriger, Katy J. *Independent Justice: The Federal Special Prosecutor in American Politics*. Lawrence: University Press of Kansas, 1992.

Hart, Roderick. *The Sound of Leadership*. Chicago: University of Chicago Press, 1987.

Heclo, Hugh. *A Government of Strangers: Executive Politics in Washington*. Washington, DC: Brookings, 1977.

Heclo, Hugh, and Lester Salamon. *The Illusion of Presidential Government*. Boulder, CO: Westview Press, 1981.

Hertsgaard, Mark. *On Bended Knee: The Press and the Reagan Presidency*. New York: Schocken Books, 1989.

Hess, Stephen. *Organizing the Presidency*. Washington, DC: Brookings, 1977.

Hinckley, Barbara, and Paul Brace. *Follow the Leader: Opinion Polls and the Modern Presidents.* New York: Basic Books, 1992.

Hodgson, Godfrey. *All Things to All Men.* New York: Touchstone, 1980.

Hofstadter, Richard. *The Idea of a Party System.* Oxford, England: Oxford University Press, 1969.

Hughes, Emmet John. *The Living Presidency.* New York: Coward, McCann and Geoghegan, 1973.

Huntington, Samuel P. *American Politics: The Promise of Disharmony.* Cambridge, MA: Harvard University Press, 1981.

Issacharoff, Samuel, Pamela S. Karlan, and Richard H. Pilde. *When Elections Go Bad: The Law of Democracy and the Presidential Election of 2000.* New York: Foundation Press, 2000.

Jehl, Douglas. "Clinton Assails G.O.P. Delays in Bitter Tones." *New York Times,* July 27, 1993, Section A, p.1.

Johnson, Richard T. *Managing the White House.* New York: HarperCollins, 1974.

Jones, Charles O. *The Presidency in a Separated System.* Washington, DC: Brookings, 1994.

Kann, Mark E. "Challenging Lockean Liberalism in America: The Case of Debs and Hillquit." *Political Theory,* no. 8 (May 1980): pp. 203–222.

Karnow, Stanley. *Vietnam: A History.* New York: Viking, 1983.

Kellerman, Barbara, and Ryan J. Barilleaux. *The President as World Leader.* New York: St. Martin's Press, 1991.

Kennedy, John F. Foreword to Theodore C. Sorenson, *Decision-Making in the White House.* New York: Columbia University Press, 1963.

Kennedy, Paul. *The Rise and Fall of the Great Powers.* New York: Vintage Books, 1987.

Kernell, Samuel M. "Explaining Presidential Popularity." *American Political Science Review* 72 (1978): pp. 506–522.

———. *Going Public: New Strategies of Presidential Leadership.* Washington, DC: CQ Press, 1986.

Kernell, Samuel, and Gary W. Cox. *The Politics of Divided Government.* Boulder, CO: Westview Press, 1991.

Kernell, Samuel, and Samuel Popkin, eds. *Chief of Staff.* Berkeley: University of California Press, 1986.

Kessel, John H. *Presidential Campaign Politics.* Chicago: Dorsey Press, 1988.

Kessel, John H., George C. Edwards, and Bert A. Rockman. *Researching the Presidency: Vital Questions, New Approaches.* Pittsburgh: University of Pittsburgh Press, 1993.

King, Gary, and Lyn Ragsdale. *The Elusive Executive.* Washington, DC: CQ Press, 1988.

Koenig, Louis W. *The Chief Executive.* San Diego: Harcourt Brace Jovanovich, 1980.

Koh, Harold Kongju. *The National Security Constitution: Sharing Power After the Iran-Contra Affair.* New Haven, CT: Yale University Press, 1990.

Kozak, David C. "Some Thoughts on Clinton's Challengers." *Presidential Studies Quarterly* (Fall 1993): pp. 849–853.

Kraft, Joseph. "The Post Imperial Presidency." *New York Times,* November 2, 1980, Section 6, p. 31.

Kumar, Martha Joynt, and Michael Baruch Grossman. "Carter, Reagan, and the Media: Have the Rules Changed or the Poles of the Spectrum of Success?" Paper presented at the annual meeting of the American Political Science Association, New York, September 1981.

Kutler, Stanley, K. *The Wars of Watergate.* New York: Knopf, 1990.

Lammers, William W. *Presidential Politics: Patterns and Prospects.* New York: HarperCollins, 1976.

LeLoup, Lance T., and Steven A. Shull. *Congress and the President: The Policy Connection.* Belmont, CA: Wadsworth, 1993.

———. "Congress Versus the Executive: The 'Two Presidencies' Reconsidered." *Social Science Quarterly* 59 (March 1979): pp. 704–719.

Lerner, Max. *America as a Civilization.* New York: Knopf, 1957.

Leuchtenburg, William E. *In the Shadow of FDR: From Harry Truman to Ronald Reagan.* Ithaca, NY: Cornell University Press, 1983.

Lifton, Robert Jay. *The Protean Self: Resilience in an Age of Fragmentation.* New York: Basic Books, 1993.

Light, Paul C. *The President's Agenda.* Baltimore: Johns Hopkins University Press, 1982.

Lindblom, Charles E. "The Market as Prison." *Journal of Politics* 44 (1982): pp. 324–337.

Lindsay, James M., and Wayne P. Steger. "The Two Presidencies in Future Research: Moving Beyond Roll-Call Analysis." *Congress and the Presidency* 20, no. 2 (Autumn 1993): pp. 119–130.

Locke, John. *Treatise on Civil Government and a Letter Concerning Toleration.* New York: Appleton-Century-Crofts, 1937.

Longaker, Richard, ed. Clinton Rossiter, *The Supreme Court and the Commander in Chief,* expanded ed. (Ithaca, NY: Cornell University Press, 1976).

Lowi, Theodore J. *The Personal President: Power Invested Promise Unfulfilled.* Ithaca, NY: Cornell University Press, 1985.

Lowi, Theodore J., and Benjamin Ginsberg. *Democrats Return to Power.* New York: Norton, 1994.

Machiavelli, Niccolo. *The Prince and the Discourses.* New York: Modern Library, 1950.

Maltese, John Anthony. *Spin Control: The White House Office and Communications and the Management of Presidential News.* Chapel Hill: University of North Carolina Press, 1992.

Mansfield, Harvey C. Jr. *Taming the Prince.* New York: Free Press, 1989.

Maraniss, David. *First In His Class: The Biography of Bill Clinton.* New York: Touchstone Books, 1995.

Mayer, Jane, and Doyle McManus. *Landslide: The Unmaking of the President, 1984–1988.* Boston: Houghton Mifflin, 1988.

Mayhew, David. *Congress: The Electoral Connection.* New Haven: Yale University Press, 1974.

———. *Divided We Govern.* New Haven: Yale University Press, 1991.

McConnel, Grant. *The Modern Presidency.* New York: St. Martin's Press, 1967.

Meyers, Frank F. "Social Classes and Political Change in Western Industrial Systems." *Comparative Politics* 2 (1970): pp. 389–412.

Milkis, Sidney M. *The President and the Parties.* New York: Oxford University Press, 1993.

Mill, John Stuart. *Considerations on Representative Government.* New York: Libveral Arts Press, 1958.

Miroff, Bruce. *Icons of Democracy.* New York: Basic Books, 1993.

———. *Pragmatic Illusions.* New York: David McKay, 1976.

Moe, Terry M. "The Politicized Presidency." In *The New Direction in American Politics.* Washinton, DC: Brookings, 1985.

———. "Presidential Style and Presidential Theory." Paper presented at the Presidency Research Conference, Pittsburgh, November 1990.

Moore, Raymond A., Marcia Lynn Whicker, and James P. Pfiffner. *The Presidency and the Persian Gulf War.* Westport, CT: Pracger, 1993.

Mosley, Zelma, Joseph Pika, and Richard A. Watson. *The Presidential Contest.* Washington, DC: CQ Press, 1992.

Murray, Robert K., and Tim H. Blessing. *Greatness in the White House: Rating the Presidents, Washington Through Carter.* University Park: Pennsylvania State University Press, 1988.

————. "The Presidential Performance Study: A Progress Report." *Journal of American History* 170 (1983): pp. 535–555.

Nanus, Bert. *Visionary Leadership.* San Francisco: Jossey-Bass, 1992.

Nanus, Bert, and Warren Bennis. *Leaders: The Strategies for Taking Charge.* New York: HarperCollins, 1985.

Nathan, Richard. *The Administrative Presidency.* New York: Wiley, 1983.

Nelson, Michael. "Evaluating the Presidency." *In The Presidency and the Political System.* Washington, DC: CQ Press, 1984.

Neustadt, Richard E. *Presidential Power.* New York: Wiley, 1960.

————. *Presidential Power and the Modern Presidents.* New York: Free Press, 1990.

————. *Presidential Power: The Politics of Leadership.* New York: Wiley, 1976.

Nixon, David L., and James A. Davis. "The President's Party." *Presidential Studies Quarterly* 24, no. 2 (Spring 1994).

Novak, Robert, and Rowland Evans. *Lyndon B. Johnson: The Exercise of Power.* New York: New American Library, 1966.

Novak, William, and Thomas P. O'Neill. *Man of the House: The Life and Political Memoirs of Speaker Tip O'Neill.* New York: Random House, 1987.

Nye, Joseph. *Bound to Lead.* New York: Basic Books, 1990.

O'Connor, James. *The Fiscal Crisis of the State.* New York: St. Martin's Press, 1973.

O'Neill, Thomas P., with William Novak. *Man of the House: The Life and Political Memoirs of Speaker Tip O'Neill.* New York: Random House, 1987.

Oldfield, Duane M., and Aaron Wildavsky. "Reconsidering the Two Presidencies." *Society,* July/August 1989, pp. 54–60.

Orman, John. "Covering the American Presidency: Balanced Reporting in the Presidential Press." *Presidential Studies Quarterly* 14 (1984).

Ornstein, Norman, and Michael Robinson. "The Case of Our Disappearing Congress." *TV Guide*, January 11, 1986, pp. 7–8.

Peterson, Merrill D., ed. *The Portable Thomas Jefferson*. New York: Viking Press, 1975.

Peterson, Paul, and John Chubb. *Can the Government Govern?* Washington, DC: Brookings, 1989.

———. *The New Direction in American Politics*. Washington, DC: Brookings, 1985.

Pfiffner, James P. "The Carter-Reagan Transition: Hitting the Ground Running." *Presidential Studies Quarterly* (Fall 1983): pp. 623–645.

———. ed. *The Managerial Presidency*. Pacific Grove, CA: Brooks/Cole, 1991.

———. *The Modern Presidency*. New York: St. Martin's Press, 1993.

———. "The President's Chief of Staff: Lessons Learned." Working Paper 92:19, Institute of Public Policy, George Mason University, October 1992.

———. *The Strategic Presidency: Hitting the Ground Running*. Chicago: Dorsey Press, 1988.

Pfiffner, James P., Marcia Lynn Whicker, and Raymond A. Moore. *The Presidency and the Persian Gulf War*. Westport, CT: Praeger, 1993.

Phelps, Glen A. *George Washington and American Constitutionalism*. Lawrence: University Press of Kansas, 1993.

Phillips, Donald T. *Lincoln on Leadership*. New York: Warner Books, 1992.

Pika, Joseph A., Zelma Mosley, and Richard A. Watson. *The Politics of the Presidency*. Washington, DC: CQ Press, 1992.

Pious, Richard M. *The American Presidency*. New York: Basic Books, 1979.

Polsby, Nelson, and Fred I. Greenstein. *The Handbook of Political Theory: Micro-Political Theory*. Reading, MA: Addison-Wesley, 1975.

Polsby, Nelson W., and Aaron Wildavsky. *Presidential Elections*. New York: Free Press, 1991.

Popkin, Samuel, and Samuel Kernell. *Chief of State*. Berkeley: University of California Press, 1986.

Porter, Roger. "Gerald Ford: A Healing Presidency." In *Leadership in the Modern Presidency*, edited by Fred I. Greenstein. Cambridge, MA: Harvard University Press, 1988.

Poterba, James M., and David G. Golden. "The Price of Popularity: The Political Business Cycle Reexamined." *American Journal of Political Science* 24 (1980).

Rabkin, Jeremy A., and L. Gordon Corvitz. *The Tethered Presidency*. Washington, DC: American Enterprise Institute, 1989.

Ragsdale, Lyn. *Presidential Politics*. Boston: Houghton Mifflin, 1993.

Ragsdale, Lyn, and Gary King. *The Elusive Executive*. Washington, DC: CQ Press, 1988.

Randall, Willard Sterne. *Thomas Jefferson: A Life*. New York: Henry Holt, 1993.

Richter, Paul, and James Gerstenzang. "Clinton Lobbying Wins More Votes for NAFTA Pact." *Los Angeles Times*, November 17, 1993, Part A, p. 1.

Richter, Paul, and Karen Tamulty. "Clinton's Use of the Soft Sell Worries Allies." *Los Angeles Times*, July 31, 1993.

Rimmerman, Craig A. *Presidency by Plebiscite*. Boulder, CO: Westview Press, 1993.

Rivers, Douglas, and Nancy Rose. "Passing the President's Program: Public Opinion and Presidential Influence in Congress." *American Journal of Political Science* 29 (May 1985).

Robinson, Donald L. *To the Best of My Ability: The Presidency and the Constitution*. New York: Norton, 1987.

Robinson Michael J., and Margaret A. Sheehan. *Over the Wire and on TV*. New York: Russell Sage Foundation, 1983.

Rockman, Bert. *The Leadership Question: The Presidency and the American System*. New York: Praeger, 1984.

Rockman, Bert, and Colin Campbell. *The Bush Presidency: First Appraisals*. Chatham, NJ: Chatham House, 1991.

Rockman, Bert A., George C. Edwards, and John H. Kessel. *Researching the Presidency: Vital Questions, New Approaches*. Pittsburgh: University of Pittsburgh Press, 1993.

Rose, Nancy, and Douglas Rivers. "Passing the Pesident's Program: Public Opinion and Presidential Influence in Congress." *American Journal of Political Science* 29 (May 1985): pp. 183–197.

Rose, Richard. *The Postmodern President: The White House Meets the World*. Chatham, NJ: Chatham House, 1991.

Rossiter, Clinton. *The American Presidency*. New York: Harcourt, Brace and World, 1956.

———. *Conservatism in America*. New York: Vintage, 1962.

———. *Constitutional Dictatorship: Crisis Government in the Modern Democracy*. Princeton, NJ: Princeton University Press, 1948.

Rousseau, Jean Jacques. *Social Contract.* New York: Dutton, 1950.

Sabato, Larry. *Feeding Frenzy.* New York: Free Press, 1991.

Salamon, Lester, and Hugh Heclo. *The Illusion of Presidential Government.* Boulder, CO: Westview Press, 1981.

Salokar, Rebecca Mae. *The Solicitor General.* Philadelphia: Temple University Press, 1992.

Schlesinger, Arthur M., Jr. *The Cycles of American History.* Boston: Houghton Mifflin, 1986.

―――. *The Imperial Presidency.* Boston: Houghton Mifflin, 1973.

―――. "Leave the Constitutional Alone," in Donald Robinson, ed., *Reforming American Government: The Bicentennial Papers of the Committee on the Constitutional System.* Boulder, CO: Westview Press, 1985.

―――. *A Thousand Days: John F. Kennedy in the White House.* Boston: Houghton Mifflin, 1965.

Schlesinger, Arthur M., Jr., and Alfred de Grazia. *Congress and the Presidency: Their Role in Modern Times.* Washington, DC: American Enterprise Institute, 1967.

Schubert, Glendon. *The Presidency in the Courts.* Minneapolis: University of Minnesota Press, 1957.

Shuman, David F. *A Preface to Politics.* Itasca, IL: F. E. Peacock, 1991.

Seligman, Lester G., and Cary R. Covington. *The Coalition Presidency.* Chicago: Dorsey Press, 1989.

Shaw, David. "Covering Clinton: Did Media Rush to Judgment or Merely Reflect Reality?" *Los Angeles Times,* September 15–17, 1993.

Sheehan, Margaret A., and Michael J. Robinson. *Over the Wire and on TV.* New York: Russell Sage Foundation, 1983.

Shefter, Martin, and Benjamin Ginsberg. *Politics by Other Means.* New York: Basic Books, 1990.

Shogan, Robert. *The Riddle of Power.* New York: Dutton, 1991.

Shull, Steven A., ed. *The Two Presidencies: A Quarter Century Assessment.* Chicago: Nelson-Hall, 1991.

Shull, Steven A., and Lance T. LeLoup. "Congress Versus the Executive: The Two Presidencies Reconsidered." *Social Science Quarterly* 59 (March 1979): pp. 704–719.

Sigelman, Lee. "A Reassessment of the Two Presidencies' Thesis." *Journal of Politics* 41 (November 1979): pp. 1195–1205.

Skowronek, Stephen. *The Politics Presidents Make.* Cambridge, MA: Belknap, 1993.

————. "Presidential Leadership in Political times." In *The President and the Political System*, 3rd ed., edited by Michael J. Nelson. Washington, DC: CQ Press, 1990.

Smith, Hedrick. *The Power Game: How Washington Works.* New York: Ballantine, 1988.

Smith, J. Malcolm, and Cornelius P. Cotter. *Powers of the President During Crises.* Washington, DC: Public Affairs Press, 1960.

Sorensen, Theodore C. *Watchmen in the Night.* Cambridge, MA: MIT Press, 1975.

Speakes, Larry. *Speaking Out: The Reagan Presidency from Inside the White House.* New York: Scribners, 1988.

Spitzer, Robert J. *President and Congress: Executive Hegemony at the Crossroads of American Government.* New York: McGraw-Hill, 1993.

————. *The Presidential Veto: Touchstone of the American Presidency.* Albany: State University of New York Press, 1988.

Stegar, Wayne P., and James M. Lindsay. "The Two Presidencies in Future Research: Moving Beyond Roll-Call Analysis." *Congress and the Presidency* 20, no. 2 (Autumn 1993): pp. 103–117.

Stockman, David A. *The Triumph of Politics: The Inside Story of the Reagan Revolution.* New York: Avon, 1987.

Stuckey, Mary E. *The President as Interpreter-in-Chief.* Chatham, NJ: Chatham House, 1991.

————. *Strategic Failures in the Modern Presidency.* Cresskill, NJ: Hampton Press, 1997.

Sullivan, Terry. "Headcounts, Expectations, and Presidential Coalitions in Congress." *American Journal of Political Science* 32:3 (August 1988): pp. 567–590.

Sundquist, James L. *Constitutional Reform and Effective Government.* Washington, DC: Brookings, 1986.

————. "Needed: A Political Theory for the New Era of Coalition Government in the United States." *Political Science Quarterly* 103 (Winter 1988): pp. 613–637.

Tamulty, Karen. "Clinton Piles Up record Legislative Wins." *Los Angeles Times*, November 13, 1993, p. A23.

Tamulty, Karen, and Paul Richter. "Clinton's Use of the Soft Sell Worries Allies." *Los Angeles Times*, July 31, 1993, Section A, p. 1.

Tatalovich, Raymond, and Bryon W. Daynes. *Presidential Power in the United States*. Belmont, CA: Brooks/Cole, 1984.

Thompson, Seth, and Michael A. Genovese. "Women as Chief Executives: Does Gender Matter?" In *Women as National Leaders*, edited by Michael A. Genovese. Newbury Park, CA: Sage, 1993.

Thurber, James A. *Divided Democracy*. Washington, DC: CQ Press, 1991.

Tocqueville, Alexis de. *Democracy in America*. New York: Knopf, 1969.

Tulis, Jeffrey K. *The Rhetorical Presidency*. Princeton, NJ: Princeton University Press, 1987.

Tulis, Jeffrey, and Joseph Bessette. *The Presidency in the Constitutional Order*. Baton Rouge: Louisiana State University, 1981.

Waterman, Richard W., Wright, Robert, and Gilbert St. Clair. *The Image-Is-Everything Presidency: Dilemmas in American Leadership*. Boulder, CO: Westview Press, 1999.

Watson, Richard A. *The Presidential Contest*. New York: Wiley, 1984.

Watson, Richard A., Norman C. Thomas, and Joseph A. Pika. *The Politics of the Presidency*. Washington, DC: CQ Press, 1993.

Wayne, Stephen J. *The Road to the White House*. New York: St. Martin's Press, 1988.

Wayne, Stephen J., and George Edwards. *Presidential Leadership: Politics and Policy Making*. New York: St. Martin's Press, 1990.

Wicker, Marcia Lynn, James P. Pfiffner, and Raymond A. Moore, eds. *The Presidency and the Persian Gulf War*. Westport, CT: Praeger, 1993.

Wildavsky, Aaron, and Duane M. Oldfield. "Reconsidering the Two Presidencies." *Society* (July/August 1989): pp. 54–59.

Will, George. "The Veep and the Blatherskite." *Newsweek*, June 29, 1992, p. 72.

Williams, Phil. "The Limits of American Power: From Nixon to Reagan." *International Affairs* (Autumn 1987): pp. 575–588.

Williams, Walter. *Mismanaging America: The Rise of the Anti-Analytic Presidency*. Lawrence: University Press of Kansas, 1990.

Wilson, Woodrow. *The State*. Boston: D.C. Heath, 1903.

Wolfe, Alan. *The Limits of Legitimacy*. New York: Free Press, 1977.

Wolin, Sheldon. *Politics and Vision*. Boston: Little, Brown, 1960.

Young, James S. *The Washington Community, 1800–1828.* New York: Columbia University Press, 1966.

Zeidenstein, Harvey G. "Presidents' Popularity and Their Wins and Losses on Major Issues: Does One Have a Greater Influence over the Other?" *Presidential Studies Quarterly* (Spring 1985): pp. 287–300.

Index

Accountability, 159, 163
Adams, Henry, 65
Adams, John, 41, 72
Adams, John Quincy, 41
Adams, Sherman, 127
African-Americans, 29
Agenda, controlling, 100–101
Agnew, Spiro, 16, 116
Air Pollution Control Act, 13
American Creed, 61
Arthur, Chester A., 41
Ashcroft, John, 103
Atomic bombs, 6

Barber, Benjamin R., 158
Barber, James David, 44, 168
Barger, Harold M., 39–40, 112,
    151–152
Bay of Pigs, 7
Beirut, 92–93
Bennis, Warren, 62–63, 88, 126
"Blessed Are the Meek" era, 9, 16
Brace, Paul, 108
Breslin, Jimmy, 43
Brody, Richard A., 121
Bryce, James, 155
Buchanan, James, 41
Bunce, Valerie, 65
Bureaucracy, politicizing, 131–133

Burns, James MacGregor, 12, 40,
    59, 68, 69, 70, 72, 85–86, 87,
    93, 103, 104, 152
Busch, Andrew, 27
Bush, George H.
    Congress and, 123, 124
    economy, 136
    foreign policy, 78, 85, 136,
        138–139
    historians' assessment, 36, 38
    ideology, 28
    leadership qualities, 3, 4, 19–20,
        34, 89
    media coverage, 114
    news, managing, 117
    political experience, 92
    popularity, 110, 111
    promises kept, 32, 33
    skill, 58, 90
Bush, George W.
    election of 2000, 25–28, 28–31
    historians' assessment, 36, 38
    management style, 131
    news, managing, 117
    political experience, 92
    political parties, 103
    popularity, 105
    after terrorist attacks, 31, 62, 90,
        91, 107, 147, 162

Business. *See* Economy;
  Market-oriented systems

Camelot president, 7–8
Campaigning, need for constant,
  71–72, 114–115
Camp David peace accords, 17
Capitalist state, 73
Carter, Jimmy
  Congress and, 16, 56, 96–97, 102
  foreign policy, 91
  fortune, 99, 100
  historians' assessment, 35, 38, 41,
    140
  ideology, 28
  leadership qualities, 3, 4, 17, 34
  media coverage, 113
  political experience, 92
  popularity, 110
  promises kept, 32, 33
  public, view of, 62, 64, 109
  skill, 58
Ceaser, James, 27
Celebrity in chief, 112–113
Checks and balances, 10, 52, 137,
  157–158, 161–163
Chief of staff, 126–127
China, 14, 91
Civil Rights Act, 13, 37
Civil War, 147
Cleveland, Grover, 41
Clinton, Bill
  Congress and, 95, 96–97, 104,
    120, 123–125
  economy, 76, 136, 168
  foreign policy, 136
  gun control, 91
  historians' assessment, 36, 38
  ideology, 28, 101
  interest groups, 103
  leadership qualities, 3, 4, 34

management style, 130, 131
news, managing, 117
political experience, 92–93
popularity, 110, 111
promises kept, 33
scandals and leadership, 20–24,
  159
skill, 58, 90–91
after terrorist attacks, 107
Clinton, Hillary, 21
Coalition
  builders, 167
  electoral, 71, 102
  governing, 71, 102–104
Cold War, 37–38
  containment policy, 6
  and importance of presidency,
    153
  post-Cold War period, 4, 18–19,
    19, 78, 166
Community, sense of, 60, 63
Congress, 118–125
  administrative strategy,
    presidential, 130–133
  coalition building, 104
  consensus-building, 102
  Democratization of, 14
  divided government, 7, 8, 27,
    35–36
  domestic versus foreign policy,
    133–136
  honeymoon period, 95–100
  Johnson and, 13
  leadership, 69, 70, 86
  negative power, 81
  powers determined by
    Constitution, 49, 53, 54, 167
  presidential-curbing era, 16, 17,
    139–140
  presidential popularity, 105
  Reagan and, 18

Supreme Court and, 138–139
terms, 168
Consensus, 63, 69–70, 101–104,
165–169
Conservative(s), 21–22, 28, 101,
141, 162, 167
Constitutional Convention, 51
Constitutional dictatorship, 142,
143–145
Constitution (United States), 3, 13.
See also Founding
Fathers/Framers of
Constitution
Article 1, 53
Article 2, 53
emergency powers, 141
power sharing, 43, 49–50, 52–57,
119–120
Containment, 6
Coolidge, Calvin, 5, 41, 66
Corvitz, L. Gordon, 141
Corwin, Edward, 52, 119, 144,
170
Cotter, Cornelius P., 143
Crisis
community, sense of, 63
emergency powers, 31, 141–147
presidential leadership and, 59,
64–65, 120
Cronin, Thomas, xii, 3, 5, 12, 40,
43, 60, 61, 67, 69, 76, 82, 102,
113–114, 154, 155, 162, 166,
171–172,
Crozier, Michel, 62
Cuba, 7
Cuban missile crisis, 7
Cult of the presidency, 1–2, 5, 9,
113
Culture, political, 59–63
Cunliffe, Marcus, 15
Cutler, Lloyd, 162

Cycle, presidential
of decreasing popularity, 65
of growing effectiveness, 65
normal versus crisis, 64–65
roots of, 66–67
succession, 65
Cynicism, 15, 64, 167

Dahl, Robert, 83
Davis, James, 115–116
Deaver, Michael, 114
Debs, Eugene, 154
"Deliver Us from Presidents" era,
9, 16
Democracy, 108–109, 160–161,
166–167
Democratic party, xiii, 3, 16, 21–22,
97, 104
Democratization of the Congress,
14, 34, 56, 97
Department of Housing and Urban
Development, 13
Department of Transportation, 13
Détente, 38
Dialogue, national, 166
Dispersal of power. *See* Power
Dole, Robert, 95, 123
Domestic policy, 34, 37–38,
133–136, 157
Donaldson, Sam, 117
Drucker, Peter, 44
Durant, Robert, 129

Eastland, Terry, 141, 162
Economic policy, 37–38, 97, 123, 157
Economy
Clinton period, 23
international, 78, 100
presidential success linked to,
75–76, 111, 136
Reagan and, 18

Edwards, George, 105, 106, 112, 121
Egypt, 17
Ehrlichman, John, 131–132
Einstein, Albert, 87
Eisenhower, Dwight D.
  historians' assessment, 35, 37, 41
  leadership qualities, 7
  management style, 127
  popularity, 110
  presidential cycles, 66
Election of 2000, 25–31
Electoral coalition. *See* Coalition
Elementary and Secondary Education Act, 13
Emergency power. *See* Power
Emerson, Ralph W., 65, 160
Ensor, James, x – xi
Europe, 159, 161–162
European Recovery Program. *See* Marshall Plan
Evans, Rowland, 122
Executive Office of the President (EOP), 125
Executive orders, 130–131
Ex parte Milligan, 147

Fair Deal, 37
Family Leave Bill, 24
Federalist Papers
  Federalist 10, 52
  Federalist 51, 50, 56, 158
  Federalist 70, 50
Fillmore, Millard, 41
Financing, campaign, 72
Finer, Herman, 12
Fishel, Jeff, 32–33
Florida, 2000 presidential election, 28–31
Followership, key tasks, 59–60

Ford, Gerald
  Congress and, 16–17, 95
  failure, 64, 140
  historians' assessment, 35, 38, 41
  leadership qualities, 3, 4, 34
  popularity, 110
  promises kept, 33
  skill, 58
Foreign policy
  Clinton, 24
  Cold War approach, 34
  presidential effectiveness, 37–38, 91, 133–136, 157
  presidential experience, 59
  Supreme Court and, 137–138
Formal power. *See* Power
Fortas, Abe, 144
Fortune, 90, 99–100
Foster, Vince, 22
Founding Fathers/Framers of Constitution
  ambition and power, checks on, 140, 162, 163
  antileadership design, 49–52, 153
  democracy, mixed feelings about, 115
  emergency powers, 141
  government structure, 52–57, 84, 118
  leaders, listed, 72
  separation of powers, 108
Franck, Thomas M., 40
Franklin, Benjamin, 3, 72

Gallup poll, presidential, 109–110
Gardner, John, 59
George III, king of England, 49, 55
Gingrich, Newt, 21, 28, 86
Ginsberg, Benjamin, 3, 20, 102
Globalization, 77–79
Gore, Albert, 25–29

Governing coalition. *See* Coalition
Grant, Ulysses S., 41
Great Depression, 2, 4, 66, 147
"Great Society," 8, 37
Greenberg, Edward S., 75
Greenstein, Fred, 91, 107
Gridlock, 43, 141, 164
Gulf War. *See* Persian Gulf War
Gun control, 91, 124–125

Haig, Alexander M., Jr., 96
Haiti, 110
Haldeman, Bob, 115, 116, 127
"Hallowed Be the President" era, 8, 9, 16, 19
Hamilton, Alexander, 3, 12, 43, 50, 72
Harding, Warren G., 41, 66
Hargrove, Erwin C., 66–67, 91
Harrison, Benjamin, 41
Hayes, Rutherford B., 41
Health care legislation, 125
Heclo, Hugh, 10, 48
"Heroic" model of the presidency, 5, 61, 162
Hinckley, Barbara, 108
Hodgson, Godfrey, 40
Hollywood-on-the-Potomac, 113
Honeymoon period, 95–100
Hoover, Herbert, 41, 66
House of Representatives, 22, 27
Human rights, 38, 91
Humphrey, Hubert H., 72
Huntington, Samuel, 56–57, 63
Hyde, Henry, 21, 22

Ideology, 34–36
Impeachment, Clinton, 22–23, 28, 34, 159
Imperial Presidency, 8, 15, 16
Imperiled presidency, 16, 40
Impossible presidency, 39–40
Individualism, 61–63

INF. *See* Intermediate-range
Nuclear Forces treaty
Informal powers. *See* Power
Intermediaries, decline of, 69–71
Intermediate-range Nuclear Forces
treaty, 18–19
Iran, hostages in, 17
Iran-Contra scandal, 18, 19, 138, 159
Israel, 17

Jackson, Andrew, 41, 61
Jackson, Justice Robert, 120, 138
Japan, 6
Jefferson, Thomas
antiauthoritianism, 61
goal, 12
on political parties, 70
power, mistrust of, 51, 153
presidency of, 3, 41
Jeffersonian goal, 155–157, 166
Jeffords, Jim, 27
job approval ratings, 28
Johnson, Andrew, 41
Johnson, Lyndon, xiii
Congress and, 8, 70, 96, 121–123, 124
frustration at office, 48
historians' assessment, 35, 37, 41
leadership qualities, 3, 4, 34
political experience, 92
popularity, 110
presidential cycles, 66
promises kept, 32, 33
skill, 58
strong-presidency model, 12–14
war on poverty, 91
Jones, Paula, 22
Judeo-Christian ethos, 60

Kemell, Samuel, 115

Kennedy, John F.
  business, relationship with,
    75–76
  Congress and, 7–8
  historians' assessment, 35, 37, 41
  leadership qualities, 88
  management style, 127
  news, managing, 113, 116
  popularity, 110
  on presidency, 48, 86
  presidential cycles, 66
  promises kept, 32, 33
King, Martin Luther, Jr., 88
Klein, Joe, 21
Koh, Harold, 162
Korean War, 6, 13, 131

Law, temptation to break, 139–141
Leadership
  democracy and, 153–154
  management versus, 126
Learning curve, 65
L'Enfant, Pierre, 118
Lerner, Max, 61
Lewinsky, Monica, 22
Liberalism, 167
Liberals, 21–22, 28
Liberty
  Founding Fathers, 49, 51–52
  modern obsession, 60–61
Light, Paul, 40, 96, 97–98
Limited government, 52
Lincoln, Abraham
  democracy, definition of, 156
  emergency powers, 147
  historians' assessment, 41
  leadership qualities, 61
  popularity, 106
Lind, Michael, 169
Lindblom, Charles, 73–74, 77
Locke, John, 142, 143

Longaker, Richard, 147
Lowi, Theodore, 3, 20, 108

Machiavelli, Nicolo, 99, 143
Madison, James
  human nature, view of, 63
  powers, separation of, 49–50, 51,
    52, 54, 56, 158
  presidency, 3, 41
Madisonian model (system), 51–52
Management style, 37–38, 94,
    125–133
Mand, Louis, 27
Mandate, 99, 120
Mansfield, Harvey C., Jr., 141, 162
Market-oriented systems, 73–77
Marshall Plan, 6
Marx, Groucho, 13
Mayhew, David, xii
McClosky, Herbert, 65
McConnell, Grant, 12
McKinley, William, 41
Media, 71, 112–118
Medicaid, 13
Medicare, 13
Mill, John Stuart, 143
Miller, Dennis, 28
Miroff, Bruce, 77, 108–109, 155,
    157
Mobocracy, 49
Moe, Terry, 5
Monarchy, 49
Mondale, Walter, 16, 116
Monroe, James, 41
Morris, Dick, 132
Murray-Blessing poll, 34–36, 40–42

NAFTA. *See* North American Free
    Trade Agreement
Nanus, Burt, 87–88
Nathan, Richard, 132

NATO. *See* North Atlantic Treaty
Organization
Nelson, Michael, 19
Neustadt, Richard, xiii,10, 11, 58,
76, 85, 105–106, 110, 121
New Deal, 37
New Frontier, 37
news management, 115–118
New World Order, 20
Nicaragua, 140
Nixon, Richard M., xiii. *See also*
Watergate
character, 14–15, 20, 58
emergency powers, 147
foreign policy, 91
historians' assessment, 35, 38, 41
leadership qualities, 3, 4, 34
management style, 127, 129,
131–132
news, managing, 116, 117
political experience, 92
popularity, 110
presidential cycles, 66
promises kept, 33
skill, 93
Noriega, Manuel, 85
North American Free Trade
Agreement (NAFTA), 23, 38,
124
North Atlantic Treaty Organization
(NATO), 6
Novak, Robert, 122

Organization of Petroleum
Exporting Countries (OPEC),
99
Orman, John, 113
O'Toole, James, xi

Paine, Thomas, 3, 49, 155
Panama, 85

Parliament (British System),
161–162, 164
Parties, political, 104
divided government, 123
opposition, consulting with, 124
relative weakness, 69, 159
role of, 69, 70–71
Patriotism, 63
Peace Corps, 8
Persian Gulf War, 20, 138
Pfiffner, James P., 55, 95, 127
Pierce, Franklin, 41
Pious, Richard M., 145 116
Political experience, 92–93
Political parties. *See* Parties,
political
Polk, James K., 41
Popularity, 37–38, 104–111, 121
Powell, Jody, 106–107
Power, dispersal of
accountability and, 157–159
emergency
("supraconstitutional"),
141–147
evaluation of, 161–162
formal, 53, 153
fragmentation of, 55–56
illusion versus reality, 47–48
informal, 53, 54, 85, 153
negative, 81
Supreme Court and, 137 139
Promises, presidential, 32–33

Rabkin, Jeremy, 141, 162
Ragsdale, Lyn, 53
Ratings, presidential by historians,
37–38, 40–42
Reagan, Ronald
administrative strategy, 132–133
coalition building, 104
Congress and, 86, 96, 98–99, 123

Reagan, Ronald *(continued)*
  economy and, 136, 168
  emergency powers, 147
  foreign policy, 134
  fortune, 99–100
  historians' assessment, 35, 41
  ideology, 28, 100–101
  image, 107, 108, 109, 114–115
  Iran-Contra scandal, 140
  leadership qualities, 3, 4, 18–19,
    34, 88–89
  management style, 127, 129–130
  news, managing, 113, 116, 117
  political experience, 92–93
  popularity, 105, 106, 110
  promises kept, 33
  skill, 58, 94
Regan, Donald, 127
Republicanization of the
  presidency, 34, 56
Republican party, 3, 14, 21, 22–23,
  28, 104
Rockman, Bert, 53–54, 55–57, 64,
  72, 163
Roosevelt, Franklin D.
  emergency powers, 145, 147
  historians' assessment, 35, 37, 41
  Kennedy's comments about,
    75–76
  leadership qualities, 2–3, 4–6, 34,
    61, 82–83
  management style, 127, 131
  media coverage, 113
  popularity, 65, 106
  on presidency, 161
  presidential cycles, 66
  skill, 59, 93
Roosevelt, Theodore, 41, 66, 87,
  106, 136
Rossiter, Clinton, 10–11, 60–61,
  137, 142, 143–144, 147

Rousseau, Jean-Jacques, 142–143
Rule of Law, 52

Sacrifices, 62
Salamon, Lester, 48, 89
Schlesinger, Arthur M., Jr., 15, 44,
  57, 65–66, 68–69, 155
Schubert, Glendon, 137
Schuman, David F., 63
"Search for a Savior" era, 9, 18
Senate, U.S., 15, 22–23, 27
Separation of powers, 52, 165–169
September 11, 2001, 31
Shefter, Martin, 102
Skill, leadership, 57–59, 82, 89–94,
  121
Smith, Hedrick, 104, 113, 115
Smith, J. Malcolm, 143
Smithers, Peter, 40
Somalia, 92–93
Sorensen, Theodore, 40
South Africa, 86
Soviet Union, 6, 15, 153
Spitzer, Robert, 6, 119–120, 162
Starr, Ken, 21–23
State government, 27
States rights, 30
Stevens, Justice John Paul, 31
Stockman, David, 98–99, 123
Succession cycle. *See* Cycle
Sundquist, James L., 40
Sununu, John, 127
"Superman," 5, 15, 19, 39, 171
Superpower, 77–79
Supreme Court, 137–139
  emergency powers and, 144–145,
    147
  on executive orders, 130
  negative power, 81
  presidential election of 2000, 26,
    29–31

Sutherland, Justice George, 138

Taft, William Howard, 41, 66
Taylor, Zachary, 41
Terrorism, war against, 62
Terrorist attacks, 31, 38
  crisis presidency, 107, 147, 166
  patriotism following, 63
Textbook presidency, 12
Theatrical presidency, 113–114
Tocqueville, Alexis de, 61–62
Transition period, 94–95
Truman, Harry S
  effectiveness, 6–7
  executive orders, 131
  foreign policy, 134
  historians' assessment, 35, 37, 41
  popularity, 110, 111
  presidential cycles, 66
Twenty-second Amendment, 168
Tyler, John, 41

U.S. Civil Rights Commission, 29
U.S. v. Curtiss-Wright Export Corp.,
  138

Van Buren, Martin, 41
Vietnam War, 4, 13–14, 15–16, 37,
  64, 134
Vision, 19, 87–89, 161, 167

Warber, Adam, 129
War on Poverty, 13, 91
War Powers Act, 16, 135

Washington, D.C., 103–104
Washington, George
  executive orders, 130
  historians' assessment, 41
  leadership qualities, 3, 61
  presidency, role in shaping, 52,
    153
Watergate, 4, 14–15, 15–16, 139,
  159
Watt, James, 133
Wayne, Stephen J., 106, 112
Welfare reform, 38, 74–75
"Where There Is No Vision, the
  People Perish" era, 9
White House, 4, 34, 125–133
Whitewater scandal, 22
Wildavsky, Aaron, 40, 133–134
Will, George, 19
Williams, Phil, 3
Williams, Walter, 127, 128
Wills, Garry, 21
Wilson, Woodrow, 41, 43, 66, 163,
  168
Wimpyman, 19, 39
Wizard of Oz, 4, 18, 108, 168–169
World War II, 4, 6, 37

*Youngstown Sheet and Tube Co. v.
  Sawyer*, 138

Zaller, John, 65
Zapata, Emiliano, 154